UGC NET Paper I Unlocked

Volume VIII

Higher Education System

ANKIT SHARMA

A Complete Guide for UGC NET

TO THE POINT NOTES BASED ON PREVIOUS YEARS QUESTION PAPERS

Table of Contents

Volume VIII: Higher Education System

Foreword

*The **UGC NET Paper I Unlocked Volume VIII: Higher Education System** is an **indispensable resource** for aspirants preparing for the **UGC NET Paper I** examination. This book stands apart from the outdated materials available in the market, as it is **meticulously updated**, aligning with the latest trends, **exam patterns**, and **recent policy changes** in the higher education sector.*

*Higher education plays a **pivotal role** in shaping societies, economies, and national development. This volume delves deep into **India's educational history**, covering its **ancient foundations, colonial transformations, post-independence reforms, and contemporary advancements under the National Education Policy (NEP) 2020**. The book provides a structured overview of **institutions, policies, governance, accreditation, and global influences** on India's education system, making it a **must-have** for every aspirant.*

What Makes This Book Unique?

***Comprehensive Question Analysis** – We have thoroughly analyzed **past UGC NET questions**, examined **patterns**, and provided **detailed explanations** not just for the correct answer but also for **other options**, ensuring a deeper understanding.*

***Exam-Oriented Approach** – Unlike traditional books filled with unnecessary details, this volume contains **to-the-point notes**, summarizing key concepts concisely while retaining **depth and clarity**.*

***Trend-Based Content** – The **UGC NET exam pattern evolves constantly**, and so does this book! Instead of relying on outdated content, we have meticulously studied **recent question trends** and **curated updated notes** to help you stay ahead.*

***Structured & Easy-to-Understand Format** – Topics are presented in a **logical sequence**, making it easier to grasp complex ideas like **education governance, regulatory frameworks, funding mechanisms, accreditation, and higher education reforms**.*

Chronological Sequencing *– The book* ***systematically arranges historical developments****, ensuring clarity in understanding the* ***timeline of higher education policies*** *and key institutions.*

Extensive Coverage of NEP 2020 *– As the* **National Education Policy (NEP)** ***2020*** *reshapes India's education landscape, this book provides* **detailed** ***insights*** *into its* **vision, implementation, and impact** *on higher education.*

Practice-Oriented Learning *– Each section includes* ***exam-based questions, topic-wise classification, and previous year question discussions****, allowing aspirants to* ***test their knowledge and refine their preparation****.*

With this book, we aim to ***bridge the gap between outdated resources and current exam requirements****. The* **Higher Education System** *is a* **dynamic** *and* ***ever-evolving domain****, and this book ensures that* ***you are well-equipped*** *with* ***accurate, relevant, and up-to-date*** *knowledge.*

Whether you are an ***aspirant, educator, researcher, or policymaker****, this volume will* ***serve as a reliable guide****, providing* ***concise yet impactful learning material****.*

Wishing you all success in your UGC NET journey!

Best Regards,

Ankit Sharma
(Author & Educator)

Unit-X Higher Education System

- Institutions of higher learning and education in ancient India.
- Evolution of higher learning and research in Post Independence India.
- Oriental, Conventional and Non-conventional learning programmes in India.
- Professional, Technical and Skill Based education.
- Value education and environmental education.
- Policies, Governance, and Administration.

CHAPTER I

Institutions of higher learning and education in ancient India

Institutions of higher learning and education in ancient India.

Introduction to Unit X: The Higher Education System in India

The first rays of dawn painted the sky over Nalanda, where scholars once debated under the shade of ancient banyan trees. Here, in the heart of India's intellectual past, seekers from distant lands gathered—not for wealth, not for power, but for knowledge. It was a time when learning was a sacred pursuit, when wisdom flowed like the Ganges, nourishing minds and shaping civilizations.

As centuries passed, empires rose and fell, and the great seats of learning—Takshashila, Vikramashila, and others—became echoes of a glorious past. The arrival of colonial rule brought a new era, one where Western education systems merged with India's deep-rooted traditions. The corridors of institutions like Calcutta University and Banaras Hindu University saw the birth of modern academic thought, a bridge between ancient wisdom and contemporary disciplines.

Independence in 1947 was more than political freedom—it was a chance to reimagine education, to mold a system that could uplift a newly awakened nation. Universities expanded, research institutions flourished, and policies took shape, ensuring that education became a tool of empowerment rather than privilege. But challenges remained: How could India balance its rich heritage with the demands of a rapidly changing world?

This evolution of **higher education in India** is not just a historical study; it is a crucial component of the **UGC NET Paper I syllabus**, where aspirants must understand how education has shaped and been shaped by time. The syllabus delves into key areas such as:

- ***Ancient Institutions of Higher Learning*** – tracing the roots of Indian academia.
- ***Post-Independence Reforms*** – understanding the policies that built modern education.
- ***Conventional and Non-Conventional Learning*** – exploring the diverse modes of knowledge dissemination.
- ***Professional, Technical, and Skill-Based Education*** – analyzing the role of education in workforce development.
- ***Value and Environmental Education*** – recognizing education as a tool for ethical and sustainable progress.
- ***Policies, Governance, and Administration*** – examining the frameworks that sustain academic institutions.

From **traditional Gurukuls to AI-driven classrooms**, from **Vedic studies to professional and technical education**, from **environmental awareness to value-based learning**, India's higher education system is a vast and evolving landscape. Governance and policy decisions continue to shape the destiny of millions of students, while alternative learning models push the boundaries of conventional academia.

For UGC NET aspirants, understanding this journey is not just about passing an exam—it is about engaging with the very foundation of India's academic and research ecosystem. **The Higher Education System in Paper I** is more than a topic; it is an invitation to explore the past, analyze the present, and contribute to the future of learning in India.

This chapter unfolds the **story of India's higher education system**, tracing its journey from the ancient to the modern, from the **Gurukuls of the past to the digital universities of the future**. It is a tale of resilience, adaptation, and the eternal quest for knowledge—a journey that every scholar, every teacher, and every student continue to walk today.

Institutions of higher learning and education in ancient India.

Imagine a time long before smartphones, tablets, or even printed books. A world where knowledge was so revered that it was etched into stones, inscribed on copper plates, and carefully written on delicate palm leaves. India, our very own land, has been a beacon of learning since ancient times, nurturing some of the greatest minds and ideas in human history.

Have you ever wondered how people studied in those distant days? What did their classrooms look like? Did they have textbooks like we do today? How did they decide what to learn, or how were they tested on their knowledge?

In this chapter, we embark on a fascinating journey to uncover the roots of our education system. We'll travel back in time to explore how our ancestors valued and preserved knowledge, passing it down through generations. From ancient inscriptions carved into stone to meticulously handwritten manuscripts, we'll delve into the tools and techniques that shaped learning in a world vastly different from our own.

We'll visit the gurukuls, where students lived and learned under the guidance of their gurus. We'll discover how subjects like mathematics, astronomy, medicine, and philosophy were taught, and how these ancient systems laid the foundation for modern education. Along the way, we'll meet some of the great scholars and teachers who made India a cradle of knowledge.

INTRODUCTION

Close your eyes for a moment and imagine you are a traveller from a distant land. You've heard tales of a mystical place called India—a land of immense wealth, vibrant culture, and profound wisdom. Your curiosity burns brightly, and you set out on a journey to this land of wonder. When you arrive, what you discover surpasses even your wildest dreams.

Welcome to ancient India, where the education system was as legendary as the country itself. Picture this: travelers from far and wide, each hailing from unique climates and cultures, flocked to India, drawn by its reputation as a beacon of knowledge and tradition. What they found was a land where education was not merely about memorizing facts or passing exams—it was about the holistic development of a person, nurturing the mind, body, and soul.

From the time of the Rigveda onwards, India's education system evolved into something extraordinary. It was designed to cultivate not just intellectual prowess but also moral integrity, physical vitality, and spiritual depth. Imagine a system where students were taught to think critically, live harmoniously with nature, and uphold values like humility, truthfulness, discipline, self-reliance, and respect for all living beings.

In those days, education was not confined to the four walls of a classroom or the pages of a textbook. It was everywhere—in the open fields, under the shade of ancient trees, and within the serene spaces of ashrams. The teachings of the Vedas and Upanishads guided students to fulfill their duties—not just to themselves, but to their families, their communities, and the world at large. It was an education that embraced life in its entirety, weaving together the practical and the profound.

Imagine waking up at dawn to meditate, practice yoga, and engage in physical activities to keep your body strong and your mind sharp. Your day would be filled with lessons that explored not only the outer world but also the inner world of thoughts, emotions, and spirituality. You'd be encouraged to discover and nurture your unique talents, whether in music, art, science, or philosophy.

Doesn't this make you wonder how different—and how exciting—learning must have been in those times? The emphasis was on balance: a healthy mind in a healthy body, and a life lived in harmony with the world around you. This rich heritage of pragmatic, holistic education is not just a relic of the past—it is a timeless treasure that continues to inspire us today.

As we journey through this chapter, let us step into the shoes of those ancient learners and explore the roots of an education system that shaped not just individuals, but an entire civilization. Let us rediscover the wisdom of our ancestors and see how it can guide us in our modern lives.

The story of education in ancient India is not just a tale of the past—it is a legacy that lives on, waiting to be uncovered and embraced once more.

SOURCES OF EDUCATION

Imagine a time when learning was not confined to textbooks and examinations but was an immersive journey through the vast wonders of knowledge. In **ancient India**, education was not merely a means to acquire information; it was a profound pursuit of wisdom, deeply rooted in texts like the **Vedas, Brahmanas, Upanishads, and Dharmasutras**. These were not just scriptures—they were reservoirs of philosophical, scientific, and practical knowledge that shaped Indian civilization.

The contributions of scholars like **Aryabhata, Panini, Katyayana, and Patanjali** continue to influence modern academia. Aryabhata, a pioneer in mathematics and astronomy, developed concepts that laid the foundation for advanced studies in these fields. Panini's work in Sanskrit grammar remains unparalleled, while Charaka and Sushruta revolutionized ancient medicine with their treatises on Ayurveda and surgery.

The **curriculum of ancient Indian education** was remarkably diverse, covering subjects such as:

- **Itihasa (History)** - Documenting the past and learning from historical narratives.
- **Anviksiki (Logic and Philosophy)** - Analyzing reasoning and the nature of knowledge.
- **Mimamsa (Interpretation and Inquiry)** - Understanding texts through critical analysis.
- **Shilpashastra (Architecture and Arts)** - Mastering construction techniques and artistic expressions.
- **Arthashastra (Political Science and Economics)** - Governing society with strategic policies.
- **Varta (Agriculture, Trade, and Animal Husbandry)** - Ensuring economic sustainability.
- **Dhanurvidya (Military Science)** - Training in warfare and combat techniques.

Education was holistic, integrating **physical training, sports (Krida), and exercises (Vyayamaprakara)** into daily routines. Students were encouraged to develop physical and mental discipline, with **yoga** serving as a bridge between the two. Unlike today's individualistic learning approaches, ancient Indian education thrived on **interactive discussions, peer learning, and debates (Shastrartha)**, where students tested their knowledge through rigorous intellectual exchanges.

The **Gurukul system**, based on a strong **guru-shishya (teacher-student) tradition**, emphasized personal mentorship, discipline, and moral development. Older students played a vital role in guiding younger learners, fostering a collaborative environment that nurtured wisdom across generations.

This deep-rooted **heritage of higher education** laid the groundwork for India's academic traditions, influencing the evolution of modern institutions and research. Understanding these foundations is essential for **UGC NET aspirants**, as it provides insight into the historical significance and progression of the **higher education system in India**—a topic integral to **Unit X of Paper I**.

Question

In the ancient Indian education system. learners were given training in the following occupations in the fields of-

A. Architecture
B. Animal Hushandary
C. Agriculture
D. Administration
E. Dairy farming

Choose the correct option:

1. ACE
2. BCE
3. ABCE
4. BCDE

Explanations:

Answer: 3. ABCE

In the ancient Indian education system, learners received training in various practical occupations essential for societal development. These fields included architecture, where they learned the principles of building and construction; animal husbandry, focusing on the care and management of livestock; agriculture, covering crop cultivation and farming techniques; and dairy farming, which was a specialized aspect of animal husbandry dealing with the production and management of milk and dairy products. Administration was not typically part of the formal education curriculum, emphasizing instead the practical and vocational training necessary for sustaining community life.

Ancient Indian Treatises

- **Rigveda** – Oldest Vedic text, contains **hymns and rituals**.
- **Yajurveda** – Focuses on **ritual sacrifices and mantras**.
- **Samaveda** – Compilation of **chants and melodies**.
- **Atharvaveda** – Contains **spells, healing practices, and hymns**.
- **Upanishads** – Philosophical texts, basis of **Vedanta philosophy**.
- **Brahmanas** – Commentaries explaining **rituals in Vedas**.
- **Aranyakas** – Bridge between **ritualistic and spiritual teachings**.
- **Bhagavad Gita** – Philosophical discourse in **Mahabharata**.
- **Manusmriti** – Ancient Hindu **law code and ethics**.
- **Arthashastra** – Political and economic treatise by **Chanakya**.
- **Natya Shastra** – Treatise on **drama, dance, and music** by **Bharata Muni**.
- **Charaka Samhita** – Foundational text of **Ayurveda and medicine**.
- **Sushruta Samhita** – Describes **surgical techniques and treatments**.
- **Nyaya Sutras** – Logical and epistemological text by **Gautama**.
- **Mimamsa Sutras** – Discusses **Vedic interpretation and rituals** by **Jaimini**.
- **Lilavati** – **Mathematical treatise** by **Bhaskara II**, covering **arithmetic, algebra, and geometry**.
- **Panchatantra** – Collection of **animal fables and moral stories** by **Vishnu Sharma**.
- **Kathasaritsagara** – Collection of **Indian folk tales and legends** by **Somadeva**.

- **Rajatarangini** – **Historical chronicle of Kashmir**, written by **Kalhana**.
- **Brihat Samhita** – Sanskrit text by **Varahamihira**, covering **astronomy, astrology, and weather science**.
- **Surya Siddhanta** – Ancient **astronomical text** on planetary motion and timekeeping.
- **Vishnu Purana** – One of the **18 Mahapuranas**, discussing **cosmology and mythology**.
- **Shatapatha Brahmana** – Commentary on **Vedic rituals and philosophy**.
- **Garga Samhita** – Sanskrit text on **astronomy and astrology**.
- **Mudrarakshasa** – Political drama by **Vishakhadatta**, narrating **Chandragupta Maurya's rise**.

Question

Which of the following is an ancient Indian treatise on problems related to Mathematics?

(1) Nyaya Sutras
(2) Lilavati
(3) Mimamsã Sutras
(4) Pramanavärttika

Explanations:
Answer: (2) Lilavati

Līlāvatī is a treatise by **Indian mathematician Bhāskara II on mathematics, written in 1150** AD. It is the first volume of his main work, the Siddhānta Shiromani, alongside the Bijaganita, the Grahaganita and the Golādhyāya.

The Nyāya Sūtras is an ancient Indian Sanskrit text composed by **Akṣapāda Gautama**, serving as the foundational text for the Nyaya school of Hindu philosophy. The exact date of its composition and the biography of its author remain unknown, with estimates ranging from the 6th-century **BCE to the 2nd-century CE**. It is possible that the text was composed by multiple authors over time. **The Nyāya Sūtras comprises five books,** each containing two chapters, with a total of 528 aphoristic sutras. **These sutras address rules of reason, logic, epistemology, and metaphysics.**

The Nyāya Sūtras is notable for its focus on knowledge and logic, without mentioning Vedic rituals. The first book provides a general introduction and a table of contents outlining sixteen categories of knowledge. The second book deals with pramana (epistemology), the third book covers prameya (the objects of knowledge), and the remaining books discuss the nature of knowledge. This text established the Nyaya tradition's empirical theory of validity and truth, challenging uncritical reliance on intuition or scriptural authority.

The Mimamsa Sutra (Sanskrit: मीमांसा सूत्र, Mīmāṁsā Sūtra), also known as the Purva Mimamsa Sutras (circa 300–200 BCE), was written by **Rishi Jaimini** and is one of the most significant ancient Hindu philosophical texts. It serves as the foundation for Mimamsa, the earliest of the **six orthodox schools (darshanas) of Indian philosophy.** According to tradition, sage Jaimini was a disciple of sage Veda Vyasa, the author of the Mahabharata.

The Pramāṇavārttika is a Commentary on Valid Cognition; Tib. tshad ma rnam 'grel) is an influential Buddhist text on pramana (valid instruments of knowledge, epistemic criteria), a form of Indian epistemology. The Pramāṇavārttika is the magnum opus of the Indian Buddhist Dharmakirti (floruit 6-7th centuries).

ANCIENT EDUCATION SYSTEM IN INDIA

In **ancient India**, education was a unique blend of **formal and informal learning**, deeply embedded in the cultural and spiritual life of society. Learning was not confined to classrooms; instead, it thrived in **homes, temples, pathshalas (traditional schools), tols, chatuspadis, and gurukuls**. Villages and temple courtyards became vibrant centers of knowledge, where scholars and teachers guided young minds in their pursuit of wisdom.

Temples served a dual purpose—not only as places of worship but also as centers of **education, philosophy, and heritage preservation**. For higher learning, students sought knowledge in **viharas (Buddhist monasteries) and universities**, where scholars engaged in deep discussions and debates. Since teaching was primarily **oral**, students relied on **memory, meditation, and repetition** to internalize complex ideas.

The **Gurukul system**, often set in serene natural environments, provided a **residential learning experience**. These schools, also known as **ashrams**, were typically named after sages or scholars who led them. Life in a **gurukul** was a disciplined yet holistic experience, where students lived with their **guru (teacher)**, shared daily responsibilities, and dedicated themselves to gaining both **intellectual and spiritual wisdom**. In ancient India, there were both formal and informal systems of education. Education here was not restricted to boys; women in the **early Vedic period** also had access to learning, with notable scholars such as **Maitreyi, Viswambhara, Apala, Gargi, and Lopamudra** making significant contributions.

The **guru-shishya (teacher-student) relationship** was the foundation of this educational system. Unlike today's structured curricula, learning was flexible and personalized, focusing on subjects like **history, law, medicine, logic, and debate**. However, education was not merely about acquiring knowledge—it was about shaping one's **character, discipline, and self-awareness**.

For Buddhist monks and nuns, **monasteries (viharas)** became centers of meditation, scholarly discussions, and philosophical exploration. Over time, these viharas evolved into renowned institutions of higher education, attracting students from distant lands, including **China, Korea, Tibet, Burma, Ceylon (Sri Lanka), Java, and Nepal**.

This **ancient education system** laid the foundation for India's **intellectual and philosophical traditions**, influencing future institutions and pedagogical methods. Understanding these systems is crucial for **UGC NET Paper I aspirants**, as it provides key insights into the evolution of India's **higher education system**, a significant component of **Unit X**.

Question

Which of the following subjects were taught in ancient Indian Universities?

A. Journalism
B. Environmental Science
C. Logic
D. Medicine
E. Philosophy

1. ABC
2. BCD
3. CDE
4. ABE

Explanations:
Answer: 3. CDE

Logic – Taught in **Takshashila, Nalanda, and Mithila** (Nyaya philosophy). **Medicine** – Ayurveda and surgery were taught in **Takshashila, Nalanda, and Vikramshila**. **Philosophy** – Buddhist, Jain, and Hindu philosophy were key subjects.

Journalism and **Environmental Science** were **not formal subjects** in ancient universities.

Question

The Buddhist women monks and learners were hailed as:

1. Sanghmitras
2. Sanginis
3. Viharikas
4. Bhikshunis

Explanations:
Answer: 4. Bhikshunis

Bhikshunis – **Female Buddhist monks (nuns)** who followed monastic rules.

- **Sanghmitras** – Refers to **Sanghamitra**, Ashoka's daughter, who spread Buddhism.
- **Sanginis** – General term for **female companions** or **associates**.
- **Viharikas** – **Residents of Buddhist viharas**, not specific to monks.

Question

Statement 1: In ancient India only the informal system of education was in existence.

Statement II: In ancient India the Indigenous education was imparted at home, in temples, pathshalas and gurukulas.

1. Both Statement I and Statement Il are correct.
2. Both Statement I and Statement Il are incorrect.
3. Statement I is correct but Statement Il incorrect.
4. Statement I is incorrect but Statement Il is correct.

Explanations:
Answer: 4. Statement I is incorrect but Statement Il is correct.

Statement I: In ancient India only the informal system of education was in existence.

Incorrect: In ancient India, there were both formal and informal systems of education. Formal education was provided in institutions like temples, pathshalas, and gurukulas, while informal education often took place at home.

Statement II: In ancient India the Indigenous education was imparted at home, in temples, pathshalas, and gurukulas.

Correct: Indigenous education in ancient India was indeed provided in a variety of settings, including at home, in temples, pathshalas (traditional schools), and gurukulas (residential schools).

Therefore, the correct answer is:
4. Statement I is incorrect but Statement II is correct.

Question

Statement I: It is said that in the early Vedic period, women had equal rights to get any type of education.
Statement II: In the last phase of Vedic period, as there were no separate gurukuls for girls of 12 a the age 12 years and above, they could not receive higher education.

1. Both Statement I and Statement Il are true.
2. Both Statement I and Statement Il are false.
3. Statement I is true but Statement Il is false.

4. Statement I is false but Statement Il is true.

Explanations
Answer: 1. Both Statement I and Staterent Il are true

Statement I: It is said that in the early Vedic period, women had equal rights to get any type of education.

True: In the early Vedic period, women had more opportunities and rights to pursue education. Texts from this period indicate that women, especially those who underwent the Upanayana ceremony, could engage in Vedic studies and other educational pursuits.

Statement II: In the last phase of Vedic period, as there were no separate gurukuls for girls of 12 years and above, they could not receive higher education.

True: By the later Vedic period, societal changes led to a decline in the educational opportunities for women. There were no separate gurukuls for older girls, which limited their access to higher education.

Therefore, the correct answer is **Both Statement I and Statement II are true**.

Question

Identify the distinctive feature of traditional method of Indian education from the following list :

1. "Direct perception of truth' - both as means and end
2. Making everything on Trust'
3. Evolving own way of learning
4. Following Nyaya Philosophy with Deductive - Inductive Process

Explanations:
Answer: 1. "Direct perception of truth' - both as means and end

The traditional method of Indian education places a strong emphasis on the direct perception of truth, both as a means and an end. This approach is deeply embedded in the spiritual and philosophical traditions of India, where knowledge is not just about theoretical understanding but about experiencing and realizing the ultimate truths directly. This method is often associated with the practice of meditation, contemplation, and direct experiential learning under the guidance of a guru.

VIHARAS AND UNIVERSITIES

The Indian subcontinent has long been a center of education and intellectual pursuit, with its roots tracing back to the **Indus Valley Civilization**. Throughout history, India was home to some of the world's earliest and most renowned institutions of higher learning. Among the most celebrated were **Takshashila, Kashmir Smast, Nalanda, Valabhi University, Sharada Peeth, Pushpagiri Vihara, Odantapuri University, Vikramashila, Somapura Mahavihara, Bikrampur Vihara, and Jagaddala Mahavihara**. These institutions flourished under the patronage of rulers and scholars who valued knowledge as a cornerstone of civilization.

Historical texts such as the **Jataka Tales** and the travelogues of **Chinese scholars Xuanzang (Hiuen Tsang) and I-Qing (Yijing)** provide fascinating insights into the grandeur of these institutions. These accounts highlight how **kings and society actively supported the advancement of education**, leading to the establishment of renowned centers of learning. Many of these universities, such as **Takshashila, Nalanda, Valabhi, Vikramashila, Odantapuri, and Jagaddala**, emerged around **Buddhist viharas**, serving as monastic learning centers. Others, like the universities in **Benaras, Navadeep, and Kanchi**, grew around **temples**, becoming vital hubs of intellectual and spiritual discourse.

Unlike elementary learning centers, these **ancient universities catered to advanced students**, who engaged in **deep discussions and philosophical debates** with eminent scholars. Education here was not limited to textbooks or lectures; it was a dynamic process that encouraged critical thinking and intellectual exchanges.

In addition to daily academic life, grand scholarly assemblies were often organized by **kings and rulers**, where scholars from different viharas and universities would convene. These gatherings were **intellectual festivals**, filled with spirited debates, exchanges of ideas, and the pursuit of greater understanding. They played a crucial role in shaping the **intellectual and philosophical traditions** of ancient India.

Question

Statement I: According to the ancient Hindu system of Education an aspect of education which is emphasized by the upholders of education in democratic society is that education should be free as far as practicable.
Statement II: According to the ancient Hindu system of education an aspect of education which is emphasized by the upholders of education in democratic society is that education should be compulsory as far as practicable.

1. Both Statement I and Statement Il are true.
2. Both Statement I and Statement Il are false.
3. Statement I is true but Statement Il is false.
4. Statement I is false but Statement Il is true.

Explanations:
Answer: 1. Both Statement I and Statement Il are true.

Statement I is True: In ancient Hindu educational systems, it was common for education to be provided without fees, as the relationship between the guru and shishya (student) was considered sacred, and the education was often supported by public donations.

Statement II is also true: Although the concept of compulsory education as understood in modern democratic societies may not be directly found in ancient texts, the emphasis on the Upanayana rite and the structured educational journey for children indicates a strong societal expectation for education, aligning with the idea of making education accessible and encouraged for all eligible individuals.

Therefore, the correct answer is:
Both Statement I and Statement II are true.

Question

Some of the most notable universities that evolved during the ancient period in India were situated at.

A. Takshashila
B. Vikramshila
C. Jagaddala
D. Odantapuri
E. Nalanda

Choose the correct pair:

1. A B C D and E
2. A B and E only
3. A B C and E only
4. A B D and E only

Explanations:
Answer: 1. A B C D and E

All these universities were significant centers of learning and have been recognized for their contributions to education in ancient India.

Question

Some of the most notable universities that evolved during the ancient period in India were situated at.

A. Takshashila
B. Vikramshila
C. Jagaddala
D. Odantapuri
E. Nalanda

Choose the correct answer from the options given below:

1. A B C D and E
2. A B and E only
3. A B C and E only
4. A B D and E only

Explanations:
Answer: 1. A B C D and E

The ancient period in India saw the evolution of several notable universities, each of which made significant contributions to education and learning:

Takshashila: One of the earliest universities, known for a wide range of subjects including medicine, politics, and military science.

Vikramshila: A major center for Buddhist learning, especially known for its focus on Tantric Buddhism.

Jagaddala: Another important Buddhist center of learning.

Odantapuri: An ancient university in Bihar, known for its Buddhist teachings.

Nalanda: Perhaps the most famous ancient university, renowned for its extensive curriculum and international student body.

TAKSHASHILA OR TAXILA:

- **Ancient Indian** center of **higher learning**
- Flourished until its **destruction (5th century CE)**
- Located in **north-west Pakistan** (present-day)
- Offered studies in **law, medicine, astronomy**
- Taught **military science** and **eighteen arts**
- **Panini, Jivaka, Chanakya** studied here
- **Panini** wrote **Ashtadhyayi** (grammar text)
- **Jivaka** was a famous **ancient physician**
- **Chanakya** wrote **Arthashastra** on statecraft
- Students came from **Kashi, Kosala, Magadha**
- Learning was **oral, discussion-based**
- **Teachers** had complete **academic freedom**
- **Courses ended** when students were **ready**
- Admission was **at teacher's discretion**
- **Advanced students** assisted in **teaching**
- **UNESCO World Heritage Site (1980)**
- Ruins discovered by **Alexander Cunningham**
- **Major archaeological site** of ancient India
- Teachers designed **custom courses** for students

- **Debate and discussions** were teaching methods

Important Teachers:

- **Panini**: The great 5th century BCE Indian grammarian.
- **Chanakya**: The influential Prime Minister of Chandragupta Maurya, founder of the Mauryan Empire.
- **Kumāralāta**: According to the 3rd century Chinese Buddhist monk and traveler Yuan Chwang, Kumāralāta founded the Sautrāntika school.
- **Vasubandhu**: Founder of Tibetan Buddhism, with famous pupils like Dharmakirti and Dignaga.

Important Students:

- **King Pasenadi of Kosala:** A close friend of the Buddha.
- **Jivaka**: Court doctor at Rajagriha and personal doctor of the Buddha.
- **Charaka**: The "father of medicine" in India and a leading authority in Ayurveda.
- **Chandragupta Maurya:** The future founder of the Mauryan Empire.

Chandragupta Maurya, the future **founder of the Mauryan Empire**, is believed to have received his education at **Takshashila** under **Chanakya (Kautilya)**. According to **Buddhist literature**, Chandragupta was born near **Patna (Bihar)** in **Magadha**, but **Chanakya took him to Takshashila** for formal training.

At Takshashila, he studied **various sciences, arts, and military strategies** for **eight years**, preparing for his future role as a ruler. Both **Greek and Hindu texts** support the claim that **Chanakya, originally from the northwest Indian subcontinent**, mentored Chandragupta at this renowned center of learning. This account aligns with **Plutarch's** assertion that **Alexander the Great** encountered the young Chandr Gupta during his **Punjab campaign**.

Question

Which amongst the following is not a Buddhist monastic University?

1. Nalanda
2. Takshashila
3. Vikramshila
4. Odantpuri

Explanations:
Answer: 2. Takshashila

Takshashila – **Not a Buddhist monastic university**, but an **ancient learning center** (600 BCE) covering various disciplines, including Vedic and secular education.

- **Nalanda** – Major **Buddhist monastic university** (5th–12th century CE).
- **Vikramshila** – Established by **Pala rulers**, focused on Buddhist education.
- **Odantpuri** – Another **Buddhist monastic university** in Bihar.

Question

Match the column:

List I (Ancient University)	List II (Well-known Student)
A. Takshasila	(I) Nagarjuna
B. Nalanda	(Il) Gangesha Upadhyaya
C. Mithila	(III) Kumarajeeva
D. Sharadapeeth	(IV) Chanakya

1. A-I B-II C-III D-IV
2. A-II B-III C-IV D-I
3. A-I|I B-IV C-I D-II
4. A-IV B-I C-II D-III

Explanations:
Answer: A-IV B-I C-II D-III

A. Takshashila → IV. Chanakya (Studied politics and authored *Arthashastra*).
B. Nalanda → I. Nagarjuna (Philosopher of Mahayana Buddhism, developed Sunyata).

C. Mithila → II. Gangesha Upadhyaya (Scholar of Nyaya philosophy, *Tattvachintamani*).
D. Sharadapeeth → III. Kumarajeeva (Buddhist scholar, translated Sanskrit texts into Chinese).

Question

Which of the following statements are true regarding Takshashila?

A. The great grammarian Panini had his education there.
B. Kautilya was a learner there
C. It had its gates open to all providing free education
D. Students had to pay for their education

1. BD
2. ABC
3. AD
4. ABD

Explanations:
Answer: 4. ABD

- **Panini** studied at **Takshashila**, where he developed **Sanskrit grammar** (*Ashtadhyayi*).
- **Kautilya (Chanakya)** studied and taught there, later advising **Chandragupta Maurya**.
- **Students had to pay** for their education, as there was no system of free education.

It did not provide free education to all; students paid fees based on their learning.

Question

Match the column:

A. Takshila	I. Tantric Buddhism
B. Nalanda	II. Brahminical centre of learning
C. Vikramshila	III. Principle seats of Sanskrit learning
D. Benares and Navadwib	IV. Buddhist centre of learning

1. A-IV B-III C-II D-I
2. A-I B-II C-III D-IV
3. A-III B-I C-IV D-II
4. A-II B-IV C-I D-III

Explanations:
Answer: 4. A-II B-IV C-I D-III

A. Takshashila → II. Brahminical centre of learning: Ancient university offering **Vedic studies, medicine, law, and military science**.

B. Nalanda → IV. Buddhist centre of learning: A **major Buddhist monastic university** (5th–12th century CE).

C. Vikramshila → I. Tantric Buddhism: Established by **Dharampala (Pala dynasty)**, focused on **Vajrayana Buddhism**.

D. Benares and Navadwip → III. Principal seats of Sanskrit learning Centers for Sanskrit, Hindu philosophy, and classical learning.

Question

Arrange the following chronologically according to their year of foundation:

A. Takshashila
B. Vikramshila
C. Nalanda
D. Pushpagiri
E. Navadwip

1. ABCDE
2. ADCBE
3. ECBDA
4. BDAEC

Explanations:
Answer: 3. ECBDA

- **Takshashila (600 BCE)** – Ancient Brahminical learning center.

- **Nalanda (5th Century CE)** – Buddhist monastic university.
- **Vikramshila (8th Century CE)** – Tantric Buddhist education center.
- **Pushpagiri (3rd–11th Century CE)** – Buddhist Mahavihara in Odisha.
- **Navadwip (11th–12th Century CE)** – Sanskrit and Hindu learning hub.

Question

Takshashila is an important archaeological site and UNESCO declared it to a world Heritage Site in the year

1. 1980
2. 1990
3. 1992
4. 1978

Explanations:
Answer: 1. 1980

Takshashila, also known as Taxila, is an important archaeological site located in modern-day Pakistan. It was declared a UNESCO World Heritage Site in the year 1980.

Question

At which of the following ancient places of higher learning did the famous royal physician Jivaka, who had cured the king Bimbisara study?

1. Takshashila
2. Kanchi
3. Jayender Vihar
4. Vallabhi

Explanations:
Answer: 1. Takshashila

The famous royal physician Jivaka, who cured King Bimbisara, studied at Takshashila. Takshashila (Taxila) was one of the most renowned centers of learning in ancient India, attracting students from various regions for its diverse curriculum, including medicine.

Question

Who among the following are said to have had their education at Takshashilla?

A. Sri Chaitanya
B. Panini
C. Nagarjuna
D. Chanakya

Choose the correct answer from the options given below:

1. (A) and (C) only.
2. (B), (C) and (D) only.
3. (A), (B) and (C) only.
4. (B) and (D) only.

Explanations:
Answer: 4. (B) and (D) only.

Takshashila, also known as Taxila, was an ancient center of learning where many notable scholars received their education. Among those listed, Panini and Chanakya are said to have had their education at Takshashila.

Panini: The renowned Sanskrit grammarian who authored the Ashtadhyayi.
Chanakya: Also known as Kautilya, he was a teacher, philosopher, and royal advisor, best known for his work "Arthashastra."

Sri Chaitanya and Nagarjuna were not associated with Takshashila.

Question

The oldest university in India was:

1. Nalanda
2. Takshashila
3. Vikramshila

4. Mithila

Explanations:
Answer: 2. Takshashila

The oldest university in India is Takshashila (Taxila). It is considered one of the earliest centers of higher learning in the world, dating back to at least the 5th century BCE, if not earlier. It attracted students from across India and beyond, offering a diverse curriculum that included subjects like medicine, law, military science, and politics.

Question

In ancient India, the eligibility criterion in respect of age for students seeking admission to Takshashila University was set at

1. 22 years
2. 20 years
3. 18 years
4. 16 years

Explanations:
Answer: 4. 16 years

In ancient India, the eligibility criterion in respect of age for students seeking admission to Takshashila University was typically set at 16 years. This was the age when students were considered mature enough to undertake higher education in various subjects such as medicine, law, military science, and politics.

Question

Statement I: Reputed scholars like Panini and Chanakya had their education from Nalanda university
Statement II: Thakshashila was a university known for its education in Indian arts and science especially medicine.

In the light of the above statements, choose the correct answer from the options given below:

1. Both Statement I and Statement I are true

2. Both Statement I and Statement II are false
3. Statement I is true but Statement II is false
4. Statement I is false but Statement II is true

Explanations:
Answer: 4. Statement I is false but Statement II is true

Statement is False: Panini and Chanakya were educated at Takshashila, not Nalanda. Takshashila was known for its diverse curriculum, including grammar and statecraft, which were the fields of Panini and Chanakya, respectively.

Statement II is True: Takshashila (Taxila) was indeed a renowned center for various fields of study including arts, sciences, and especially medicine. Notable scholars like Jivaka, Panini, and Chanakya are associated with Takshashila.

NALANDA UNIVERSITY

- **Nalanda** was an **ancient center of higher learning**.
- Also known as **Nala**, it gained global fame.
- **Xuan Zang** visited in the **7th century CE**.
- **I-Qing and Xuan Zang** documented its history.
- Daily **100+ discourses** through debates/discussions.
- **Shilabhadra** was its chancellor and **yoga authority**.
- Curriculum included **Vedas, arts, medicine, and math**.
- **Astronomy, politics, and warfare** were also taught.
- Located in **Magadha** (modern-day **Bihar**).
- Recognized as a **Mahavihara** (great monastery).
- Established in the **4th century CE**.
- Flourished from **5th century to 1200 CE**.
- Played a key role in **India's intellectual history**.
- Attracted scholars from **China, Korea, Tibet, Persia**.
- **Xuan Zang** studied **Yogashastra** at Nalanda.
- Known for its **strict admission standards**.
- Destroyed by **Bakhtiyar Khilji in 1200 CE**.
- Rediscovered in the **19th century** by archaeologists.
- Declared a **UNESCO World Heritage Site (2009)**.
- Considered one of the **world's greatest universities.**

Question

Statement (I) : The Nalanda University of ancient India attracted students from various parts of Asia.
Statement (Il) : The Nalanda University was overshadowed by the universities in Europe and Arabia immediately after its establishment.

In the light of the above statements, choose the correct answer from the options given below:

1. Both Statement I and Statement Il are correct.
2. Both Statement I and Statement Il are incorrect.
3. Statement I is correct but Statement Il is incorrect.
4. Statement l is incorrect but Statement Il is correct.

Explanations:
Answer: 3. Statement I is correct but Statement Il is incorrect.

Statement I is Correct: Nalanda University was a major center of learning in ancient India and attracted students from various parts of Asia, including China, Korea, Japan, Tibet, Mongolia, Turkey, Sri Lanka, and Southeast Asia.

Statement II is Incorrect: Nalanda University thrived as a prominent center of learning for many centuries before the rise of significant universities in Europe and Arabia. It was not immediately overshadowed by these institutions; instead, it continued to be a leading educational institution until its decline.

Question

Statements I: In Ancient times, Nalanda attained greatest and most brilliant achievements in the field of logic.
Statement II: Each professor in Nalanda had charge of one subject only.

In the light of the above statements, choose the correct answer from the options given below:

1. Both Statement I and Statement Il are correct
2. Both Statement I and Statement Il are incorrect
3. Statement I is correct but Statement Il is incorrect
4. Statement I is incorrect but Statement Il is correct

Explanations:
Answer: 1. Both Statement I and Statement II are correct

Statement I is Correct: Nalanda University was renowned for its contributions to various fields of study, including logic (Nyaya), which was a significant area of achievement and scholarship.

Statement II is Correct: In the Nalanda system, it was common for professors to specialize and take charge of a specific subject, ensuring in-depth knowledge and expertise in that particular area.

Question

Statement I: Curriculum at Taxila was varied and included technical sciences.
Statement II: Curriculum of Nalanda excluded technical sciences.

In the light of the above statements, choose the correct answer from the options given below:

1. Both Statement I and Statement II are correct
2. Both Statement I and Statement II are incorrect
3. Statement I is correct but Statement II is incorrect
4. Statement I is incorrect but Statement II is correct

Explanations:
Answer: 1. Both Statement I and Statement II are correct

Statement I is Correct: Taxila (Takshashila) was known for its diverse curriculum that included various subjects such as medicine, politics, warfare, astronomy, and technical sciences.

Statement II is Correct: Nalanda was primarily focused on Buddhist studies, philosophy, logic, metaphysics, and religious scriptures. It did not emphasize technical sciences to the extent that Taxila did.

Question

University of the ancient period which has been declared by UNESCO as a heritage site is:

A. Mithila
B. Vallabhi
C. Pushpagiri
D. Takshashila
E. Nalanda

Choose the correct pair:

1. A and B only
2. B and C only
3. C and D only
4. D and E only

Explanations:
Answer: 4. D and E only

Among the universities listed, the ones that have been declared UNESCO World Heritage Sites are:

- Takshashila (Taxila)
- Nalanda

Both of these ancient universities have been recognized by UNESCO for their historical
significance and contributions to education.

A. Mithila- The headquarter of the Ancient Mithila University was at the court of King Janaka in Mithila. Therefore, Balirajgadh is also the possible site of the Ancient Mithila University.

B. Vallabhi- Valabhi was the capital of the Maitraka empire from 480-775 CE and served as a vital international trade port located in **Saurashtra (now Vallabhipur in Bhavnagar district, Gujarat).**

C. Pushpagiri - Pushpagiri (Odia: ପୁଷ୍ପଗିରି) was an ancient Indian mahavihara or monastic complex located atop Langudi Hill (or Hills) in Jajpur district of Odisha, India.

D. Takshashila - Located in what is now north-western Pakistan, Takshashila was not just an educational hub but also an important archaeological site. **UNESCO declared it a World Heritage Site in 1980.**

E. Nalanda - Located in the ancient kingdom of Magadha, which is modern-day Bihar,
Today, it's recognized as a UNESCO World Heritage Site on January 9th, 2009.

Question

Given below are two statements:

Statement I: Universities of Nalanda, Taxsila and Vikramshila of ancient India are now
all located in the Indian Territory.
Statement II: The entrance test of its own kind was prevalent in the ancient seats of
learning of India.

In the light of the above statements, choose the most appropriate answer from the options given below:

1. Both Statement I and Statement II are correct
2. Both Statement I and Statement II are incorrect
3. Statement I is correct but Statement II is incorrect
4. Statement I is incorrect but Statement II is correct

Explanations:
Answer: 4. Statement I is incorrect but Statement II is correct

Statement I is Incorrect: While Nalanda and Vikramshila are located in present-day India, Taxila (Takshashila) is located in present-day Pakistan.

Statement II is Correct: Ancient seats of learning like Nalanda and Vikramshila had rigorous entrance examinations to ensure that only the most qualified students were admitted.

Question

Which of the following modes of admission was prevalent in Nalanda University in ancient

1. Entrance Examination
2. Good Academic Credentials
3. Interview
4. Peer Discussion

Explanations:
Answer: 1. Entrance Examination

In ancient Nalanda University, a rigorous entrance examination was required for admission. This process was designed to ensure that only the most capable and knowledgeable students were admitted. The entrance examination tested various aspects of the students' prior knowledge and understanding, making it a selective and competitive process.

Mithila University

- **Mithila University** was famous for **Nyaya Sutra**.
- Specialized in **logical sciences and philosophy**.
- Originated from **philosophical conferences** in Mithila.
- Established by **Seeradhwaja Janaka**, an **Ikshwaku king**.
- **Janaka** was the father of **Goddess Sita**.
- Mentioned in the **Ramayana** as Sita's father.
- **Kingdom of Videha** was in **Mithila region**.
- Janaka's real name was **Seeradhwaja**.
- Had a **brother, Kushadhwaja**, in Videha dynasty.
- Their father **Hrasvaroman** descended from **King Nimi**.
- Mithila was a **hub of intellectual discourse**.
- Evolved into a **renowned center of learning**.
- Focused on **logic, reasoning, and philosophy**.
- Contributed to the **development of Nyaya philosophy**.
- Became a **significant seat of Indian education**.

Valabhi University

- **Valabhi University** was a **Buddhist learning center**.

- Promoted **Hinayana Buddhism (600–1200 CE)**.
- Located in **Saurashtra (Vallabhipur, Gujarat)**.
- **Capital of Maitraka Empire (480–775 CE)**.
- Served as an **important international trade port**.
- **Rivaled Nalanda University** in educational excellence.
- Attracted **students from India and abroad**.
- Known for **Buddhist and secular studies**.
- **Destroyed around the 12th century CE**.
- In **2017, plans emerged for its revival**.

Sharada Peeth

- **Sharada Peeth** was a **Hindu temple university**.
- Located in **Pakistan-administered Jammu and Kashmir**.
- Flourished between the **6th–12th centuries CE**.
- One of the **major temple universities** in India.
- Had an **impressive library with rare texts**.
- Attracted **scholars from across the subcontinent**.
- Played a key role in **popularizing the Sharada script**.
- Known for **academic excellence and Sanskrit studies**.
- **Vaishnava saint Ramanuja** studied here (11th century).
- Ramanuja wrote **Sri Bhasya** after studying Brahma Sutras.
- **Jain scholar Hemachandra** needed texts for his work.
- **Prabhāvakacarita** records Hemachandra's request.
- Hemachandra needed **eight Sanskrit grammar texts**.
- **King Jayasimha Siddharaja** retrieved the texts for him.
- **Sharada Peeth library housed complete rare texts**.
- Considered one of the **greatest centers of learning**.
- Connected scholars from **India, Nepal, and Tibet**.
- One of **three holiest sites** for Kashmiri Hindus.
- **Now in ruins**, but historically significant.
- Efforts have been made to **revive its legacy**.

Important Students

- **Vaṭeśvara**
    - **10th-century Indian mathematician** known for **trigonometric identities**.

  - Wrote **Vaṭeśvara-siddhānta (904 AD)** on **astronomy and applied mathematics**.
- **Kumarajiva**
  - Born to a **Kashmiri father** and a **Chinese mother**.
  - Studied **Buddhism in Kashmir** under a **Sarvastivada scholar**.
- **Thonmi Sambhota**
  - **7th-century Tibetan scholar** sent to **Kashmir** for linguistic studies.
  - Created the **Tibetan script**, influenced by the **Sharada alphabet**.
- **Rinchen Zangpo**
  - **Translator of Sanskrit Buddhist texts** into **Tibetan**.
  - Studied at **Sharada Peeth**, mastering **Sanskrit scriptures**.
- **Kalhana Pandit:**
  - The famous Kashmiri historian.
- **Adi Shankara:**
  - The renowned Hindu philosopher also studied here.

Pushpagiri Vihara

- **Pushpagiri** was an **ancient Buddhist Mahavihara**.
- Located atop **Langudi Hill, Jajpur district, Odisha**.
- Mentioned by **Chinese traveler Xuanzang (602–664 CE)**.
- Initially thought to be part of **Lalitgiri-Ratnagiri-Udayagiri**.
- **Excavations (1996–2006)** revealed its true location.
- Inscriptions referred to it as **"Puṣpa Sabhar Giriya."**
- Confirmed as **Pushpagiri by modern scholars**.
- The site contains **ruins of stupas and monasteries**.
- **Artifacts, sculptures, and inscriptions** were discovered.
- **Flourished from the 3rd to 11th centuries CE**.
- Ranked among **India's major Buddhist learning centers**.
- Comparable to **Nalanda, Vikramashila, and Takshashila**.
- Now a **protected site and tourist attraction**.
- Played a key role in **Buddhist education and culture**.
- Artifacts from **Pushpagiri are preserved in museums**.

Odantapuri University

- **Odantapuri (Odantapura/Uddandapura)** was a **Buddhist Mahavihara**.
- Located in **Magadha (modern Bihar, India)**.
- **Founded by Gopala I** in the **8th century CE**.
- Considered **India's second-oldest Mahavihara** after **Nalanda**.
- A **major center of Buddhist learning** in ancient India.
- Attracted **scholars and students from distant regions**.
- **Flourished under the Pala dynasty's patronage**.
- Had a **large monastic complex with stupas and temples**.
- **Destroyed in the 12th century CE** by Bakhtiyar Khilji.
- Played a **key role in spreading Buddhist philosophy**.

Question

Which of the following universities have their locations in Bihar?

A. Vallabhi
B. Vikramshila
C. Shridhanya katak
D. Odantapuri

Choose the correct answer from the options given below:

1. AD
2. BD
3. AB
4. BC

Explanations:
Answer: 2. BD

Among the listed universities, those that are located in Bihar are:

Vikramshila: An ancient university located in Bihar, known for its emphasis on Tantric Buddhism.

Odantapuri: Another ancient university located in Bihar, which was an important center of learning in ancient India.

Vallabhi and Shridhanya Katak are not located in Bihar.

Vikramashila

- **Vikramashila** was a **major center of learning** under the **Pala Empire**.
- Located in **Antichak village, Bhagalpur district, Bihar**.
- **Founded by Emperor Dharmapala (783–820 AD)**.
- Established due to a **decline in Nalanda's scholarship**.
- **Atiśa**, a renowned **Buddhist pandita**, was an abbot.
- Specialized in **Buddhist philosophy and tantric teachings**.
- Attracted **scholars from India, Tibet, and beyond**.
- Had a **large monastic complex with temples and stupas**.
- **Destroyed in 1193** by **Muhammad bin Bakhtiyar Khalji**.
- Considered one of **India's greatest Buddhist universities**.

Question

The University of Vikramasila was a well-known centre of-

1. Arabic language
2. Chinses philosophy
3. Tantric Buddhism
4. Japanese Art

Explanations:
Answer: 3. Tantric Buddhism

The University of Vikramashila was a renowned center of learning in ancient India, primarily known for its emphasis on Tantric Buddhism. It was one of the major centers of Buddhist learning alongside Nalanda, specializing in the teachings and practices related to Vajrayana or Tantric Buddhism.

Question

Vikramashila was a renowned centre of-

1. Physical education
2. Pictorial art

3. Tantric Buddhism
4. Culinary art

Explanations:
Answer: 3. Tantric Buddhism

Question

Statement (I): The monastery of Vikramasila, possessed a University with six colleges.
Statement (II): Vikramasila was a well-known centre of Tantric Buddhism and attracted students from other countries.

In the light of the above statements, choose the correct answer from the options given below:

1. Both Statement I and Statement Il are correct
2. Both Statement I and Statement Il are incorrect
3. Statement I is correct but Statement Il is incorrect
4. Statement I is incorrect but Statement Il is correct

Explanations:
Answer: 1. Both Statement I and Statement Il are correct

Statement I is Correct: Vikramashila was indeed a significant center of learning, and historical accounts mention that it had six colleges, each specializing in different subjects.

Statement II is Correct: Vikramashila was renowned for its teachings in Tantric Buddhism and attracted scholars and students from various regions, including other countries.

Question

Which of the following universities have their locations in Bihar?

A. Vallabhi
B. Vikramshita
C. Shridhanya katak
D. Odantapuri

Choose the correct pair from the given option below:

1. AD
2. BD
3. AB
4. BC

Explanations:
Answer: 2. BD

A. **Vallabhi:** Located in Gujarat.
B. **Vikramashila:** Located in Bihar.
C. **Shridhanya katak:** Not a known historical university, possibly a distractor.
D. **Odantapuri:** Located in Bihar.

Therefore, the correct pair of universities located in Bihar is: **2. BD**

Bikrampur Vihara

- **Bikrampur Vihara** was an **ancient Buddhist monastery**.
- Located in **Raghurampur village, Munshiganj, Bangladesh**.
- A **significant center of Buddhist learning** in Bengal.
- Associated with **Buddhist scholars and monks**.
- **Archaeological excavations** have revealed its ruins.

Jagaddala Mahavihara

- **Jagaddala Mahavihara** was a **Buddhist monastery and learning center**.
- Flourished between the **late 11th to mid-12th century**.
- Located in **Varendra (modern north Bengal, Bangladesh)**.
- **Founded by Pala king Ramapala (c. 1077–1120)**.
- Situated near **Jagdal village, Dhamoirhat Upazila**.
- Close to the **Bangladesh-India border near Paharpur**.
- Some texts spell it as **Jaggadala**.
- A major **center for Mahayana Buddhist studies**.
- Part of the **five great Mahaviharas** under the Palas.
- **Destroyed during the 12th century invasions**.

Other Centers:

There were many other significant centers of learning, such as Telhara in Bihar, which is probably older than Nalanda, and Kanchipuram in Tamil Nadu. Other notable centers included **Manyakheta in Karnataka**, **Ujjain in Madhya Pradesh**, **Nagarjunakonda in Andhra Pradesh, and Varanasi in Uttar Pradesh,** which has been a center of learning from the eighth century to modern times. Additionally, Abhayagiri Vihāra and Jetavanaramaya in Sri Lanka were also prominent educational centers.

Gurukula:

A **gurukula** (or **gurukulam**) was a **residential education system** in **ancient India**, where students (**śiṣyas** or disciples) lived with their **guru** (teacher). Unlike modern schools, education in a **gurukula** was not limited to classrooms but was an **immersive experience**, emphasizing **holistic learning, discipline, and spiritual growth**.

The word **"gurukula"** comes from **Sanskrit**, combining **"guru" (teacher)** and **"kula" (family/home)**, signifying that students were not just learners but members of the guru's household. This tradition is referenced in **the Upanishads (1000–800 BCE)**, which mention various **gurukulas**, such as the one led by **Guru Drona in Gurgaon**. Another example is the **Bhrigu Valli**, a discourse on **Brahman** that took place at **Guru Varuni's gurukula**.

Structure and Learning in Gurukulas

- **Admission Age:** According to **Vedic tradition**, children joined a **gurukula** before the age of **8 or by 12** and remained students until 25.
- **Subjects Taught:** Students studied **Vedas, philosophy, grammar, mathematics, medicine, astronomy, and military science**, depending on the guru's expertise.
- **Holistic Training:** Learning was not just academic but included **self-discipline, humanism, politeness, and spirituality**.
- **Practical Education:** Students helped with **daily household chores**, which taught **responsibility and humility**.

Role of the Guru and Student-Guru Relationship

The **guru** was a **revered figure**, and the **student-guru relationship** was considered **sacred**. Unlike modern education, **gurus did not charge fees**, as **education was seen as a noble duty rather than a profession**. Instead, students offered **guru dakshina** at the end of their studies—a **gesture of gratitude**, which could be **monetary, a special service, or fulfilling a task assigned by the guru**.

Public Support and Legacy

Gurukulas were often **supported by donations from the public**, making them **one of the earliest forms of public education**. Students lived away from home for **years**, fully dedicating themselves to **learning and self-improvement**. This system laid the foundation for **India's traditional education model**, influencing later learning institutions and **monastic schools**.

Though the **gurukula system declined**, its **philosophy of immersive education, discipline, and respect for teachers** continues to inspire **modern residential schools and monastic learning traditions**.

- **Gurukula** was an **ancient Indian education system**.
- Students (**śiṣyas**) lived with their **guru**.
- Education was **holistic, practical, and spiritual**.
- The word **gurukula** means **"teacher's home"**.
- Mentioned in **Upanishads (1000–800 BCE)**.
- **Guru Drona's** gurukula was in **Gurgaon**.
- **Bhrigu Valli** discourse occurred at **Guru Varuni's**.
- Students joined **before 8 or by 12**.
- Stayed until **age 25 for learning**.
- Subjects included **Vedas, medicine, astronomy, war**.
- Learning involved **debates, practical work, discipline**.
- Education was **free; no fixed fees**.
- **Guru dakshina** was given after studies.
- Supported by **public donations and patronage**.
- Influenced **modern monastic and residential schools**.

Question

Given below are two statements:

Statement I: In ancient India, education was free
Statement II: In ancient India, education was centralized

In light of the above statements, choose the most appropriate answer from the options given below:

1. Both Statement I and Statement II are correct.
2. Both Statement I and Statement II are incorrect.
3. Statement I is correct but Statement II is incorrect.
4. Statement I is incorrect but Statement II is correct.

Explanations:
Answer: 3. Statement I is correct but Statement II is incorrect.

Statement I: In ancient India, education was free.

This statement is generally considered true. In ancient India, education was often provided free of charge or at very minimal costs. Education was seen as a noble pursuit, and it was considered a responsibility of the society to provide education to all individuals, irrespective of their socio-economic background.

Statement II: In ancient India, education was centralized.

This statement is not correct. In ancient India, education was decentralized and varied across different regions and kingdoms. There were multiple centers of learning and educational institutions across the country. Some famous centers of education included Takshashila, Nalanda, and Vikramshila, among others. These centers of learning attracted students and scholars from various parts of the Indian subcontinent and beyond. Education was not controlled or centralized under a single authority.

Therefore, while Statement I is correct, Statement II is incorrect.

Question

The purpose of Gurukul system of education is to

1. Promote equality and excellence
2. Empowering for future learning

3. Minimise stress in learning
4. Encourage self-help

Explanations:
Answer: 1. Promote equality and excellence

The Gurukul system of education in ancient India was designed to promote holistic development, emphasizing the values of equality, excellence, and character building. Students from various social backgrounds lived together in the Gurukul (a residential schooling system), learning not just academic subjects but also life skills, moral values, and practical knowledge under the guidance of a guru (teacher). This environment fostered a sense of equality among students and aimed for excellence in all aspects of life, including academics, physical health, and moral integrity.

Upanayana

- **Upanayana** is a **Hindu educational sacrament**.
- Marks **acceptance of a student by a guru**.
- A **traditional saṃskāra (rite of passage)**.
- Considered a **spiritual rebirth** for the student.
- Transforms a child into a **dvija (twice-born)**.
- Begins the **brahmacharya (student) stage of life**.
- Represents **commitment to education and discipline**.
- Associated with **learning the Vedas and scriptures**.
- Mainly performed for **Brahmin, Kshatriya, Vaishya boys**.
- Symbolizes **spiritual growth and pursuit of knowledge**.

Question

Statement I: The Upanayana ceremony which marked the initiation of a child into a study of the Vedas was performed for boys as well as for girls.
Statement II: Both boys and girls received education in Ashrams' and 'Gurukulas' in ancient India.

1. Both Statement I and Staterent II are true
2. Both Statement I and Statement II are false
3. Statement I is true but Statement II is false
4. Statement I is false but Statement II is true

Explanations
Answer: 1. Both Statement I and Staterent Il are true

Statement I: The Upanayana ceremony which marked the initiation of a child into a study of the Vedas was performed for boys as well as for girls.

True: In some regions and texts from ancient and medieval times, such as the Harita Dharmasutras, Asvalayana Grhya Sutra, and Yama Smriti, it is suggested that girls could also undergo the Upanayana rite and begin Vedic studies. These girls were called Brahmavadini.

Statement II: Both boys and girls received education in Ashrams and Gurukulas in ancient India.

True: Although it was more common for boys to receive education in Ashrams and Gurukulas, there are references in ancient texts indicating that girls, particularly those who underwent the Upanayana ceremony, also had access to education. Girls who did not go to a Gurukula were called Sadyovadhu and underwent a symbolic Upanayana during wedding rituals.

Therefore, both statements reflect the historical nuances and are true.

Question

In the age of four Vedas, students were admitted to the Vedic schools after the performance of which ceremony, among the following:

1. Upanayana ceremony
2. Utsarjana ceremony
3. Satapatha ceremony
4. Dhanurvidya ceremony

Explanations:
Answer: 1. Upanayana ceremony

In the age of the four Vedas, students were admitted to the Vedic schools after the **performance of the Upanayana ceremony.** Upanayana is an important initiation ceremony in Hinduism, also known as the sacred thread ceremony. It marks the formal beginning of the student's education and signifies their readiness to receive Vedic education. During the

Upanayana ceremony, a sacred thread called the "Yajnopavita" is worn by the student, symbolizing their initiation into the study of the Vedas. This ceremony is typically performed during childhood or early adolescence and is considered a significant milestone in a person's spiritual and educational journey.

Patanjali Yogpeeth

- **Patanjali Yogpeeth** is a **yoga institute in Haridwar**.
- Founded in **2006 by Ramdev and Balkrishna**.
- Named after **sage Rishi Patanjali**.
- Focuses on **yoga, Ayurveda, and research**.
- Includes a **hospital, pharmacy, and trusts**.
- Home to **University of Patanjali and Yog Gram**.
- Balkrishna is the **General Secretary**.
- **Ramdev is the Vice-Chancellor**.
- Aims to **promote yoga and traditional medicine**.
- A major center for **Ayurvedic research and practice**.

Acharyakulam

- **Acharyakulam** is a **residential school in Haridwar**.
- Combines **Vedic and modern education**.
- Open for **students from grades 5 to 12**.
- **Affiliated with CBSE (Central Board of Secondary Education)**.
- Located near **Patanjali Yogpeeth**.
- Inaugurated on **April 26, 2013**.
- Opened by **Narendra Modi (then Gujarat CM)**.
- Focuses on **spiritual and intellectual growth**.
- Promotes **Indian culture and traditional knowledge**.
- Encourages **holistic education and self-discipline**.

Question

Given below are two statements:

Statement I: Holistic education in ancient India was not just about the acquisition of knowledge or preparation for life in this world and beyond, but also for the complete realization and liberation of the self.

Statement II : Values of pluralism, mutual understanding and peace constituted the foundation of holistic education during ancient education.

In the light of the above statements, choose the correct answer from the options given below:

1. Both Statement I and Statement II are true
2. Both Statement I and Statement Il are false
3. Statement I is correct but Statement II is false
4. Statement I is incorrect but Statement II is true

Explanations:
Answer: 1. Both Statement I and Statement II are true

Statement I is True: In ancient India, education aimed at the overall development of an individual, focusing not just on intellectual growth but also on spiritual realization and self-liberation.

Statement II is True: Ancient Indian education emphasized values like pluralism, mutual understanding, and peace, which were integral to the holistic educational approach.

Ancient Thinkers

Panini

- **Sanskrit grammarian** who structured the language.
- Developed **scientific phonetics, phonology, and morphology**.
- Wrote **Ashtadhyayi**, a comprehensive grammar treatise.
- Considered the **founder of Sanskrit's structured form**.
- Influenced **linguistics and grammar studies worldwide**.

Bhartrihari

- **Renowned grammarian and philosopher** of language.
- Known for **Speech Theory (Vakyapadiya)**.
- Explored **grammar, logic, and semantics**.
- Divided speech into **four stages of expression**.

- Linked **language to metaphysical and cognitive processes**.

Question

Match the column:

List I (Authors)	List II (Treatises)
A. Panini	I. Mahabhasya
B. Bhatrhari	Il. Vaishishika-Sutras
C. Kanada	III. Vakyapadiya
D. Patanjali	IV. Ashtashyayi

Choose the correct answer:

1. A-IV B-II C-III D-I
2. A-IV B-III C-II D-I
3. A-III B-IV C-II D-I
4. A-IV B-III C-I D-II

Explanations:
Answer: 2. A-IV B-III C-II D-I

A. Panini - IV. Ashtadhyayi
B. Bhatrhari - III. Vakyapadiya
C. Kanada - II. Vaisheshika-Sutras
D. Patanjali - I. Mahabhasya

Question

Who among the following ancient scholars was a proponent of grammarian tradition?

1. Ishwar Krishna
2. Bhartrhari
3. Gautama
4. Kanada

Explanations:
Answer: 2. Bhartrhari

Kapila

- Founder of **Sankhya philosophy** in Hindu tradition.
- **Emphasized Vedic supremacy** and spiritual knowledge.
- Explained **concepts of prakriti (nature) and purusha (spirit)**.
- His philosophy influenced **Vedanta and Yoga schools**.
- Considered an **incarnation of Lord Vishnu** in texts.

Patanjali

- Wrote the **Yoga Sutras**, foundational text on yoga.
- Authored **Mahabhashya**, a commentary on Panini's grammar.
- Integrated **philosophy, linguistics, and health sciences**.
- **Yoga Sutras focus on self-discipline and meditation**.
- His teachings influence **modern yoga and Sanskrit studies**.

Question

Who among the following ancient thinkers wrote treatise about Grammar (Vyzkayana)

A. Panini
B. Shartrnan
C. Kapila
D. Patanjali

Choose the correct answer:

1. C and D only
2. A C and D only
3. A B and D only
4. B and C only

Explanations:
Answer: 3. A B and D only

Among the ancient thinkers listed, the following wrote treatises on the subject of Grammar (Vyakarana):

Panini: Known for his work "Ashtadhyayi," which is a foundational text in Sanskrit grammar.

Shartrnan: There seems to be a typo here. If it's referring to Shakatayana, he was indeed an ancient grammarian.
Patanjali: Known for his work "Mahabhashya," which is a commentary on Panini's Ashtadhyayi.

***Kapila** is known for founding the Samkhya school of philosophy and did not write on grammar.*

Question

Match the column:

A. Bharatha	I. Grammar
B. Bharathrahari	II. Sadharanikaran
C. Bhattanayaka	III. Rasa theory
D. Panini	IV. Speech theory

Choose the correct answer:

1. A-I B-II C-III D-IV
2. A-II B-III C-IV D-I
3. A-III B-IV C-II D-I
4. A-IV B-I C-III D-II

Explanations:
Answer: 3. A-III B-IV C-II D-I

Let's match the authors with their corresponding contributions:

A. Bharatha - III. Rasa theory
B. Bharathrahari - IV. Speech theory
C. Bhattanayaka - II. Sadharanikaran
D. Panini - I. Grammar

Rishi Gautama

- Author of **Nyaya Sutras**, a logical philosophy text.
- Stressed **rational verification of knowledge**.
- His **Nyaya school influenced Indian epistemology**.
- Wrote **Dharma Sutra**, discussing ethics and morality.

- Advocated **logical reasoning and debate for truth-seeking**.

Bharata Muni

- Author of **Natya Shastra**, a text on performing arts.
- Developed **Rasa Theory** in drama and aesthetics.
- Classified **nine rasas (emotions) in art and literature**.
- Influenced **Indian classical dance and theatre**.
- His work is **foundational for Indian aesthetics**.

Kanada

- Founder of **Vaisheshika school of philosophy**.
- Proposed **atomic theory (Anu-Vada) 2500 years ago**.
- Considered **atoms as eternal and indivisible**.
- Connected **metaphysics with physical sciences**.
- His work influenced **early Indian physics**.

Question

Who among the following thinkers observed that light and heat are only different forms of the same essential substance and also speaks of gravity as the cause of falling?

1. Nagarjuna
2. Jivaka
3. Kanad
4. Ramanuj

Explanations:
Answer: 3. Kanad

Kanad, an ancient Indian philosopher and founder of the Vaisheshika school of philosophy, observed that light and heat are only different forms of the same essential substance. He also spoke of gravity as the cause of falling objects. His contributions to early physics and atomic theory are significant in the history of Indian philosophy.

Jivaka

- **Legendary ancient physician and surgeon**.
- Specialized in **abdominal surgery and herbal medicine**.
- Known for **treating intestinal obstructions**.
- Personal physician to **Buddha and Magadha kings**.
- His methods laid the **foundation for Ayurveda**.

Charaka

- **Father of Indian medicine and Ayurveda**.
- Authored **Charaka Samhita**, a key medical text.
- Focused on **diagnosis, treatment, and prevention**.
- Emphasized **diet, lifestyle, and holistic healing**.
- His work influenced **modern Ayurvedic practices**.

Question

Which of the following are the ancient treatises on the science of medicine?

A. Carak Samhita
B. Sulva Sutras
C. Susruta Samhita
D. Yoga Satras

Choose the correct answer:

1. BD
2. BCD
3. AC
4. ABCD

Explanations:
Answer: 3. AC

The ancient treatises on the science of medicine are:

Carak Samhita: An ancient Indian text on Ayurveda (the science of life) and a foundational text on medicine.

Susruta Samhita: Another foundational text on Ayurveda, focusing on surgery and surgical techniques.

The Sulva Sutras are texts on geometry and construction, and the Yoga Sutras (which seem to be incorrectly referenced as Yoga Satras) are texts on the philosophy and practice of Yoga.

Brahmagupta (598–668 CE)

- **Renowned mathematician and astronomer** of ancient India.
- Wrote **Brahmasphutasiddhanta**, an important astronomical text.
- **Introduced zero** as a number and rules for its operations.
- Developed methods for **solving quadratic equations**.
- Proposed formulas for **arithmetic and geometric progressions**.

Kautilya (Chanakya) (4th Century BCE)

- Author of **Arthashastra**, a treatise on statecraft and economics.
- Advisor to **Chandragupta Maurya**, shaping the Mauryan Empire.
- Laid the foundation for **economic and political strategies**.
- Discussed **taxation, administration, and espionage** in governance.
- Emphasized **diplomacy and military strategies** for state control.

Patanjali (2nd Century BCE)

- Compiler of **Yoga Sutras**, a foundational text on yoga.
- Developed the **eightfold path (Ashtanga Yoga)**.
- Linked **yoga with mental and physical well-being**.
- Also contributed to **Sanskrit grammar (Mahabhashya)**.
- His work influenced **Hindu and Buddhist meditation practices**.

Charaka (1st–2nd Century CE)

- Known as the **Father of Indian Medicine (Ayurveda)**.
- Wrote **Charaka Samhita**, a key text in Ayurveda.
- Classified **diseases and their treatments** systematically.
- Stressed **diet and lifestyle** as crucial for health.

- Emphasized **preventive healthcare and ethics** in medicine.

Question

Match the column:

List I (Scholar)	List II (Subject)
A. Brahmagupta	I. Political Strategist
B. Kautilya	II. Yoga
C. Patanjali	III. Physician
D. Charaka	IV. Mathematician

1. A-I B-II C-III D-IV
2. A-II B-III C-IV D-I
3. A-III B-IV C-I D-II
4. A-IV B-I C-II D-III

Explanations:
Answer: 4. A-IV B-I C-II D-III

A. Brahmagupta → IV. Mathematician (Introduced zero, advanced arithmetic).
B. Kautilya → I. Political Strategist (*Arthashastra*, statecraft, and governance).
C. Patanjali → II. Yoga (*Yoga Sutras*, foundation of yoga practice).
D. Charaka → III. Physician (*Charaka Samhita*, Ayurveda and medicine).

Sushruta

- Known as the **"Father of Indian Surgery"**.
- Wrote **Sushruta Samhita**, a surgical treatise.
- Developed **plastic surgery and cataract operations**.
- Described **over 300 surgical procedures**.
- His work influenced **modern surgical techniques**.

Nagarjuna

- **Founder** of Madhyamaka school of Mahayana Buddhism.
- Developed the philosophy of **Sunyata** (emptiness).
- Major work: **Mūlamadhyamakakārikā** on Buddhist logic.

- Contributed to **alchemy** and early chemical sciences.
- Influenced **Indian and Tibetan Buddhist traditions**.

Question

Match the column:

List I (Scholar)	List II (Contribution)
A. Aryabhata	I. Atomic theory
B. Kanad	II. Surgery
C. Sushruta	III. Alchemy
D. Nagarjuna	IV. Astronomy

1. A-I B-II C-III D-IV
2. A-II B-III C-IV D-I
3. A-III B-IV C-I D-II
4. A-IV B-I C-II D-III

Explanations:
Answer: 4. A-IV B-I C-II D-III

A. Aryabhata → IV. Astronomy (*Aryabhatiya*, Earth's rotation, planetary motion).
B. Kanad → I. Atomic Theory (Founder of *Vaisheshika* philosophy, early atomic concepts).
C. Sushruta → II. Surgery (*Sushruta Samhita*, Father of Surgery, plastic surgery).
D. Nagarjuna → III. Alchemy (Metallurgy, chemical processes, early alchemy).

Jaimini

- Founder of **Purva Mimamsa school of philosophy**.
- Wrote **Mimamsa Sutras**, analyzing Vedic rituals.
- Advocated **ritualistic interpretation of the Vedas**.
- Emphasized **karma (action) and dharma (duty)**.
- His philosophy influenced **Hindu legal traditions**.

Question

Match the column:

A. Samkhya	I. Gautam
B. Nyaya	II. Kanada
C. Vaisheshika	III. Kapila
D. Purvamimansa	IV. Jamni

Choose the correct answer:

1. A-I B-III C-IV D-II
2. A-II B-I C-IV D-II
3. A-III B-I C-II D-IV
4. A-IV B-III C-II D-I

Explanations:
Answer: 3. A-III B-I C-II D-IV

A. Samkhya - III. Kapila
B. Nyaya - I. Gautam
C. Vaisheshika - II. Kanada
D. Purvamimansa - IV. Jaimini

Sulva and Grihya Sutras

- **Sulva Sutras deal with early Indian geometry.**
- Describe **construction of altars using mathematical rules.**
- **Grihya Sutras focus on household rituals.**
- Cover **marriage, birth, and domestic ceremonies.**
- Both texts are **important for Vedic traditions.**

Question

Which of the following ancient texts relate to Law?

A. Grihya Sutra
B. Nyaya Sutra
C. Dharma Sutra
D. Sarnkhya pravacana Sutra

Choose the correct answer:

1. ACD
2. AC
3. ABCD
4. BD

Explanations:
Answer: 2. AC

The ancient texts that relate to Law are:

Grihya Sutra: These are part of the Kalpa Sutras and deal with domestic rituals and the legal aspects of household duties and ceremonies.

Dharma Sutra: These are part of the Smriti literature and provide guidelines on law, ethics, and morality.

The Nyaya Sutra and Samkhya Pravacana Sutra are primarily philosophical texts dealing with logic and epistemology (Nyaya) and metaphysics (Samkhya), respectively, rather than law.

Question

Which of the following is an ancient treatise on mathematics?

1. Nyaya Sutras
2. Samkhya Karika
3. Samkhya pravacana sutras
4. Sulva sutras

Explanations:
Answer: 4. Sulva sutras

The Sulva Sutras are ancient Indian texts that form part of the larger body of texts known as the Kalpa Sutras. They are primarily concerned with geometry and mathematics, providing instructions for constructing altars and geometrical shapes necessary for Vedic rituals. The other texts mentioned are related to philosophy and logic rather than mathematics.

Question

Match the column:

A. Siksha	I. Metre
B. Nirukta	Il. Phonetics
C.Kalpa	III. Etymology
D. Chhandas	IV. Religious Practices

Choose the correct answer:

1. A-III, B-II, C-IV, D-I
2. A-I, B-II, C-VI, D-III
3. A-Il, B-III, C-IV, D-I
4. A-IV, B-III, C-II, D-I

Explanations:
Answer: 3. A-Il, B-III, C-IV, D-I

Let's match the terms with their corresponding fields:

A. Siksha - II. Phonetics
B. Nirukta - III. Etymology
C. Kalpa - IV. Religious Practices
D. Chhandas - I. Metre

Sattvika Values

Sattvika values are derived from **Sattva**, one of the three **Gunas (qualities)** in **Samkhya philosophy**, alongside **Rajas (activity, passion)** and **Tamas (ignorance, inertia)**. **Sattva** represents **purity, wisdom, balance, and truthfulness**, and individuals who embody **Sattvika values** are believed to cultivate a **peaceful, enlightened, and selfless life**.

Key Sattvika Values

- **Truthfulness (Satya)** – Commitment to honesty in thought, speech, and action.
- **Compassion (Karuna)** – Kindness and empathy toward all living beings.

- **Self-discipline (Dama)** – Control over desires and emotions.
- **Non-violence (Ahimsa)** – Avoidance of harm to others in any form.
- **Purity (Shaucha)** – Cleanliness of body, mind, and soul.
- **Contentment (Santosh)** – Satisfaction with what one has.
- **Forgiveness (Kshama)** – Letting go of grudges and embracing patience.
- **Wisdom (Jnana)** – Seeking knowledge and higher consciousness.
- **Faith (Shraddha)** – Deep devotion and belief in righteous living.
- **Selfless Service (Seva)** – Helping others without expecting rewards.
- **Equanimity (Samata)** – Maintaining balance in happiness and sorrow.
- **Detachment (Vairagya)** – Freedom from materialistic attachments.
- **Meditation (Dhyana)** – Practicing mindfulness and spiritual focus.
- **Humility (Vinaya)** – Respectful and modest attitude toward life.
- **Non-possessiveness (Aparigraha)** – Living with minimal material desires.

Importance of Sattvika Values

- **Promote inner peace and self-realization**.
- **Encourage ethical and responsible behavior**.
- **Help in attaining spiritual progress and enlightenment**.
- **Lead to a balanced, harmonious, and happy life**.

Question

Paravidya, according to the vedic tradition. implies :

1. Knowledge based on human experience
2. Knowledge that transcends human experience
3. Knowledge acquired from teachers
4. Knowledge acquired from texts.

Explanations:
Answer: 2. Knowledge that transcends human experience

In the Vedic tradition, Paravidya refers to the higher knowledge that transcends human experience and pertains to spiritual wisdom and understanding. It is contrasted with Aparavidya, which is the knowledge of the material world and is based on human experience. Paravidya is concerned with the ultimate truths and spiritual realization.

Question

Identify from the following those values which are called "Sattvika Values"

A. Compassion
B. Jealousy
C. Respect
D. Falsehood

Choose the correct answer:

1. (A) and (B) only
2. (B) and (C) only
3. (C) and (D) only
4. (A) and (C) only

Explanations:
Answer: 4. (A) and (C) only

"Sattvika values" are those that are considered pure, harmonious, and virtuous according to Hindu philosophy.

Compassion (A): This is a sattvika value as it involves empathy and kindness towards others.

Respect (C): This is also a sattvika value as it involves honoring and valuing others.

Jealousy (B) and Falsehood (D) are not sattvika values as they involve negative emotions and dishonest behavior, respectively.

Vedas

The Vedas are a vast collection of religious writings from ancient India, composed in Vedic Sanskrit. They represent the earliest texts in both Sanskrit literature and Hinduism.

- **Rigveda**:
    - This is the oldest, largest, and most important of the Vedas according to scholars.
    - It consists of hymns and praises dedicated to various deities.
- **Yajurveda**:
    - A collection of mantras used in performing yajnas (sacrifices).
- **Samaveda**:
    - Comprising chants and melodies.
    - It is meant to be sung during worship and the performance of yajna.
- **Atharvaveda**:
    - Contains hymns, mantras, and incantations related to everyday life.

Question

The medium of instruction in the vedic system of education has been,

1. Sanskrit
2. Hindi
3. Pali
4. Urdu

Explanations:
Answer: 1. Sanskrit

The medium of instruction in the Vedic system of education was Sanskrit. Sanskrit was the language in which the Vedas, Upanishads, and other ancient Indian scriptures and texts were composed. It was the primary language used for teaching and learning during the Vedic period.

There are two important bodies of supplementary literature closely related to the Vedas:

Vedangas: The Vedangas explain the sciences required to understand and apply the Vedas:

- **Kalpa**: Religious practices
- **Siksha**: Pronunciation/phonology
- **Vyakarana**: Grammar
- **Nirukti**: Etymology
- **Chandas**: Metre
- **Jyotisha**: Astronomy/astrology

Upavedas: The Upavedas deal with four traditional arts and sciences:

- **Ayurveda**: Medicine, associated with Atharvaveda
- **Gandharva-Veda:** Music and dance, associated with Samaveda
- **Dhanur-Veda:** Warfare, associated with Yajurveda
- **Shilpa-Veda:** Architecture, associated with Rigveda

Vedic Commentaries:

Brahmanas:

- Ancient Hindu texts that provide prose commentaries on the four Vedas.
- These texts explain the mantras and hymns found in the Vedas.

Upanishads:

- **Late Vedic and Post-Vedic texts** mark **transition from Vedic ritualism**.
- Document emergence of **new Hindu religious ideas**.
- Introduce **central concepts of Hindu philosophy**.
- **Vedanta means "conclusion of the Vedas"**.
- **Upanishads elaborate on Vedic teachings**.
- Form the basis of **Vedanta school of philosophy**.
- Shift focus from **rituals to metaphysical inquiry**.

Question

The ancient system of education in India included education of which of the following ancient texts?

A. Vedas
B. Brahmanas
C. Upanishads
D. Dharma sutras

Choose the most appropriate answer from the options given below:

1. A and C Only
2. B and D Only
3. A, C and D Only
4. A, B, C and D

Explanations:
Answer: 4. A, B, C and D

The ancient system of education in India included the education of all the mentioned ancient texts:

A. Vedas: The Vedas are considered the oldest scriptures of Hinduism, and they were an important part of ancient Indian education. Students would study the Vedas, which were composed of hymns, rituals, and philosophical teachings.

B. Brahmanas: The Brahmanas are prose texts that provide explanations and instructions for performing rituals and ceremonies. They were an integral part of Vedic education and provided insights into the rituals and their symbolic meanings.

C. Upanishads: The Upanishads are philosophical texts that explore the nature of reality, consciousness, and the self. They were studied by advanced students who sought deeper knowledge and understanding of spiritual and metaphysical concepts.

D. Dharma sutras: Dharma sutras are ancient texts that provide guidelines and rules for ethical and moral conduct. They formed an important part of the education system, teaching students about societal norms, duties, and righteous behavior.

Question

During the Vedic period, the higher level of education had-

1. Professional curriculum
2. General curriculum
3. Specialised curriculum
4. Technical curriculum

Explanations:
Answer: 3. Specialised curriculum

During the Vedic period, the higher level of education had:

The higher level of education in the Vedic period focused on specialized curricula, which included in-depth studies of various subjects such as the Vedas, philosophy, medicine, astronomy, and more. This specialized approach allowed students to gain profound knowledge and expertise in specific fields.

- **Agriculture**: Study of farming practices and crop management.
- **Architecture**: Knowledge of construction and design of buildings.
- **Coinage**: Understanding of monetary systems and currency.
- **Demographics**: Study of population characteristics and statistics.
- **Dynasties**: Historical records of ruling families and their reigns.
- **Economy**: Analysis of economic systems, trade, and commerce.

CHAPTER II

Pre-Independence Education System of India

Pre-Independence Education System of India

Education Policy in Pre-Independent India

The education policy in pre-independent India can be split into two main periods: the Pre-British period and the British period.

Pre-British Period

In this time frame, we look at educational policies from the beginning of ancient times up until the British arrived. Throughout India's history, those in power have influenced education, but it was only in modern times that a scientific approach to formulating educational policies began.

Unfortunately, there are no literary sources that provide a clear picture of educational policies in ancient India. However, texts from 1000 A.D. onwards, like the Rigveda, the Aranyakas, the Upanishads, the Epics, and the Puranas, give us a decent understanding of how education was managed back then.

The Aryans, who entered India around the 2nd millennium B.C., were the first to significantly shape education policies in India. They had a well-defined educational system, and the native people, referred to as 'Dasyus,' had to follow the norms set by the Aryans.

Ancient Indian thinkers saw education as a tool to transform an ignorant person into an intellectual, progressive, moral, and virtuous individual. Students were not only expected to learn practical skills for life but also to engage in research and contribute to the advancement of knowledge. As a result, learned individuals were highly respected. Education in ancient India was deeply influenced by religion.

After the Vedic period, large kingdoms emerged with powerful kings who wanted to advance their societies. These kings supported higher education by giving donations and land to scholars and enacted policies to develop the education system. Major universities like Nalanda and Taxila became renowned for their scholarship.

Between 400 BCE and 1000 CE, there was a struggle between Buddhism and Brahmanism for dominance in interpreting the world. Buddhism, which was more people-centric and egalitarian, differed from the hierarchical Brahminical system and did not rely on Vedic studies or Brahmin teachers. Buddhist education was more radical and opened knowledge to all castes. Buddhist monks lived in Viharas, which spread across India and became centers of higher learning. Nalanda was the most important Buddhist center of learning, attracting foreign travelers like Fa-Hien, Hiuen-Tsang, and Itsing, who stayed there to study Buddhism. Nalanda provided free education, boarding, and lodging to its students.

During the Mughal period, the rulers didn't focus on universalizing education but aimed to spread Islamic education. Any Muslim could study at a 'Madrasa,' where higher education was taught in Arabic by Moulvis. Islamic education was divided into 'Maktabas' (primary schools often attached to mosques or run in private houses) and 'Madrasas' (schools for higher learning generally attached to monasteries). Initially, these were limited to Muslims, but eventually, Hindus and Muslims began learning each other's languages, leading to the creation of Urdu. Both Hindu and Muslim educational institutions in pre-British India emphasized religion over other subjects.

In ancient India, the primary objective of education was religious. There were no significant efforts to make education universal and inclusive. Education remained monopolized by a few groups, with caste and gender largely determining access to educational opportunities.

Question

The methods of learning in Higher Education in India in the past consisted of

1. Memorization, Brainstorming procedure and Seminar
2. Memorization, Critical Analysis and Storytelling
3. Critical Analysis, Assignment Writing and Oral reports
4. Story Telling, Brainstorming procedure and Seminar

Explanations:
Answer: 2. Memorization, Critical Analysis and Storytelling

The methods of learning in higher education in ancient India included:

Memorization: Students often memorized large portions of texts, such as the Vedas and other scriptures, as oral transmission was a key part of education.

Critical Analysis: There was a strong emphasis on understanding and critically analyzing texts and philosophical ideas, encouraging deep engagement with the material.

Storytelling: Storytelling was an essential method to impart moral lessons, historical knowledge, and cultural values.

These methods collectively aimed at a holistic development of the individual, combining rote learning with critical thinking and engaging narratives.

Question

In which era given below, higher education in India got a set back?

1. British Era
2. Mughal Era
3. Buddhist Era
4. Post-Independence Era

Explanations:
Answer: 2. Mughal Era

Higher education in India experienced a setback during the Mughal Era. While the Mughals contributed significantly to the cultural and architectural heritage of India, the period saw a decline in the emphasis on the traditional Indian systems of higher education, such as the universities of Nalanda and Vikramashila which had flourished during the Buddhist Era. The Mughal focus was more on Persian culture and literature, and less on the indigenous systems of higher learning.

Question

Identify from the following, features which describe most appropriately the Indian values

A. Emphasis on individual ambition
B. Emphasis on collectivism
C. Emphasis on social progress
D. Emphasis on social stability
E. Emphasis on unity in diversity

Choose the correct answer from the options given below:

1. A, B and C only
2. B, C and D only
3. C, D and E only
4. B, D and E only

Explanations:
Answer: 4. B, D and E only

Indian values are deeply rooted in the cultural and social fabric of the country, emphasizing the importance of community, stability, and unity. The features that describe these values most appropriately include:

Emphasis on collectivism (B): Indian culture traditionally values community and collective well-being over individual ambition.

Emphasis on social stability (D): Maintaining social order and harmony is a key aspect of Indian values.

Emphasis on unity in diversity (E): India is known for its cultural, religious, and linguistic diversity, and there is a strong emphasis on maintaining unity despite these differences.

British Period

The introduction of Western education in India during the British period was a big deal. Before this, education was pretty much limited to a small section of the population, mostly those higher up in the social hierarchy. People from lower castes and classes had very little access to education. The early work in education under British rule was mainly done by missionaries. While they did try to spread education, their efforts were often driven by a desire to spread Christianity among Indians. However, their efforts did push governments in both England and India to realize the importance of educating the people they ruled (Keay 1972).

The Charter of 1698 said that English ministers of religion should provide education along with spreading the Gospel. But the East India Company, understanding the political importance of religious neutrality, avoided following these directions strictly. Instead, the Company encouraged education by giving grants to establish schools. For instance, St. Mary's School was set up in Madras in 1715, followed by two more charity schools by Danish missionaries in 1717. In 1718, a charity school opened in Bombay, and another in Calcutta in 1731. By 1787, two charity schools for boys and girls were established in Madras (Singh 2005). These schools mostly focused on the basics: reading, writing, arithmetic, and Christian teachings.

In 1781, Sir Warren Hastings, the first Governor-General of India, established the Calcutta Madrasa to promote Arabic and Persian studies. He also founded the Benares Sanskrit College in 1791 to encourage classical studies in Sanskrit. One main reason for setting up these institutions was to train Indian assistants for English judges, to help explain the principles of Hindu and Muslim laws (Basu 1982).

In the early 18th century, Christian missionaries started offering education to the masses in India. However, they were officially allowed to teach and preach only after the Charter Act of 1813. Before this, the East India Company was hesitant to let missionaries carry out educational activities due to fears of resistance from Indians who were wary of religious conversion efforts.

Supporters of the missionaries in England protested against the Company's anti-missionary stance. Their efforts eventually paid off, leading to the Charter Act of 1813. This Act committed the British government to allocate 1 lakh rupees for the education of Indians, marking the first time a formal educational policy was established in India.

The Act, however, was vague about its objectives, leading to a debate between Classicists and Anglicists. The Classicists wanted education in Sanskrit, Arabic, and Persian, while the Anglicists pushed for English education. Unfortunately, the potential of using Indian mother tongues as mediums of education was overlooked, a decision that still impacts Indian education today.

Indian reformers like Raja Ram Mohan Roy supported the idea of English education, believing it would usher in a renaissance for the country.

In 1823, the Committee of Public Instruction was set up to shape and implement the new educational policy. The Committee had two main goals: winning the confidence of the educated and influential classes by promoting the literature they respected, and using limited funds to support the higher education of the upper classes, with a focus on keeping them appeased.

By the mid-19th century, a big debate was raging between the Anglicists and the Orientalists. The Orientalists, who loved traditional Indian culture, wanted education to be taught in classical languages like Sanskrit, Arabic, or Persian. On the flip side, the Anglicists believed education should be in English, arguing that modern knowledge could only be effectively taught in English. This debate dragged on until the end of 1834, stalling any clear educational policy.

Enter Lord T.B. Macaulay, who came to India as the President of the Committee of Public Instruction. A staunch Anglicist, Macaulay pushed hard for Western education to be taught in English. He argued that teaching sciences and modern subjects could only be done through English, dismissing Indian languages as unsuitable for this purpose. He didn't think Arabic or Sanskrit could compete with English in this regard.

Macaulay's harsh criticism of classical Indian languages was largely due to his lack of understanding of their richness. This caused widespread resentment among those who admired these languages and knew their value. Nevertheless, Macaulay firmly believed that English education would positively impact Indian minds and advocated for its strong implementation.

Question

Identify the correct chronological order of the following institutions of higher learning?

A. Rajkot College, Rajkot
B. Civil Engineering College, Roorkee
C. Sanskrit College, Calcutta
D. Sanskrit College, Benaras
E. Fort Williams College, Calcutta

1. A, B, E, D, C
2. C, A, B, E, D
3. D, E, C, B, A
4. B, C, A, D, E

Explanations:
Answer: 3. D, E, C, B, A

- **Sanskrit College, Benaras (D) - 1791**
- **Fort William College, Calcutta (E) - 1800**
- **Sanskrit College, Calcutta (C) - 1824**
- **Civil Engineering College, Roorkee (B) - 1847** *(Later became IIT Roorkee)*
- **Rajkot College, Rajkot (A) - 1868**

Question

Statement I: In the Vedic age both men and women had access to education.
Statement II: Woods Despatch (1854) recognized for the first time that the Government should give 'frank and cordial support to female education.

1. Both Statement I and Statement II are true
2. Both Statement I and Statement II are false
3. Statement I is true but Statement II is false

4. Statement I is false but Statement II is true

Explanations:
Answer: 1. Both Statement I and Statement II are true

Statement I is True: In the Vedic age, both men and women were provided with opportunities for education. Women scholars such as Gargi and Maitreyi are well-known examples from this period.

Statement II is True: Wood's Despatch, also known as the Magna Carta of English Education in India, emphasized the importance of education for all, including women, and recommended government support for female education.

Macaulay's Arguments for English Education:

Macaulay believed that English was a modern language and way more useful than Arabic or Sanskrit. He argued that English was the leading language of the West and was already the language of the ruling classes in India. He thought that English had a bright future as the language of commerce in the East.

He compared English to Greek and Latin, which brought about the Renaissance in Europe, and believed English could do the same for India. He noticed that native Indians were more eager to learn English rather than Sanskrit or Arabic, and he believed that it was possible to make Indians good scholars in English.

Macaulay also believed that English education could create "a class of persons Indian in blood and colour but English in taste, in opinions, in morals and intellect." This class would act as a bridge between the British and the masses, helping to spread English ideas and culture.

In 1835, Lord William Bentinck, the then Governor General, approved Macaulay's suggestions. This led to a major shift in educational policy, making English the primary language of instruction in high schools and colleges under government control. This decision had a long-lasting impact on Indian education, bringing Indians closer to Western ideas of government and democracy and eventually contributing to the rise of Indian nationalism.

The Charter of the East India Company had to be renewed every 20 years. When it was time to renew the Charter in 1833, the British Parliament decided to increase the budget for education in India from one lakh (in 1813) to one million rupees annually. Realizing that India had many educational problems, the Parliament decided during the 1853 Charter renewal to create a clear education policy to develop a well-organized education system in the country.

To achieve this, a committee led by Charles Wood was formed to suggest educational reforms. The report they produced became known as the Wood's Education Dispatch. This document, often called the 'Magna Carta of English Education in India,' had a huge impact on the development of the country's education system. Spanning 100 paragraphs, it covered various aspects of educational reform in India. It aimed to spread the arts, science, philosophy, and literature of Europe, encouraged the study of Indian languages, and promoted teaching English where there was demand for it. Essentially, both English and Indian languages were to be used to spread European knowledge.

One of the most significant outcomes of the Wood's Despatch was the decision to establish universities in India. The first modern university in India was set up in Calcutta in 1857, followed by universities in Bombay and Madras.

Fast forward to 1944, the Sargent Commission was set up under Sir John Sargent to review and improve the education system in India. Their report, known as the 'Sargent Scheme,' laid out plans for the post-war development of education in India. This report played a crucial role in shaping the future of the Indian education system.

Before independence, the British government played a major role in shaping the education system in India. They established numerous schools and colleges across the country, producing a large number of educated Indians well-versed in modern subjects. While their main goal was to train clerks for their administration, the spread of modern education (both liberal and technical) by the British had a progressive impact on India.

Question

Statement I: The earliest part of the British policy on education was to withdraw from higher education
Statement II: The British policy completely supported the idea of mother tongue as the medium of instruction as against English.

1. Both Statement I and Statement Il are true
2. Both Statement I and Statement Il are false
3. Statement I is true but Statement Il is false
4. Statement I is false but Statement Il is true

Explanations:
Answer: 3. Statement I is true but Statement Il is false

Statement I is True: Initially, the British policy on education in India did not focus on higher education, aiming instead to prioritize other areas.

Statement II is False: The British policy, especially after Macaulay's Minute on Indian Education in 1835, emphasized English as the medium of instruction, considering it superior to native languages for education.

Therefore, the correct answer is:
3. Statement I is true but Statement II is false.

Policies

Macaulay's Minute (1835)

- Presented by **Thomas Babington Macaulay** on **February 2, 1835**.
- Advocated for **English education over Indian knowledge systems**.
- Considered **Indian literature and sciences inferior**.
- Aimed to create a **class of English-educated Indians**.
- Supported **Western science and literature** in India.
- Rejected **funding for Sanskrit, Arabic, and Persian studies**.
- Promoted English as the **medium of instruction**.
- Favored education only for **upper-class Indians**.
- Believed English would be a **link language** for governance.

- Criticized **vernacular languages as inadequate for modern learning**.
- Influenced Lord **William Bentinck's education policies**.
- Opposed **Orientalist approaches to Indian education**.
- Encouraged **translation of European works into English**.
- Led to the **Anglicist vs. Orientalist debate** in India.
- Served as the **basis for the English Education Act of 1835**.

Question

Which of the following statements are true regarding Macaulay?

A. He succeeded in replacing Persian with English as the administrative language
B. He promoted training of English Speaking Indians as teachers.
C. He was inspired by Utilitarian ideas.
D. He promoted "useful learning".

Choose the correct answer from the options given below:

(1) A and B only
(2) B and C only
(3) A and C only
(4) A, B, C and D

Explanations:
Answer: 4. A, B, C and D

A. He succeeded in replacing Persian with English as the administrative language: The passage states that English became the language of administration and of the higher law courts, replacing Persian, as under the Mughal Empire.

B. He promoted training of English-speaking Indians as teachers: Macaulay's Memorandum emphasized the need to produce "a class of persons, Indian in blood and colour, but English in taste, in opinions, in morals and in intellect," implying the training of English-speaking Indians.

C. He was inspired by Utilitarian ideas: Macaulay urged Lord William Bentinck to reform secondary education on utilitarian lines to deliver "useful learning," indicating his inspiration from Utilitarian ideas.

D. He promoted "useful learning.": Macaulay equated "useful learning" with Western culture and argued for its promotion through the education system.

Therefore, the correct answer from the given options is: **4. A, B, C and D**

Question

The infamous minutes of 1834 can be associated with-

1. Charles Wood
2. William Bentuick
3. Thomas Babington Macaulay
4. Charles Grant

Explanations:
Answer: 3. Thomas Babington Macaulay

English Education Act (1835)

- Passed by the **Council of India in 1835**.
- Implemented **Macaulay's recommendations on English education**.
- Enforced by **Governor-General Lord William Bentinck**.
- Reallocated British funds **towards English education**.
- Discontinued state support for **Sanskrit and Persian institutions**.
- Established English as the **official medium of instruction**.
- Encouraged **Western-style education and curricula**.
- Introduced **government funding for English schools and colleges**.
- Aimed to create an **English-educated elite** in India.
- Marked the **beginning of formal British education policy**.
- Laid the groundwork for **colonial administration training**.
- Strengthened **missionary and government-run schools**.
- Shifted focus from **Indian to European knowledge systems**.
- Provided limited education to **select groups, not mass education**.

- Contributed to **India's socio-political divide in education**.

Wood's Dispatch (1854)

- Issued by **Sir Charles Wood in 1854**.
- Sent to **Governor-General Lord Dalhousie**.
- Recommended **vernacular language in primary schools**.
- Promoted **Anglo-vernacular education in high schools**.
- Introduced **English as the medium for college education**.
- Stressed the importance of **teacher training institutions**.
- Encouraged **female education for the first time**.
- Called for **government support in expanding women's education**.
- Suggested **government and private cooperation in education**.
- Recommended **professional training in Law, Medicine, and Engineering**.
- Led to the **foundation of universities in Calcutta, Bombay, and Madras**.
- Proposed a **Department of Public Instruction** for India.
- Introduced **government scholarships for deserving students**.
- Emphasized **moral and secular education**.
- Considered the **Magna Carta of Indian education policy**.

The Outcome of Wood's Dispatch:

As a result of Sir Charles Wood's departure, the Universities of Calcutta, Bombay, and Madras were established in 1857, modeled after the University of London. These universities were set up during the tenure of Lord Canning as the Governor-General of India.

Following these, the Universities of Punjab, Lahore, and Allahabad were also established. The main reason for their establishment was the increasing demand for higher education in these regions.

Question

The well-known *'Wood's despatch'* is often described as the of English education in India.

1. Bill of Rights

2. People's Charter
3. Preamble
4. Magna Carta

Explanations:
Answer: 4. Magna Carta

Question

Match the column

List I (Document)	List II (Recommendation)
A. Macaulay's minute	I. Promotion of Science knowledge among inhabitants
B. Dispatch of 1854	II. Establishment of a Sanskrit College at Calcutta
C. Rajaram Mohan Roy Memorandum	III. Establishment of a college in Nadiea
D. Lord Minto's minute	IV. Clousre of oriental learning institutions

1. A-I, B-II, C-III, D-IV
2. A-II, B-III, C-IV, D-I
3. A-III, B-IV, C-I, D-II
4. A-IV, B-I, C-II, D-III

Explanations:
Answer: 4. A-IV, B-I, C-II, D-III

A. Macaulay's Minute → IV. Closure of Oriental learning institutions Favored **English education** over traditional **Indian learning**.

B. Dispatch of 1854 → I. Promotion of Science knowledge Known as **Wood's Dispatch**, emphasized **scientific and technical education**.

C. Raja Ram Mohan Roy Memorandum → II. Establishment of a Sanskrit College at Calcutta Supported **modern and Western education** alongside Sanskrit learning.

D. Lord Minto's Minute → III. Establishment of a college in Nadiya Encouraged **expansion of higher education institutions**.

Question

Which of the following Indian universities were modelled on the lines of University of London?

A. Calcutta
B. Bombay
C. Madras
D. Andhra
E. Mysore

Choose the correct answer from the options given below:

1. A, B and C only
2. B, C and D only
3. C, D and E only
4. A, B and D only

Explanations:
Answer: 1. A, B and C only

The universities of Calcutta, Bombay, and Madras were established in 1857 and were modeled on the lines of the University of London. These universities were among the first modern universities in India and aimed to provide a broad and liberal education similar to the University of London.

Question

The Education/Despatch of 1854 suggested professional training in-

A. Library science
B. Law
C. Medicine
D. Civil Engineering
E. Material science

Choose the correct answer from the options given below:

1. ABC
2. BCD
3. CDE

4. ABE

Explanations:
Answer: 2. BCD

The Education Despatch of 1854, also known as Wood's Despatch, recommended the establishment of institutions for professional education in India, specifically focusing on the fields of law, medicine, and civil engineering. These fields were considered essential for the administration and development of the country under British rule.

Question

Which of the following universities were established in the year 1857?

A. Calcutta University
B. Bombay University
C. Madras University
D. Allahabad University

Choose the correct pair:

1. A, B and D Only
2. A, B and C Only
3. B, C and D Only
4. A, C and D Only

Explanation:
Answer: 2. A, B and C Only

The universities established in the year 1857 were:

1. Calcutta University
2. Bombay University
3. Madras University
4. Allahabad University was established later, in 1887.

Therefore, the correct pair is: 2. A, B and C Only

Question

Which one of the following has been described as the Magna Carta of Indian education?

1. The Indian universities Act, 1904
2. Hunter commission report
3. Sargent plan
4. The Education Dispatch of 1854

Explanations:
Answer: 4. The Education Dispatch of 1854

The Education Dispatch of 1854, also known as Wood's Despatch, is often referred to as the Magna Carta of Indian education. It was a comprehensive plan to reform and expand the education system in India. The Despatch outlined the establishment of a widespread education system, the introduction of English as a medium of instruction, and the creation of universities in Calcutta, Bombay, and Madras. It laid the foundation for modern education in India, similar to how the Magna Carta laid the foundation for modern constitutional governance.

Question

Which of the following recognised for the first time that the government should give 'frank and cordial support to female education and take effective measures for its expansion?

1. Women's Indian Association
2. All India Women's Conference
3. The Woods Despatch
4. National Council of Women

Explanations:
Answer: 3. The Woods Despatch

The Wood's Despatch of 1854, also known as the Magna Carta of English Education in India, was the first official document to recognize the need for the government to support female education and take effective measures for its expansion. It emphasized the importance of educating women and recommended that the government provide encouragement and support for female education.

Question

The period between 1200 and 1764 AD was remarkable in India for the highest distinction attained by:

1. Popular literature
2. Vernacular literature
3. English literature
4. French literature

Explanations:
Answer: 2. Vernacular literature

The period between **1200 and 1764 AD** in India was significant for the **rise and flourishing of vernacular literature** in various regional languages.

Medieval Bhakti and Sufi Movements played a crucial role in promoting **vernacular languages** like Hindi, Bengali, Tamil, Marathi, and Kannada. Notable works include **Kabir's dohas (Hindi), Tulsidas' *Ramcharitmanas* (Awadhi), Surdas' *Sur Sagar* (Braj Bhasha), and Mirabai's devotional poetry**. **Persian and Urdu literature** also developed, especially under Mughal patronage. **Regional literary traditions** flourished, with notable works in Bengali (Chandidas), Assamese, and Telugu (Krishnadevaraya's *Amuktamalyada*).

Act of Incorporation (1857) by Lord Canning

- **Passed in February 1857** to establish **modern universities**.
- Led to the creation of **Calcutta, Bombay, and Madras Universities**.
- Modeled on the **London University system**.
- Aimed at **higher education expansion in India**.
- Marked the **beginning of formal university education**.

Question

The Act of Incorporation passed by lord Canning in February, 1857, provided for the establishment of which of the following universities?

A. Calcutta
B. Delhi
C. Bombay
D. Madras

Choose the correct answer from the options given below:

1. BCD
2. AD
3. ACD
4. ABD

Explanations:
Answer: 3. ACD

The Act of Incorporation passed by Lord Canning in February 1857 provided for the establishment of the first three universities in India:

- **Calcutta University**
- **Bombay University**
- **Madras University**

Question

Act of Incorporation, passed by Lord Canning in January 1857, provided for the establishment of which of the following Universities?

A. University of Calcutta
B. University of Delhi
C. University of Madras
D. Bombay University

1. ABC
2. ACD
3. BD
4. ABCD

Explanations:
Answer: 2. ACD

Question

Which among the following was not part of the triad of first three universities established in 1857?

1. Bombay
2. Calcutta
3. Madras
4. Allahabad

Explanations:
Answer: 4. Allahabad

Hunter Commission (1882-83)

- Led by **William Hunter** for education review.
- Emphasized **expansion of primary education**.
- Suggested **local control of primary schools**.
- Encouraged **female and rural education**.
- Supported **vocational training in schools**.
- Recommended **better pay for teachers**.
- Proposed **diversified secondary education**.
- **Higher education** should be **managed by Indians**.
- **Government colleges** only where **demand exists**.
- **Generous grants** for **non-government colleges**.
- Left **religious education to local bodies**.
- Faced **implementation challenges**.
- Focused on **quality over quantity**.

Question

What were the recommendations of the Hunter commission on higher education in India?

A. The Government should leave the management of higher education to Indians themselves.
B. Government colleges should be established only where the demand existed.
C. The Government should provide grants to non-government colleges generously.

D. Students should study the prescribed subjects without any option.
E. There was no need for moral education in colleges.

Choose the correct pair:

1. A, B, C Only
2. B, C, D Only
3. C, D, E Only
4. A, D, E Only

Explanations:
Answer: 1. A, B, C Only

The recommendations of the Hunter Commission on higher education in India included:

A. The Government should leave the management of higher education to Indians themselves.
B. Government colleges should be established only where the demand exists.
C. The Government should provide grants to non-government colleges generously.

The recommendations did not include that students should study the prescribed subjects without any option or that there was no need for moral education in colleges.

Therefore, the correct pair is: **A, B, C Only.**

Question

The Hunter Commission was the brainchild of-

1. Lord Curzan
2. Lord Ripon
3. Lord Auckland
4. Lord Dufferin

Explanations:
Answer: 2. Lord Ripon

Hunter Commission (1882) was formed by **Lord Ripon**. Aimed at **improving primary and secondary education** in India. Recommended **local bodies (municipalities & district boards)** to manage education.

Question

What were the recommendations of the Hunter commission on higher education in India?

A. The Government should leave the management of higher education to Indians themselves.
B. Government colleges should be established only where the demand existed.
C. The Government should provide grants to non-government colleges generously.
D. Students should study the prescribed subjects without any option.
E. There was no need for moral education in colleges.

Choose the correct answer from the options given below:

1. A, B, C Only
2. B, C, D Only
3. C, D, E Only
4. A, D, E Only

Explanations:
Answer: 1. A, B, C Only

The Hunter Commission, officially known as the Indian Education Commission of 1882, made several recommendations regarding higher education in India. Some of the key recommendations were:

A. The Government should leave the management of higher education to Indians themselves.
B. Government colleges should be established only where the demand existed.
C. The Government should provide grants to non-government colleges generously.

The recommendations aimed to encourage the involvement of Indians in the management of higher education, establish colleges based on demand, and support non-government institutions through grants.

Indian Universities Act (1904)

- The first Indian Universities Commission (1902) was headed by Thomas Raleigh
- Introduced by **Lord Curzon** for reform.
- Reduced **university autonomy** significantly.
- Increased **government control over universities**.
- Tightened **college affiliation rules**.
- Implemented **regular inspections in education**.
- Focused on **higher education standardization**.
- Promoted **research and postgraduate studies**.
- Provided **financial aid for institutions**.
- Criticized for **suppressing academic freedom**.
- Influenced **later university governance**.

Question

The first Indian Universities Commission (1902) was headed by:

1. Gurudas Bannerjee
2. Syed Hasan Bilgrami
3. William Adam
4. Thomas Raleigh

Explanations:
Answer: 4. Thomas Raleigh

The first Indian Universities Commission was appointed in 1902 to examine the condition of higher education in India and to suggest reforms. This commission was headed by Thomas Raleigh, a British official.

Question

In 1902, in a telegram to Hamilton, who among the following proposed to appoint an Indian Universities commission with six permanent members?

1. S.H. Wood
2. A. Abbott
3. Lord Curzon
4. Lord Macaulay

Explanations:
Answer: 3. Lord Curzon

In 1902, Lord Curzon, the then Viceroy of India, proposed the appointment of the Indian Universities Commission in a telegram to Hamilton. This commission was intended to investigate and recommend reforms for higher education in India. The commission eventually led to the Indian Universities Act of 1904.

Question

The Indian university Act, 1904, was passed during the period of

1. Lord wellesly
2. Lord Ripon
3. Lord Curzon
4. Lord Chelmsford

Explanations:
Answer: 3. Lord Curzon

The Indian University Act, 1904, was passed during the period of Lord Curzon, who was the Viceroy of India from 1899 to 1905. The act aimed to bring about significant reforms in the higher education system in India, focusing on improving the quality of education and administration in universities.

Question

Who among the following was behind the enactment of the Indian Universities Act in the early 20th century?

1. Lord Canning
2. Lord Curzon
3. Charles Budd
4. Lord Dalhousie

Explanations:
Answer: 2. Lord Curzon

Lord Curzon, who served as the Viceroy of India from 1899 to 1905, was the driving force behind the enactment of the Indian Universities Act in 1904. The act aimed to reform and regulate the universities in India, improving their administration and educational standards.

Sadler Commission (1917-19)

- Investigated **Calcutta University's education system**.
- Focused on **higher education reforms**.
- Suggested **separating school from university education**.
- Proposed **intermediate colleges system**.
- Recommended **women's education expansion**.
- Encouraged **regional languages in universities**.
- Stressed **vocational and technical education**.
- Suggested **university autonomy improvement**.
- Promoted **teacher training programs**.
- Influenced **future university policies**.

Hartog Committee (1929)

- Examined **education efficiency in India**.
- Recommended **reducing school dropout rates**.
- Favored **quality over rapid expansion**.
- Suggested **curriculum reforms and exams**.
- Supported **vocational education development**.
- Focused on **teacher training improvements**.
- Recommended **girls' education expansion**.
- Proposed **limited university admissions**.
- Addressed **inefficiencies in education system**.
- Had **partial implementation in policies**.

Wardha Scheme (1937)

- Proposed by **Mahatma Gandhi**.
- Called **Nai Talim (New Education)**.

- Introduced **free education for ages 7-14**.
- Used **mother tongue as instruction medium**.
- Included **craft-based learning system**.
- Focused on **self-sufficient education model**.
- Encouraged **moral and value-based learning**.
- Opposed **early English education**.
- Criticized as **rural-centric and impractical**.
- Influenced **post-independence education policies**.

Sargent Plan (1944)

- Blueprint for **universal education in India**.
- Proposed **free schooling for ages 6-14**.
- Suggested **multi-stream secondary education**.
- Recommended **expansion of university education**.
- Emphasized **vocational training importance**.
- Stressed **women's education equality**.
- Proposed **special education for differently-abled**.
- Called for **better teacher training programs**.
- Suggested **state investment in education**.
- Faced **non-implementation due to independence movement**.

UGC Plan (1945-46)

- Modeled on **UK's University Grants Committee**.
- Proposed for **higher education improvement**.
- Ensured **uniformity in education policies**.
- Provided **funding for universities**.
- Encouraged **scientific and social research**.
- Focused on **university autonomy and governance**.
- Linked **education with industrial needs**.
- Became basis for **post-independence UGC (1956)**.
- Promoted **teacher training programs**.
- Strengthened **higher education infrastructure**.

Indian Educational Reformers:

Lord Curzon's Contribution to Indian Education

- **Viceroy** of India (1899–1905), education reforms.
- **Indian Universities Act** (1904), stricter control.
- **Founded Imperial Library** in **1903, Kolkata**.
- Inspired by **Bodleian and British Museum**.
- Later became **National Library of India**.
- **Largest university** in India during **Curzon's tenure**.
- Established in **1857**, key in **higher education**.
- Had **many affiliated colleges** and **students**.
- Reduced **university autonomy**, increased supervision.
- Improved **higher education** and research standards.
- Introduced regular **university inspection** system.
- Restricted **college affiliations**, ensured quality.
- Promoted **technical** and **agricultural education**.
- Strengthened **teacher training** programs.
- Increased **financial grants** for education.
- Criticized for restricting **Indian education freedom**.

Question

Which one of the following Universities was the largest in the initial years of Lord Curzon's regime?

1. Calcutta
2. Madras
3. Bombay
4. Punjab

Explanations:
Answer: 1. Calcutta

During the initial years of Lord Curzon's regime, the University of Calcutta was the largest among the universities in India. Established in 1857, it played a central role in higher education and had a significant number of affiliated colleges and students.

Question

Who among the following founded the Imperial Library which he wanted to see as a Future Bodleian Library or a British Museum of the East?

1. Lord Curzon
2. Lord Canning
3. Charles Wood
4. Lord Mountbatten

Explanations:
Answer: 1. Lord Curzon

Lord Curzon, during his tenure as Viceroy of India, founded the Imperial Library in 1903. He envisioned it as a premier institution, akin to the Bodleian Library in Oxford or the British Museum in London, to serve as a major repository of knowledge and culture in the East. The Imperial Library later became the National Library of India, located in Kolkata.

Question

Find out the chronological order of the following British Authorities/Persons who took interest in higher education in India.

A. Lord Curzon
B. Lord Ripon
C. Lord Canning
D. Lord Dalhousis

1. ABCD
2. BDAC
3. DCBA
4. CDAB

Explanations:
Answer: 3. DCBA

Lord Dalhousie (D) - 1848 to 1856: Introduced the **Wood's Despatch of 1854**, which laid the foundation for **modern education in India**. Advocated for the establishment of **universities in Calcutta, Bombay, and Madras**.

Lord Canning (C) - 1856 to 1862: Established the **Calcutta, Bombay, and Madras Universities in 1857** based on the Wood's Despatch. Encouraged **Western education and administrative reforms**.

Lord Ripon (B) – 1880 to 1884: Introduced **Hunter Commission (1882)**, which emphasized **primary and secondary education**. Advocated for **local self-government in education**.

Lord Curzon (A) – 1899 to 1905: Appointed the Indian Universities Commission in 1902, leading to the **Indian Universities Act (1904)**. Focused on **improving the quality of higher education and university administration**.

Final Order: **DCBA** (Dalhousie → Canning → Ripon → Curzon)

Raja Ram Mohan Roy

- Founder of **Brahmo Samaj (1828)**, a socio-religious reform movement.
- Known as the **"Father of Modern India"**.
- Advocated for **women's rights and abolition of Sati**.
- Promoted **English education and Western scientific learning**.
- Supported the founding of **Hindu College (1817), later Presidency College**.
- Established **Vedanta College (1825)** for Indian and Western education.
- Opposed **idol worship and rigid caste system**.
- Advocated for **freedom of speech and press**.
- Inspired reforms in **education, religion, and women's empowerment**.
- Believed **English education was superior to traditional Indian methods**.
- Played a role in **modernizing the Indian education system**.
- Promoted **rational thinking and scientific inquiry**.
- Supported the British government's efforts in **educational reform**.
- Advocated for **religious tolerance and monotheism**.
- His efforts laid the foundation for **modern Indian social reform movements**.

Question

Raja Ram Mohan Roy was responsible for the establishment of:

1. Agra college, Agra

2. Hindu College, Kolkata
3. Banaras Sanskrit College, Banaras
4. Serampore College, Serampore

Explanations:
Answer: 2. Hindu College, Kolkata

Raja Ram Mohan Roy was instrumental in the establishment of Hindu College in Kolkata (now Presidency College) in 1817. The college aimed to provide modern education, including Western scientific education, to Indian youth, which was a significant step towards educational reform in India.

Bhimrao Ambedkar

- Principal architect of the **Indian Constitution**.
- Fought against **untouchability and caste discrimination**.
- Advocated for **education as a tool for social upliftment**.
- Established **Siddharth College and Milind College in Maharashtra**.
- Promoted education for **weaker sections, Dalits, and women**.
- Founded the **People's Education Society (1945)**.
- Earned a **doctorate in economics from Columbia University**.
- Advocated for **secularism and fundamental rights**.
- Played a key role in **Hindu Code Bill reforms**.
- Converted to **Buddhism in 1956**, inspiring mass conversions.
- Wrote **"Annihilation of Caste"** challenging social hierarchies.
- Stressed the importance of **technical and higher education**.
- Believed in **constitutional rights for marginalized groups**.
- Supported **affirmative action and reservation policies**.
- His work continues to inspire **social justice movements in India**.

Question

B.R. Ambedkar was associated with the efforts in establishing:

1. Milind College
2. Aurangabad college
3. Maha Bodhi college
4. Nagpur college

Explanations:
Answer: 1. Milind College

B.R. Ambedkar was instrumental in the establishment of Milind College in Aurangabad. He was a strong advocate for the education of marginalized communities and played a significant role in promoting higher education among them.

Annie Besant

- A **British theosophist, social reformer, and educationist**.
- Founded **Central Hindu Girls School (1904) in Banaras**.
- Established **Hindu College in Banaras** for religious and moral education.
- Opposed **Western-style education's impact on Indian culture**.
- Promoted **Indian nationalism and Home Rule Movement**.
- First woman to serve as **President of the Indian National Congress (1917)**.
- Strong advocate for **women's education and rights**.
- Supported **Vedic and moral education alongside modern studies**.
- Worked with **Theosophical Society to promote Indian spirituality**.
- Founded **Theosophical Education Trust for schools in India**.
- Established several **institutions for women's education**.
- Played a role in **reviving Indian traditional knowledge systems**.
- Encouraged **freedom of thought and rational thinking**.
- Inspired **Indian self-governance and social reform movements**.
- Her contributions helped shape **modern education policies in India**.

Question

Who among the following opposed the implementation of western system of education in India?

1. William Adam
2. Lord Canning
3. Mrs. Annie Besant

4. BL Rice

Explanations:
Answer: 3. Mrs. Annie Besant

Mrs. Annie Besant was a strong proponent of traditional Indian education and opposed the implementation of the Western system of education in India. She believed in the value of Indian culture and heritage and worked to promote Indian educational institutions that reflected traditional values and teachings.

Bethune College

- **India's first women's college**, established in **1849 as a school.**
- Became a **college in 1879**, affiliated with **Calcutta University**.
- Founded by **John Elliot Drinkwater Bethune**.
- Aimed at **women's empowerment through education.**
- Started as a **girls' school to educate Indian women.**
- First college to **offer higher education for girls** in India.
- Promoted **literacy and social upliftment of women.**
- Influenced the rise of **women's education movements.**
- Supported by **Ishwar Chandra Vidyasagar and social reformers**.
- Encouraged **women's participation in professional careers**.
- Helped in breaking **social taboos against female education**.
- Played a key role in **women's rights and empowerment**.
- Offered **Western and traditional Indian education.**
- Inspired the establishment of **more women's colleges in India**.
- Continues to be a **leading institution for women's education**.

Important universities in pre-independent India

Hindu College of Calcutta (1817)

- **Established in 1817** by **Raja Ram Mohan Roy** and others.
- Later became **Presidency College, now Presidency University**.
- Promoted **Western education alongside Indian knowledge**.
- Played a key role in the **Bengal Renaissance**.
- Focused on **English, science, and liberal arts**.

Question

The Hindu college of Calcutta was later renamed as

1. Surendranath college
2. Ram Mohan Roy college
3. University/College
4. Presidency college

Explanations:
Answer: 4. Presidency college

The Hindu College of Calcutta, established in 1817, was later renamed Presidency College. This institution played a significant role in the educational and intellectual awakening of India during the 19th century and became a prominent center for higher education.

Question

The Anglo- Indian Vidyalaya (college) was founded in Calcutta in 1816 by-

1. The Christian missionaries
2. The local government
3. The East India company
4. The people of Calcutta

Explanations:
Answer: 4. The people of Calcutta

The **Anglo-Indian Vidyalaya** was founded in **Calcutta in 1816** by a group of **Indian intellectuals and reformers**, primarily led by **Raja Rammohan Roy** and **David Hare**. It was later renamed **Hindu College (1817)** and became one of the first institutions in India to impart Western education.

The institution was not founded by **Christian missionaries, the local government, or the East India Company**, but by the **progressive citizens of Calcutta** who wanted to modernize education.

Calcutta University (1857)

- Established under the **Indian Universities Act (1857)**.
- First **modern university in India**, modeled on **London University**.
- Promoted **English education and Western sciences**.
- Key player in the **Bengal Renaissance** and reform movements.
- One of the **three earliest universities in India**.

Question

The Universities of Calcutta, Bombay and Madras were to be set up on the model of:

1. Oxford University
2. Cambridge University
3. University of London
4. University of Edinburgh

Explanations:
Answer: 1. Oxford University

The Universities of Calcutta, Bombay, and Madras, established in 1857, were actually set up on the model of the University of London, not Oxford University. These universities were designed to serve as examining bodies and affiliates for various colleges, similar to the University of London's model at that time, which focused on examination and affiliation rather than direct teaching.

Bombay University (1857)

- Founded under the **Indian Universities Act (1857)**.
- Promoted **Western-style education and research**.
- Introduced the Anglo-vernacular **education system**.
- Pioneered **scientific and technical education**.
- Played a vital role in **industrial and medical education**.

Madras University (1857)

- Established under the **Indian Universities Act (1857)**.
- Focused on **higher education in humanities and sciences**.
- Encouraged **vernacular education alongside English**.

- Contributed to **South Indian intellectual movements**.
- Paved the way for **modern educational institutions** in South India.

Banaras Hindu University (1916)

- Established through the **BHU Act of 1915**.
- The Hindu College in Banaras, set up by Annie Besant
- Founded by **Pandit Madan Mohan Malaviya**.
- Blended **traditional Indian and modern education**.
- Focused on **science, engineering, and Vedic studies**.
- One of India's **largest residential universities**.

Question

The Hindu College in Benares set up by Annie Besant before Independence proposed to impart:

1. Physical education
2. Religious and moral education
3. Western education
4. Medical education

Explanations:
Answer: 2. Religious and moral education

The Hindu College in Banaras, set up by Annie Besant before Independence, aimed to impart religious and moral education. Annie Besant was deeply involved in promoting Indian culture and values and established educational institutions to preserve and teach these traditional values alongside modern education.

Question

The Banaras Sanskrit college was set up by-

1. Jonathan Duncan
2. Pandit Madan Mohan Malaviya
3. Bishop Middleton
4. Surendranath Banerjee

Explanations
Answer: 1. Jonathan Duncan

Banaras Sanskrit College was established in **1791** by **Jonathan Duncan**, who was the **British Resident of Benares** at that time. The institution was set up to promote **Sanskrit learning and traditional Indian education**. Later, it became a part of **Sampurnanand Sanskrit University** in **1958**.

Aligarh Muslim University (1920)

- Upgraded to a university under the **AMU Act of 1920**.
- Evolved from **Mohammedan Anglo-Oriental College (1875)**.
- Founded by **Sir Syed Ahmed Khan**.
- Promoted **modern education among Muslims**.
- Encouraged **scientific and secular learning**.

Question

Statement 1: University of Punjab at Lahore and University of Allahabad were established during colonial rule in India.
Statement II: The main reason for their establishment was the increasing demand in these places for higher education including 'Oriental as well as modern European education.

1. Both Statement I and Statement Il are true
2. Both Statement I and Statement Il are false
3. Statement I is true but Statement Il is false
4. Statement 1 is false but Statement Il is true

Explanations:
Answer: 1. Both Statement I and Statement Il are true

Statement I is True: Both the University of Punjab at Lahore and the University of Allahabad were established during British colonial rule in India. The University of Punjab was established in 1882 and the University of Allahabad in 1887.
Statement II is True: The establishment of these universities was driven by the increasing demand for higher education in these regions, which included both traditional Oriental education and modern European education.

Therefore, the correct answer is: **Both Statement I and Statement II are true.**

Milind College

- **Founded by Dr. B.R. Ambedkar** in **1950**.
- Aimed at **educating Dalits and underprivileged**.
- Located in **Aurangabad, Maharashtra**.
- Promoted **higher education and social equality**.
- Focused on **arts, commerce, and science disciplines**.

Question

Match the column:

List I (Institutions)	List II (Propounders)
A. Milind College	I. BR Ambedkar
B. Rajghat Besant School	II. Sri Aurobindo
C. Banasthali Vidyapeeth	III. Hiralal Shastri
D. Auroville	IV. Jiddu Krishnamurti

1. A-IV, B-III, C-II, D-I
2. A-III, B-II, C-I, D-IV
3. A-II, B-I, C-IV, D-III
4. A-I, B-IV, C-III, D-III

Explanations:
Answer: 4. A-I, B-IV, C-III, D-III

Milind College → I. B.R. Ambedkar (Founded by Dr. Ambedkar in 1950 to promote education among Dalits).

Rajghat Besant School → IV. Jiddu Krishnamurti (Established by Krishnamurti Foundation in Varanasi).

Banasthali Vidyapeeth → III. Hiralal Shastri (Founded in 1935 to promote women's education).

Auroville → II. Sri Aurobindo (An experimental township inspired by Sri Aurobindo's vision).

University Education Commission (1948-49)

- **Formed in 1948** under **Dr. S. Radhakrishnan.**
- First **post-independence education reform commission.**
- Aimed to **restructure Indian university education.**
- **Education Aims** - Intellectual, cultural, and moral growth.
- **Medium - Mother tongue for UG, English higher.**
- **Teacher Training** - Better pay, research, and facilities.
- **University Autonomy** - Reduce political interference.
- **Education Balance** - Liberal arts and technical courses.
- **Research** - Promote scientific and industrial studies.
- **Exams** - Suggested continuous evaluation system.
- **Moral Education** - Value-based, non-sectarian learning.
- **Women's Education** - Equal opportunities in universities.
- **Rural Literacy** - Adult and rural education promotion.
- Led to **formation of UGC (1956).**
- Strengthened **higher education system in India.**

Question

Statement I: Before Independence, the Britishers failed to create a national system of higher education in India.
Statement II: After 1947. The University Education Commission (1948-49) was mandated to suggest improvement to suit the needs of higher education in India.

1. Both Statement 1 and Statement II are true.
2. Both Statement I and Statement II are false.
3. Statement 1 is true but Statement II is false.
4. Statement I is false but Statement II is true.

Explanations:
Answer: 1. Both Statement I and Statement II are true

Statement I is True: The British colonial administration did not establish a cohesive national system of higher education in India. Their efforts were more fragmented and focused on specific regions and institutions rather than creating a unified national system.

Statement II is True: After independence, the University Education Commission (1948-49), chaired by Dr. S. Radhakrishnan, was set up to propose improvements to the higher education system in India to better meet the country's needs.

Therefore, the correct answer is:

Both Statement I and Statement II are true.

Universities established in the early years of the 20th century.

The foundation of higher education in **India** has a rich history that dates back to **pre-independence** times. Several universities were established in the **19th and early 20th centuries**, shaping modern education and serving as centers of learning, research, and cultural exchange. These universities played a crucial role in producing intellectuals, leaders, and reformers who contributed significantly to India's **freedom movement and socio-economic development**.

The **University of Calcutta, Mumbai, and Madras**, founded in **1857**, were the first modern universities in India, modeled on the **British education system**. Over time, other prestigious institutions like **Aligarh Muslim University (1875), Panjab University (1882), and Allahabad University (1887)** emerged, expanding access to **higher education**.

In the **early 20th century**, universities such as **Banaras Hindu University, University of Mysore, Patna University, and Osmania University** were established, reflecting the growing demand for **education in regional languages, sciences, humanities, and professional fields**. These institutions emphasized **a blend of traditional Indian knowledge with Western education**, fostering academic excellence across disciplines.

The establishment of universities like **Visva-Bharati University (1921), University of Delhi (1922), and Andhra University (1926)** further strengthened India's **higher education system**, encouraging innovation, scientific research, and intellectual discourse. These universities remain active today, continuing their legacy of **nurturing scholars, professionals, and nation-builders**.

This **historical evolution of Indian universities** highlights their role in **shaping India's education system**, making them **important for UGC NET aspirants** studying the **development of higher education in India**.

Science education in India was first started in Calcutta in 1817 at Hindu College.

List of Oldest Active Universities in India

Rank	University	Established	Located
1	Senate of Serampore College (University)	1818 / 1829	Serampore
2	University of Calcutta	1857	Kolkata
3	University of Mumbai	1857	Mumbai
4	University of Madras	1857	Chennai
5	Aligarh Muslim University	1875	Aligarh
6	Panjab University, Chandigarh	1882	Chandigarh
7	Allahabad University	1887	Allahabad
8	Banaras Hindu University	1916	Varanasi
9	University of Mysore	1916	Mysore
10	SNDT Women's University	1916	Mumbai
11	Patna University	1917	Patna
12	Osmania University	1918	Hyderabad
13	Mahatma Gandhi Kashi Vidyapeeth	1921	Varanasi
14	Rangoon University	1920	Myanmar
14	University of Lucknow	1921	Lucknow
15	Visva-Bharati University	1921	Santiniketan
16	University of Delhi	1922	New Delhi
17	Nagpur University	1923	Nagpur
18	Andhra University	1926	Visakhapatnam
19	Dr. B.R. Ambedkar University (Agra University)	1927	Agra
20	Annamalai University	1929	Chidambaram

21	University of Roorkee / Indian Institute of Technology, Roorkee	1847 / 1949	Roorkee

Question

Identify the correct chronological order of the establishment of the following universities:

A. SNDT Women's University
B. Allahabad University
C. Patna University
D. Calcutta University
E. Punjab University

1. A, B, C, D, E
2. B, C, E, D, A
3. C, D, B, A, E
4. D, E, B, C, A

Explanations:
Answer: 4. D, E, B, C, A

- **Calcutta University (D) - 1857** (First modern university in India).
- **Punjab University (E) - 1882** (One of the oldest universities in India).
- **Allahabad University (B) - 1887** (Fourth oldest university in India).
- **Patna University (C) - 1917** (First university in Bihar).
- **SNDT Women's University (A) - 1916** (First women's university in India).

Question

Identify the correct chronological sequence of the establishment of the following universities:

A. Osmania
B. Patna
C. Lucknow
D. Annamalai

E. Rangoon

1. ACEBD
2. DEACB
3. CABED
4. BAECD

Explanations:
Answer: 4. BAECD

- **Patna University (B) - 1917** (First university in Bihar).
- **Annamalai University (A) - 1929** (One of the largest residential universities in India).
- **Osmania University (E) - 1918** (Established in Hyderabad by Nizam Mir Osman Ali Khan).
- **Rangoon University (C) - 1920** (One of the oldest universities in Myanmar, then British India).
- **Lucknow University (D) - 1921** (Established in Uttar Pradesh).

Question

Identify the correct sequence from (earliest to latest) of the universities established in the early years of the 20th century.

A. Osmania University
B. Aligarh Muslim University
C. SNDT Women's University
D. Nagpur University
E. Patna University

1. B, C, E, A, D
2. A, C, D, E, B
3. A, B, C, D, E
4. E, D, C, B, A

Explanations:
Answer: 1. B, C, E, A, D

Aligarh Muslim University (1875) – Established as **Mohammedan Anglo-Oriental College** by **Sir Syed Ahmed Khan**, later became AMU in **1920**.

SNDT Women's University (1916) – First **women's university in India**, founded by **Dhondo Keshav Karve** in **Mumbai**.

Patna University (1917) – First **university in Bihar**, known for **arts, sciences, and law**.

Osmania University (1918) – Founded by **Nizam of Hyderabad**, first university to **adopt Urdu as a medium**.

Nagpur University (1923)

Question

Which of the following is the first University established in 1951 exclusively for women?

1. Banasthali Vidyapeeth, Tonk
2. Kashi Vidyapeeth, Benaras
3. SNDT University, Mumbai
4. Savitribai Phule Pune University

Explanations:
Answer: 3. SNDT University, Mumbai

Question

Which of the following universities were set up in 1916?

A. Osmania University
B. S.N.D.T Women's University
C. Mysore University
D. Patna University
E. Banaras Hindu University

1. ABC
2. BCE
3. BCD

4. ADE

Explanations:
Answer: 2. BCE

The following universities were established in **1916**:

Osmania University (B) – Founded in **1916** in **Hyderabad**, it was the first university in India to have **Urdu as a medium of instruction**.

S.N.D.T Women's University (C) – Established in **1916** by **Dhondo Keshav Karve**, it is India's **first women's university**.

Banaras Hindu University (E) – Founded in **1916** by **Madan Mohan Malaviya**, BHU is one of the largest and most prestigious universities in India.

Other Options:

Mysore University (A) – Established earlier, in **1916**, but is not part of the most commonly accepted grouping for this question.

Patna University (D) – Established **later in 1917**, so it is not included in the correct answer.

Question

Identify the correct chronological order of the establishment of the following colleges:

A. Fort William College, Calcutta
B. Sanskrit College, Poona
C. Central Hindu College, Benares
D. Anglo-Vedic College, Lahore
E. Sanskrit College, Benares

1. ABCED
2. CDBEA
3. DEABC
4. EABDC

Explanations:
Answer: 4. EABDC

- **Sanskrit College, Benares (E) - 1791**
- **Fort William College, Calcutta (A) - 1800**
- **Sanskrit College, Poona (B) - 1821**
- **Anglo-Vedic College, Lahore (D) - 1886**
- **Central Hindu College, Benares (C) - 1898**

Question

Science education in India was first started in Calcutta in 1817 at:

1. Surendranath college
2. Ashutosh Mukherjee college
3. St Xavier college
4. Hindu college

Explanations:
Answer: 4. Hindu college

Science education in India was first started in Calcutta in 1817 at Hindu College. Hindu College was established with the aim of providing modern education, including science education, to the youth of Bengal. It played a significant role in the educational and intellectual awakening of India.

Question

The Sridhanya Katak University attained a celebrity status during the period of-

1. Sage Nagarjuna
2. Sage Sankaracharya
3. Sage Ramanuja
4. Sage Prabhakara

Explanations:
Answer: 1. Sage Nagarjuna

Sridhanya Katak University gained prominence during the time of **Sage Nagarjuna**, a great Buddhist philosopher and scholar. Nagarjuna is known for founding the **Madhyamaka school of Mahayana Buddhism**. The university was a major **center for Buddhist learning and philosophical debates**. It played a crucial role in spreading **Buddhism and Mahayana philosophy**.

Question

Which university among the following decided to start post-graduate teaching in 1916?

1. Calcutta University
2. Andhra University
3. Himachal University
4. Delhi University

Explanations:
Answer: 1. Calcutta University

Calcutta University decided to start **postgraduate teaching in 1916**. It was **one of the first universities in India** to introduce **postgraduate programs**. Established in **1857**, it played a key role in shaping India's **higher education system**.

Other universities listed were established later:

- **Andhra University** (1926)
- **Himachal University** (1970)
- **Delhi University** (1922)

English (Anglican) Missionary Societies Involved in Education in North India (Late 19th Century)

1. **The Church Missionary Society (CMS)**
2. **The London Missionary Society (LMS)**
3. **The Society for the Propagation of the Gospel (SPG)**
4. **The Cambridge Mission to Delhi**

Question

Which of the following English (Anglican) missionary societies were heavily involved in teaching in high schools and colleges throughout North India in the latter part of the 9th century?

(A) The Church Missionary Society
(B) The London Missionary Society
(C) Society for the Propagation of the Gospel
(D) The Cambridge Mission to Delhi

1. AB
2. ABCD
3. CD
4. ACD

Explanations:
Answer: 2. ABCD

During the **latter part of the 19th century**, several **English (Anglican) missionary societies** played a crucial role in establishing and managing **high schools and colleges** in **North India**:

The Church Missionary Society (A) – Actively involved in education, setting up schools and colleges, including St. John's College, Agra.

The London Missionary Society (B) – Established educational institutions, particularly in North India, to spread Christian teachings and Western education.

Society for the Propagation of the Gospel (C) – Supported the development of Christian education in India, including founding schools and colleges.

The Cambridge Mission to Delhi (D) – Founded **St. Stephen's College, Delhi** in 1881, one of India's most prestigious educational institutions.

CHAPTER III

Evolution of higher learning and research in Post Independence India.

Evolution of higher learning and research in Post Independence India.

Regulatory Framework of Indian Education

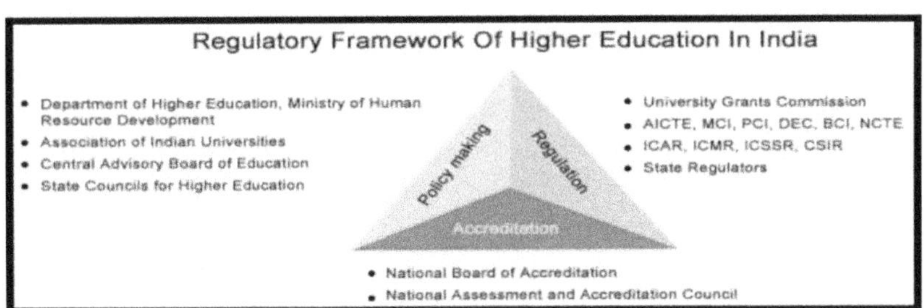

Policy Making Bodies:

Ministry of Education (India)

The Ministry of Education (MoE) is part of the Indian government and handles the implementation of the National Policy on Education. It's split into two departments: the Department of School Education and Literacy, which focuses on primary, secondary, and higher secondary education, as well as adult education and literacy; and the Department of Higher

Education, which covers university-level education, technical education, scholarships, and more.

Previously known as the Ministry of Human Resource Development (MHRD) from 1985 to 2020, it got its original name back with the introduction of the National Education Policy 2020. The current education minister is **Dharmendra Pradhan**, who is part of the Council of Ministers. India had a Ministry of Education since 1947, but it was renamed MHRD in 1985 by Rajiv Gandhi's government. In 2020, Narendra Modi's government changed the name back to the Ministry of Education when they announced the new National Education Policy.

Department of School Education and Literacy:

The Department of School Education and Literacy is responsible for the development of school education and literacy in the country.

- Central Board of Secondary Education (CBSE)
- Central Tibetan School Administration (CTSA)
- Kendriya Vidyalaya Sangathan (KVS)
- National Council of Educational Research and Training (NCERT)
- National Council for Teacher Education (NCTE)
- National Foundation for Teachers' Welfare
- National Institute of Open Schooling (NIOS)
- Navodaya Vidyalaya Samiti (NVS)
- Eklavya Model Residential School (EMRS)
- Bharatiya Shiksha Board (BSB)

Organisational structure:

- University Grants Commission (UGC)
- Indian Council of Social Science Research (ICSSR)
- Indian Council of Historical Research (ICHR)
- Indian Council of Philosophical Research (ICPR)
- 52 Central university (India) as on 11.09.2021 list issued by University Grants Commission
- All India Council of Technical Education (AICTE)
- Council of Architecture (COA)
- 23 Indian Institutes of Technology (IITs)

- 31 National Institutes of Technology (NITs)
- 25 Indian Institutes of Information Technology (IIITs)
- Indian Institute of Engineering Science and Technology, Shibpur (IIEST)
- 20 Indian Institutes of Management (IIMs)
- Indian Institute of Science (IISc)
- 7 Indian Institutes of Science Education and Research (IISERs)
- North Eastern Regional Institute of Science and Technology (NERIST)
- National Institute of Industrial Engineering (NITIE)
- National Institute of Foundry and Forge Technology (NIFFT)
- Indira Gandhi National Open University (IGNOU)
- National Institute of Educational Planning and Administration (NIEPA)
- National Book Trust (NBT)
- National Board of Accreditation (NBA)
- National Commission for Minority Educational Institutions (NCMEI)
- National Institute of Open Schooling (NIOS)
- Indian Knowledge Systems (IKS)

Question

The previous nomenclature of Ministry of Education was-

1. Ministry of Youth Affairs
2. Ministry of Human Resource Development
3. Ministry of Education and Research
4. Ministry of Central Affairs

Explanations:

Answer: 2. Ministry of Human Resource Development

- Previously called Ministry of Human Resource Development (MHRD).
- Renamed as Ministry of Education in 2020 under NEP.
- Focus shifted back to education and learning.
- Originally called Ministry of Education before 1985.

Question

According to the Department of Higher Education, Ministry of Education (GoI), which of the following are considered as the Institutions of higher learning?

A. The National Institute of Fashion Technology. New Delhi
B. National Institute of Design
C. Indian Institute of Advanced Study, Shimla
D. National University of Education Planning and Administration (Neupa), Delhi
E. Rashtriya Sanskrit Vidyapeetha, Tirupati

1. A, B, C
2. B, C, D
3. A, B, D
4. C, D, E

Explanations:
Answer: 4. C, D, E

According to the Department of Higher Education, Ministry of Education, Government of India, the following institutions are considered as Institutions of Higher Learning:

Indian Institute of Advanced Study, Shimla: Established in 1965, it serves as a residential center for advanced research in the humanities and social sciences.

National University of Educational Planning and Administration (NUEPA), Delhi: Focused on research and capacity building in educational planning and administration.

Rashtriya Sanskrit Vidyapeetha, Tirupati: A deemed university dedicated to the promotion of Sanskrit studies.

Question

Which of the following are regulatory bodies within the Department of Higher Education in the Ministry of Human Resource Development in the Central Government?

A. NUEPA
B. UGC
C. AICTE
D. DEC
E. ICSSR

Choose the correct answer from the options given below:

1. B, C and D only
2. A. B and C only
3. C. D and E only
4. A. D and E only

Explanations:
Answer: 1. B, C and D only

To determine which regulatory bodies within the Department of Higher Education in the Ministry of Human Resource Development (now known as the Ministry of Education) in the Central Government, let's look at the options:

NUEPA (National Institute of Educational Planning and Administration): It is primarily a research and training institution, not a regulatory body.

UGC (University Grants Commission): A statutory body responsible for coordinating and maintaining standards of higher education.

AICTE (All India Council for Technical Education): A statutory body responsible for the planning and coordination of technical education and the maintenance of standards.

DEC (Distance Education Council): It was responsible for the promotion and coordination of the open university and distance education system in the country (now replaced by the Distance Education Bureau under UGC).

ICSSR (Indian Council of Social Science Research): It is primarily a funding and research body, not a regulatory body.

The correct regulatory bodies are UGC, AICTE, and DEC.

Inter-University Board

The Inter-University Board, later known as the Association of Indian Universities (AIU), was established in 1925 to foster university activities by sharing information and promoting cooperation in education, culture, sports, and related fields.

Association of Indian Universities

The Association of Indian Universities (AIU) is an organization comprising major universities in India, based in Delhi. It evaluates the courses, syllabi, standards, and credits of foreign universities and equates them with various courses offered by Indian universities.

Central Advisory Board of Education

The Central Advisory Board of Education (CABE) is the top advisory body responsible for advising the Central and State Governments on educational matters. Initially established in 1920, it was later dissolved and re-established in 1935. CABE is the oldest and highest advisory board for the government in the educational sector.

Question

Which is the highest body to advise central and state governments on education?

1. UGC
2. CABE
3. NSDA
4. NIEPA

Explanations:
Answer: 2. CABE

The highest body to advise the central and state governments on education in India is the Central Advisory Board of Education (CABE). CABE is the apex advisory body responsible for advising the central and state governments on policy matters and the overall development of education in the country.

Question

Which of the following was established in 1925 to promote University activities by sharing information and cooperation in the field of education, culture, sports and allied areas

1. Inter-University Accelerator
2. Board of Higher Studies
3. Central Board of University Education
4. Inter-University Board (later known as Association of Indian Universities)

Explanations:
Answer: 4. Inter-University Board (later known as Association of Indian Universities)

- **Established in 1925** to promote university collaboration.
- **Encourages cooperation in education, culture, and sports.**
- **Later renamed as Association of Indian Universities (AIU).**
- **Plays a key role in academic exchange and policy formulation.**

Regulatory Bodies:

University Grants Commission:

The University Grants Commission (UGC) of India is a statutory body established by the Department of Higher Education, Ministry of Education, Government of India, in accordance with the UGC Act of 1956. It is responsible for coordinating, determining, and maintaining the standards of higher education. The establishment of the UGC was recommended by the Radhakrishnan Commission. In India, much of the Central Government **expenditure on general higher education** is routed through the University Grants Commission (UGC).

The UGC is mandate includes:

- Promoting and coordinating university education.
- Determining and maintaining standards of teaching, examination, and research in universities.
- Framing regulations on minimum standards of education.
- Monitoring developments in collegiate and university education and disbursing grants to universities and colleges.
- Serving as a vital link between the Union and state governments and institutions of higher learning.
- Advising the Central and State governments on measures necessary for the improvement of university education.
- To regulate the quality of higher education.
- To fund research projects of faculty
- To suggest model curriculum to the universities

Question

In India, much of the Central Government expenditure on general higher education is routed through

1. Natural Council of Teacher Education
2. All India Council for Technical Education
3. University Grants Commission
4. National Council for Educational Research and Training.

Explanations:
Answer: 3. University Grants Commission

In India, much of the Central Government expenditure on general higher education is routed through the University Grants Commission (UGC). The UGC is responsible for coordinating, determining, and maintaining the standards of higher education, and it disburses funds to universities and colleges across the country.

Question

Which among the following is NOT the responsibility of UGC?

1. To regulate quality of higher education.
2. To maintain discipline in campuses of institutions of higher education.
3. To fund research projects of faculty

4. To suggest model curriculum to the universities

Explanations:
Answer: 2. To maintain discipline in campuses of institutions of higher education.

The University Grants Commission (UGC) has several key responsibilities, including regulating the quality of higher education, funding research projects of faculty, and suggesting model curriculums to universities. However, maintaining discipline on campuses of institutions of higher education is not within the purview of the UGC; this responsibility typically falls under the administration of the individual institutions.

Question

In India, much of the Central Government expenditure on general higher education is routed through

1. Natural Council of Teacher Education
2. All India Council for Technical Education
3. University Grants Commission
4. National Council for Educational Research and Training.

Explanations:
Answer: 3. University Grants Commission

In India, much of the Central Government expenditure on general higher education is routed through the University Grants Commission (UGC). The UGC is responsible for coordinating, determining, and maintaining the standards of higher education and disburses funds to universities and colleges across the country.

Question

Which of the following come under the mandate of the University Grants Commission (UGC)?

A. Promotion and coordination of University education.
B. Determining and monitoring standards of teaching, examination and research in Universities.

C. Organising continuous professional development programmes for college and
D. University teachers
E. Framing regulations on minimum standards of education.
F. Disbursing and regulating grants to the universities and colleges.

Choose the correct answer from the options given below:

1. (A), (B) only
2. (A), (C), (D), (E) only
3. (B), (C), (D), (E) only
4. (A), (B), (D), (E) only

Explanations:
Answer: (4) (A), (B), (D), (E) only

The University Grants Commission (UGC) has the following mandates:

(A) Promotion and coordination of University education.
(B) Determining and monitoring standards of teaching, examination, and research in Universities.
(D) Framing regulations on minimum standards of education.
(E) Disbursing and regulating grants to the universities and colleges.

Organizing continuous professional development programs for college and university teachers, while important, is not specifically listed as a core function of the UGC.

Therefore, the correct answer is: **4. (A), (B), (D), (E) only**

AICTE - All India Council for Technical Education

- **Established in 1945** as an **advisory body**.
- **Gained statutory status** through **1987 AICTE Act**.
- **Regulates technical education** in **India**.
- **Approves new technical institutions** and courses.
- **Regulates intake capacity** in technical colleges.
- **Delegates diploma approvals** to **state governments**.
- **Sets norms and standards** for institutions.
- **Ensures quality** through **accreditation processes**.

- **Promotes technical education** for **women and weaker sections**.
- **Encourages research, faculty, and innovation**.
- **Provides grants** to **technical institutions**.
- Covers **engineering, pharmacy, architecture, management studies**.
- **Oversees diploma, UG, and PG programs**.
- Includes **hotel management, applied arts, crafts**.
- **Headquarters located** in **New Delhi**.
- **Has seven regional offices** across **India**.
- **New regional office** being set up in **Hyderabad**.
- **Works through an Executive Committee**.
- **Supervises training and research** in technology.
- **Focuses on quality and innovation** in education.

Question

AICTE is not dealing with the maintenance of standards in which one of the following areas?

1. Hotel Management
2. Town Planning
3. Pharmacy
4. Nursing

Explanations:
Answer: 4. Nursing

The All India Council for Technical Education (AICTE) is responsible for maintaining standards in various areas such as Hotel Management, Town Planning, and Pharmacy. However, the maintenance of standards in the field of Nursing falls under the purview of the Indian Nursing Council (INC).

Council of Architecture (COA)

- **Established** under the **Architects Act, 1972**.
- Came into force on **September 1, 1972**.
- Regulates **architectural education and practice**.
- Maintains a **Register of Architects**.
- Ensures **quality standards in architecture**.
- Conducts **inspections through expert committees**.

- Reviews **recognized architectural qualifications**.
- Can recommend **de-recognition of institutions**.
- Reports inadequacies to **Central Government**.
- Central Government **considers COA recommendations**.
- Advises on **policy matters in architecture**.
- Controls **eligibility for architecture practice**.
- Plays a role in **curriculum development**.
- Supports **architectural research and innovation**.
- Works to **protect public interest in architecture**.

Other Regulatory Bodies

MCI - Medical Council of India

- **Established in 1934** under **Indian Medical Council Act (1933)**.
- **Regulated medical education and profession** in India.
- **Set standards** for medical colleges and professionals.
- **Granted recognition** to medical qualifications.
- **Replaced by NMC (National Medical Commission) in 2020**.

PCI - Pharmacy Council of India

- **Established under the Pharmacy Act, 1948**.
- **Regulates pharmacy education and profession** in India.
- **Maintains standards** for pharmacy institutions.
- **Grants recognition** to pharmacy degrees and diplomas.
- **Ensures ethical practice** in pharmaceutical professions.

BCI - Bar Council of India

- **Established under the Advocates Act, 1961**.
- **Regulates legal education and profession** in India.
- **Sets standards** for law universities and courses.
- **Conducts All India Bar Examination (AIBE)**.
- **Maintains the roll of practicing advocates**.

Question

Match the column:

A. lay down standards of legal education	I. NCTE
B. maintaining the quality of technical education	II. AICTE
C. maintenance of standards in teacher education	I. NMC
D. Access to quality and affordable medical education	IV. BCI

1. A-IV B-II C-I D-III
2. A-I B-II C-IV D-III
3. A-II B-III C-IV D-I
4. A-III B-IV C-I D-II

Explanations:
Answer: 1. A-IV B-II C-I D-III

Let's match the institutions to their corresponding responsibilities:

A. Lay down standards of legal education - IV. BCI (Bar Council of India)
B. Maintaining the quality of technical education - II. AICTE (All India Council for Technical Education)
C. Maintenance of standards in teacher education - I. NCTE (National Council for Teacher Education)
D. Access to quality and affordable medical education - III. NMC (National Medical Commission)

NCERT - National Council of Educational Research and Training

- **Established in 1961** as an **autonomous body**.
- **Develops school curriculum and textbooks**.
- **Conducts research** on educational policies.
- **Supports teacher training programs**.
- **Provides guidance** to state and central education bodies.

Question

Statement-I: University Grants Commission (UGC) became a statutory organization of the Government of India by an act of Parliament in 1956.

Statement-II: National Council of Educational Research and Training (NCERT) is an autonomous organization set up in 1961 by the Government of India.

1. Both Statement I and Statement II are correct.
2. Both Statement I and Statement II are incorrect.
3. Statement I is correct but Statement II s incorrect.
4. Statement I is incorrect but Statement II is correct.

Explanations:
Answer: 1. Both Statement I and Statement II are correct.

Statement I is Correct: The UGC was indeed established as a statutory organization through an Act of Parliament in 1956.
Statement II is Correct: NCERT was established in 1961 as an autonomous organization by the Government of India.

Therefore, the correct answer is: **Both Statement I and Statement II are correct.**

DST - Department of Science & Technology

- **Established in May 1971** to promote **Science & Technology**.
- **Coordinates national research programs**.
- **Supports scientific institutions** like Bose Institute.
- **Funds R&D and innovation projects**.
- **Encourages technology-driven entrepreneurship**.
- The following autonomous scientific institutions come under the financial umbrella of the Department of Science and Technology (DST):
    - Bose Institute, Kolkata
    - Agarkar Research Institute, Pune
    - Wadia Institute of Himalayan Geology, Dehradun

Question

The Government of India created Department of Science and Technology in the year:

1. 1990

2. 1985
3. 1978
4. 1971

Explanations:
Answer: 4. 1971

The Government of India created the Department of Science and Technology (DST) in the year 1971 with the objective of promoting new areas of science and technology and acting as a nodal department for organizing, coordinating, and promoting S&T activities in the country.

Question

Which of the following autonomous scientific institutions come under the financial umbrella of the Department of Science and Technology?

A. Bose Institute, Kolkata
B. Agarkar Research Institute, Pune
C. Raman Research Institute, Bangalore.
D. Wadia Institute of Himalayan Geology, Dehradun
E. Indian Council of Astrological science, Banglore.

Choose the correct pair

1. ABE
2. BDE
3. CDE
4. ABD

Explanations:
Answer: 4. ABD

The following autonomous scientific institutions come under the financial umbrella of the Department of Science and Technology (DST):

- Bose Institute, Kolkata
- Agarkar Research Institute, Pune
- Wadia Institute of Himalayan Geology, Dehradun

The Raman Research Institute, Bangalore, and the Indian Council of Astrological Science, Bangalore, are not funded by the Department of Science and Technology.

DEC - Distance Education Bureau (Formerly Distance Education Council)

- **Established in 1991** by **IGNOU**.
- **Regulated open and distance learning programs**.
- **Ensured quality standards** in distance education.
- **Promoted flexible learning opportunities**.
- **Merged into UGC as Distance Education Bureau (DEB)**.

NCTE - National Council of Teacher Education

- **Established in 1995** under **NCTE Act, 1993**.
- **Regulates teacher education programs** in India.
- **Accredits teacher training institutions**.
- **Develops guidelines** for teacher eligibility.
- **Ensures quality standards** in teaching education.

Question

In pursuance of the National Council of Teacher Education Act 1993, NCTE was established in the year:

1. 1995
2. 1993
3. 1994
4. 1996

Explanations:
Answer: 1. 1995

The National Council for Teacher Education (NCTE) was established in pursuance of the National Council for Teacher Education Act, 1993. Although the act was passed in 1993, the NCTE itself came into existence on August 17, 1995.

Question

Statement I: The UGC in India has statutory responsibility for maintenance of quality and coordination of institutions of higher education

Statement II: The NCTE being a regulatory body for teacher education in India comes under the control of UGC

In light of the above statements, choose the most appropriate answer from the options given below

1. Both Statement I and Statement Il are true
2. Both Statement | and Statement Il are false
3. Statement l is correct but Statement Il is false
4. Statement I is incorrect but Statement Il is true

Explanations:
Answer: 3. Statement l is correct but Statement Il is false

Statement I is Correct: The University Grants Commission (UGC) is indeed responsible for maintaining the quality and coordination of higher education institutions in India.

Statement II is False: The National Council for Teacher Education (NCTE) is a regulatory body for teacher education, but it operates independently and does not come under the control of UGC.

Question

Pick the correctly matched pairs:

A. AICTE - Teacher Education
B. ICSSR - Social Science Research
C. NMC - Medical Education
D. NCTE - Technical Education
E. RCI - Special Education

1. BCD
2. ACE
3. AD
4. BCE

Explanations:
Answer: 4. BCE

- **ICSSR - Social Science Research** (Promotes **social science research** in India).
- **NMC - Medical Education** (Regulates **medical education and profession**).
- **RCI - Special Education** (Regulates **rehabilitation and special education**).

AICTE - Teacher Education (AICTE regulates **technical education**, not teaching).
NCTE - Technical Education (NCTE regulates **teacher education**, not technical).

Accrediting Bodies:

In India, various accreditation agencies play a crucial role in ensuring quality education. The National Board of Accreditation (NBA) oversees engineering and technology programs, while healthcare institutions are evaluated by the National Accreditation Board for Hospitals & Healthcare Providers (NABH). For higher education institutions, including universities and colleges, the National Assessment and Accreditation Council (NAAC) is responsible. Technical and management institutions are under the purview of the All India Council for Technical Education (AICTE). These agencies work diligently to assess institutions, maintain high educational standards, and contribute to the ongoing improvement of education quality across the country.

The NATIONAL ASSESSMENT AND ACCREDITATION COUNCIL (NAAC)

- **Established** under **National Policy on Education (1986)**.
- Became **independent in 1994** under **UGC**.
- Ensures **quality in higher education institutions**.
- Accredits **central, state, and private universities**.
- Covers **institutions of national importance**.
- Evaluates **affiliated and autonomous colleges**.

- Assesses **curricular aspects and teaching methods**.
- Reviews **learning resources and infrastructure**.
- Examines **student support and progression**.
- Conducts **assessment of Higher Educational Institutions (HEIs)**.
- Determines **institution's overall 'Quality Status'**.
- Encourages **continuous improvement in education**.
- Enhances **global recognition of Indian institutions**.
- Supports **policy-making in higher education**.
- Plays a key role in **higher education reforms**.
- **Evaluation by the NAAC is based on seven criteria:**
    - Curricular Aspects.
    - Teaching-Learning and Evaluation.
    - Research, Consultancy, and Extension.
    - Infrastructure and Learning Resources.
    - Student Support and Progression.
    - Governance, Leadership, and Management
    - Innovations and Best Practices

Question

Which among the following is/are not a criteria for quality assessment followed by NAAC :

A. Teaching -learning and Evaluation
B. Consultancy and Extension
C. Infrastructure and Learning Resources
D. Recruitment of Teaching Professionals
E. Governance and Leadership

1. D
2. ABD
3. BCE
4. B

Explanations:
Answer: 1. D

The criteria for quality assessment followed by the National Assessment and Accreditation Council (NAAC) include:

- Teaching-learning and Evaluation
- Consultancy and Extension
- Infrastructure and Learning Resources
- Governance and Leadership

However, "Recruitment of Teaching Professionals" is not a criterion for quality assessment followed by NAAC.

Question

Which of the following were UGC recommendations on quality assurance?

A. Dismantling unviable colleges and universities
B. Creating a parallel accreditation agency for private universities.
C. Adoption of total quality management practices
D. Sustaining quality through innovation and creativity
E. Establishment of suitable assessment and accreditation systems

1. ABC
2. BCD
3. CDE
4. ADE

Explanations:
Answer: 3. CDE

Adoption of total quality management practices – Encouraged for improving educational standards.

Sustaining quality through innovation and creativity – Essential for long-term academic excellence.

Establishment of suitable assessment and accreditation systems – Led to the creation of NAAC & NBA.

Incorrect options:

Dismantling unviable colleges and universities – Not a UGC recommendation.

Creating a parallel accreditation agency – UGC does not support multiple agencies.

Question

Which of the following are correct?

A. UGC frames regulations and sets minimum standards of education
B. NAAC ensures quality and accreditation
C. HEFA provides grant-in-Aid to higher education institutions
D. NIRF ranks Indian institutions

1. B
2. D
3. ABD
4. BCD

Explanations:
Answer: 3. ABD

A. UGC frames regulations and sets minimum standards of education – UGC regulates and maintains higher education standards.

B. NAAC ensures quality and accreditation – NAAC assesses and accredits institutions based on quality parameters.

D. NIRF ranks Indian institutions – NIRF (National Institutional Ranking Framework) ranks Indian universities and colleges.

C. HEFA provides grant-in-aid – Incorrect, HEFA provides loans, not grants, for infrastructure development.

Question

Match the column:

A. NIEPA	I. Promotion of quality in technical education
B. NAAC	II. to promote research in social sciences
C. AICTE	III. Planning and management of education
D. ICSSR	IV. Accreditation of higher education institutions

1. A-III B-IV B-II D-I
2. A-IV B-III C-II D-I
3. A-III B-IV C-I D-II
4. A-IV B-II C-I D-III

Explanations:
Answer: 3. A-III B-IV C-I D-II

A. NIEPA (National Institute of Educational Planning and Administration) - III. Planning and management of education
B. NAAC (National Assessment and Accreditation Council) - IV. Accreditation of higher education institutions
C. AICTE (All India Council for Technical Education) - I. Promotion of quality in technical education
D. ICSSR (Indian Council of Social Science Research) - II. To promote research in social sciences

So, the correct matches are:

A-III
B-IV
C-I
D-II

Question

Which of the following forms part of criteria for assessment of higher education institutions as laid down by National Assessment and Accreditation Council (NAAC)?

A. Curricular aspects
B. Teaching-learning and Evaluation
C. Continuous improvement in attainment of outcomes
D. Research, innovation and extension
E. Facilities and Technical support

Choose the correct answer from the options given below:

(1) (A). (B). (C) only

(2) (A). (B). (D) only
(3) (C). (D). (B) only
(4) (D). (B). (A) only

Explanations:
Answer: (2) (A). (B). (D) only

The criteria for assessment of higher education institutions as laid down by the National Assessment and Accreditation Council (NAAC) include:

- Curricular Aspects (A)
- Teaching-learning and Evaluation (B)
- Research, Innovation and Extension (D)

The correct answer does not include "Continuous improvement in attainment of outcomes" (C) and "Facilities and Technical support" as part of NAAC's specified criteria.

The National Board of Accreditation (NBA)

- **Established by AICTE in 1994**.
- Ensures **quality education in technical programs**.
- Accredits **engineering, pharmacy, architecture, hospitality**.
- Institutions undergo **self-assessment for accreditation**.
- Evaluates **program outcomes and curriculum**.
- Reviews **vision, mission, and educational objectives**.
- Formed under **Section 10(u) of AICTE Act**.
- Assesses **diploma to postgraduate level programs**.
- Covers **engineering, management, pharmacy, technology**.
- Focuses on **qualitative improvement in technical education**.

Question

Which of the following types of institutions come under the ambit of National Board of Accreditation (NBA)?

(1) Teacher education institutions
(3) Agriculture institutions
(2) Technical institutions
(4) Medical institutions

Explanations:
Answer:(2) Technical institutions

The National Board of Accreditation (NBA) is primarily responsible for accrediting technical institutions. This includes engineering, technology, management, architecture, pharmacy, and other technical programs. It does not typically cover teacher education, agriculture, or medical institutions.

Therefore, the correct answer is: **2. Technical institutions**

AICTE

- **Established in November 1945** as an **Apex Advisory Body**.
- **Given** statutory status by an **Act of Parliament in 1987.**
- Formed to **promote technical education in India**.
- Conducts **surveys on technical education facilities**.
- Ensures **coordinated and integrated development**.
- Oversees **engineering, technology, and management programs**.
- Regulates **architecture and town planning education**.
- Covers **pharmacy, applied arts, and hotel management**.
- Monitors **training and research in technical fields**.
- Approves **new technical institutions and courses**.
- Sets **quality standards for technical education**.
- Implements **faculty development and innovation schemes**.
- Supports **women and weaker sections in education**.
- Provides **grants to technical institutions**.
- Works through **regional offices across India**.
- Plays a key role in **technical education reforms**.
- **Objectives of AICTE:**
    - Promotion of Quality in Technical Education.
    - Planning and Coordinated Development of the Technical Education System.
    - Regulation and Maintenance of Norms and Standards.

Question

In which year. All India Council for Technical Education was set up as a statutory body by an Act of Parliament?

1. 1986
2. 1988
3. 1987
4. 1989

Explanations:
Answer: 3. 1987

The All India Council for Technical Education (AICTE) was established as a statutory body by an Act of Parliament in the year 1987.

Therefore, the correct answer is: **3. 1987**

Question

This institution that regulates all the technical education institutions in India is:

1. NPTEL
2. NCERT
3. NCTE
4. AICTE

Explanations:
Answer: 4. AICTE

Question

Match the column:

List I (Courses)	List II (Regulating Bodies)
A. B.Ed-M.Ed	(1) MCI
B. Special Education	(II) AICTE
C. B.Tech-Engineering	(III) RCI
D. MBBS	(IV) NCTE

1. A-I, B-II, C-III, D-IV
2. A-IV, B-III, C-II, D-I
3. A-III, B-I, C-II, D-IV
4. A-II, B-IV, C-II, D-III

Explanations:
Answer: 2. A-IV, B-III, C-II, D-I

B.Ed-M.Ed → IV. NCTE: National Council for Teacher Education (NCTE) regulates teacher education programs.

Special Education → III. RCI: Rehabilitation Council of India (RCI) oversees special education programs.

B.Tech-Engineering → II. AICTE: All India Council for Technical Education (AICTE) regulates engineering and technical courses.

MBBS → I. MCI: Medical Council of India (MCI) (now **NMC**) regulates medical education.

Question

Which of the following institutions was established before Indian independence?

1. ICSSR
2. AICTE
3. ICHR
4. ICPR

Explanations:
Answer: 2. AICTE

The All India Council for Technical Education (AICTE) was established in November 1945, which is before Indian independence in 1947.

The other institutions listed were established after Indian independence:

- ICSSR (Indian Council of Social Science Research) was established in 1969.
- ICHR (Indian Council of Historical Research) was established in 1972.
- ICPR (Indian Council of Philosophical Research) was established in 1977.

Question

Statement I: The All India Council of Technical Education (AICTE) was established in 1956 in order to ensure planned and coordinated development of technical education in India.
Statement II : Technical Education was defined as programmes of education in engineering, technology, architecture, town planning, management, pharmacy and applied arts and crafts.

1. Both Statement I and Statement Il are true.
2. Both Statement I and Statement Il are false.
3. Statement I is true but Statement Il is false.
4. Statement I is false but Statement Il is true.

Explanations:
Answer: 4. Statement I is false but Statement Il is true

Statement I is False: The AICTE was actually established in November 1945 as an advisory body and later gained statutory status in 1987 through an Act of Parliament, not in 1956.

Statement II is True: Technical education in India includes programs in engineering, technology, architecture, town planning, management, pharmacy, and applied arts and crafts.

Research Councils

ICAR - Indian Council of Agricultural Research

- **Established on July 16, 1929**, under **Ministry of Agriculture**.
- **Autonomous body** under **DARE, Government of India**.
- Promotes **agricultural research and education**.

Question

Which of the following are included among the Institutes of Agricultural Research?

A. Indian Council of Agricultural Research.
B. Indian Institute of Food Technology.

C. Central Agricultural Marketing Department.
D. Indian Dairy Research Institute.

1. ABCD
2. ABD
3. AB
4. AC

Explanations:
Answer: 1. ABCD

The Institutes of Agricultural Research in India include:

- Indian Council of Agricultural Research (ICAR): The apex body for coordinating, guiding, and managing research and education in agriculture.
- Indian Institute of Food Technology: Focuses on food technology and research.
- Central Agricultural Marketing Department: Deals with agricultural marketing research.
- Indian Dairy Research Institute: Conducts research in dairy science and technology.

CSIR - Council of Scientific and Industrial Research

- **Established in 1942** as an **autonomous body**.
- Focuses on **scientific and industrial research**.
- Operates **national laboratories across India**.

ICMR - Indian Council of Medical Research

- **Founded on November 15, 1911**, as **IRFA**.
- Renamed as **ICMR in 1949**.
- Promotes **biomedical research in India**.

ICSSR - Indian Council of Social Science Research

- **Established in 1969** by **Government of India**.
- Supports **social science research and funding**.

- Provides **grants and fellowships for researchers**.

Question

Match the column:

A. ICSSR	I. Philosophy
B. DST	Il. Social Sciences
C. ICMR	Ill. Sciences
D. ICPR	IV. Medicine

1. A-IV B-II C-I D-III
2. A-I B-IV C-II D-II
3. A-III B-I C-II D-IV
4. A-ll B-III C-IV D-I

Explanations:
Answer: 4. A-ll B-III C-IV D-I

Let's match the institutions to their corresponding fields:

A. ICSSR (Indian Council of Social Science Research) - II. Social Sciences
B. DST (Department of Science & Technology) - III. Sciences
C. ICMR (Indian Council of Medical Research) - IV. Medicine
D. ICPR (Indian Council of Philosophical Research) - I. Philosophy

ICHR - Indian Council of Historical Research

- **Founded in 1972** under **Indira Gandhi's tenure**.
- Promotes **historical research and publications**.
- Provides **fellowships and grants for historians**.

ICPR - Indian Council of Philosophical Research

- **Established in March 1977** under **Societies Act**.
- Encourages **philosophical research and dialogue**.
- Funds **projects, seminars, and fellowships**.

Question

Arrange the following institutions in the chronological order of their establishment.

A. ICSSR (Indian Council of Social Science Research)
B. CSIR (Council of Scientific and Industrial Research)
C. TIAS (Indian Institute of Advanced study, Shimla)
D. ICHR (Indian Council of Historical Research)
E. ICPR (Indian Council of Philosophical Research)

Choose the correct pair

1. A.C.E.B.D
2. B,C,A.D,E
3. C.D.A.E.B
4. D.A.B.E.C

Explanations:
Answer: 2. B,C,A.D,E

To arrange the institutions in chronological order of their establishment:

- CSIR (Council of Scientific and Industrial Research): Established in 1942.
- IIAS (Indian Institute of Advanced Study, Shimla): Established in 1964.
- ICSSR (Indian Council of Social Science Research): Established in 1969.
- ICHR (Indian Council of Historical Research): Established in 1972.
- ICPR (Indian Council of Philosophical Research): Established in 1977

Question

Which of the following are autonomous research institutions under various government departments and agencies in India?

A. Council of Scientific and Industrial Research
B. Indian Council of Social Science Research
C. Indian Institute of Astrophysics

D. Institute of Clinical Research, India
E. Indian Biological Sciences and Research Institute

Choose the correct pair

1. A, B and C only
2. B, C and D only
3. C, D and E only
4. A, D and E only

Explanations:
Answer: 1. A, B and C only

Among the listed institutions, the following are autonomous research institutions under various government departments and agencies in India:

- **Council of Scientific and Industrial Research (CSIR):** An autonomous body established in 1942, it is one of the largest and most diverse research and development organizations in India.
- **Indian Council of Social Science Research (ICSSR):** Established in 1969 by the Government of India to promote research in social sciences.
- **Indian Institute of Astrophysics (IIA):** An autonomous research institution devoted to the study of astronomy, astrophysics, and related sciences.

The Institute of Clinical Research, India and the Indian Biological Sciences and Research Institute are not recognized as autonomous research institutions under government departments.

Institutes

IIAS - Indian Institute of Advanced Study

- **Established in 1964** by **Ministry of Education**.
- **Began functioning on 20 October 1965**.
- Located in **Shimla, Himachal Pradesh**.
- Focuses on **higher research in humanities and social sciences**.

- Hosts **scholars for advanced interdisciplinary studies**.

NIEPA - National Institute of Educational Planning and Administration

- **Originated in 1962** as a **UNESCO initiative**.
- Taken over by **Government of India in 1970**.
- Renamed **National Staff College in 1970**.
- Became **NIEPA in 1979**.
- Specializes in **education planning and administration**.

Question

Match the column:

List I (Institutions)	**List II (Domains)**
A. NIEPA	(I) To promote quality in technical education
B. ICSSR	(II) To accredit higher education institutions
C. NAAC	(III) Education planning and management
D. AICTE	(IV) To promote social science research

1. A-I, B-II, C-III, D-IV
2. A-II, B-I, C-IV, D-III
3. A-III, B-IV, C-II, D-I
4. A-IV, B-I, C-III, D-II

Explanations:
Answer: 3. A-III, B-IV, C-II, D-I

NIEPA → III. Education planning and management National Institute of Educational Planning and Administration focuses on education policies.

ICSSR → IV. To promote social science research: Indian Council of Social Science Research funds and supports research in social sciences.

NAAC → II. To accredit higher education institutions: National Assessment and Accreditation Council evaluates and accredits universities and colleges.

AICTE → I. To promote quality in technical education: All India Council for Technical Education regulates technical education institutions.

NIOS - National Institute of Open Schooling

- **Established in November 1989.**
- Formerly known as **National Open School (NOS)**.
- Created under **National Policy on Education (1986)**.
- Provides **flexible learning for all age groups**.
- Offers **secondary, senior secondary, and vocational programs**.

NCVET - National Council for Vocational Education and Training

- **Formed on 10 October 2018.**
- Merged **NCVT and NSDA** into one body.
- Regulates **vocational education and skill training**.
- Ensures **quality standards in skill development**.
- Supports **workforce training for various industries**.

Question

Match the column:

A. NIOS	I. Teacher Education
A. NCTE	Il. Technical Education
A. AICTE	Ill. Vocational Education
A. NCVET	IV. Distance Education

1. A-IV B-I C-II D-III
2. A-I B-II C-III D-IV
3. A-Il B-III C-IV D-I
4. A-III B-IV C-I D-II

Explanations:
Answer: 1. A-IV B-I C-II D-III

Let's match the institutions to their corresponding areas of focus:

- **NIOS (National Institute of Open Schooling):** Focuses on distance education.
- **NCTE (National Council for Teacher Education):** Focuses on teacher education.
- **AICTE (All India Council for Technical Education):** Focuses on technical education.
- **NCVET (National Council for Vocational Education and Training):** Focuses on vocational education.

Types of Universities in India

India's higher education system is vast and diverse, catering to millions of students across various disciplines. The universities in India can be broadly classified into different types based on their funding, governance, and areas of specialization. The **Central Universities**, established by an Act of Parliament, receive direct funding from the **Government of India** and play a crucial role in maintaining high academic standards. **State Universities**, on the other hand, are set up by state governments and serve a larger student population by offering a wide range of courses. **Deemed-to-be Universities** enjoy autonomy in academic and administrative decisions, granted by the **University Grants Commission (UGC)** based on their excellence in education and research. **Private Universities** have emerged as significant contributors to higher education, often providing specialized courses in engineering, management, and liberal arts. **Open Universities**, such as **Indira Gandhi National Open University (IGNOU)**, cater to distance learners, making education more accessible to a broader section of society. Additionally, **Institutions of National Importance**, including **IITs, NITs, and AIIMS**, focus on advanced research and technological development. These different types of universities collectively form the backbone of India's higher education system, fostering academic growth, research, and skill development to meet global standards.

Question

Which among the following are the types of universities existing in India currently?

A. Community University
B. Deemed University
C. Research University

D. Central University
E. Private University

Choose the correct option:

1. (A), (B), (C), (D) only
2. (A, (B), (D), (E) only
3. (B), (D), (E) only
4. (A), (C), (D) only

Explanations:
Answer: 3. (B), (D), (E) only

In India, the current types of universities include:

- Deemed University
- Central University
- Private University

Community universities and research universities are not distinct categories recognized in the Indian higher education system in the same way as the above three.

Question

University and University-level institutions are categorised into:

(a) Central Universities
(b) State Universities
(c) Private Universities
(d)Deemed-to-be Universities
(e) Institutions of Higher Learning
(f) Civil Sector Institutions

Select the correct option

1. (a), (c), (e) and (f)
2. (b), (d), (e) and (f)
3. (a), (b), (c) and (d)
4. (b), (d), (e) and (f)

Explanations:
Answer: 3. (a), (b), (c) and (d)

University and university-level institutions in India are generally categorized into the following types:

Central Universities: Established by an act of Parliament and funded by the central government.

State Universities: Established by an act of the state legislature and funded by the state government.

Private Universities: Established through state legislation but funded and managed privately.

Deemed-to-be Universities: Institutions recognized by the central government upon recommendation by the UGC, having full autonomy in course and syllabus design and the ability to award degrees.

Institutions of Higher Learning and Civil Sector Institutions are not standard categories used to classify universities and university-level institutions in India.

Central University

Central universities in India are public universities set up by **an Act of Parliament and are mainly under the Department of Higher Education in the Ministry of Education.** However, **nine** universities fall under different ministries. Usually, universities in India get recognized by the University Grants Commission (**UGC**), which operates under the University Grants Commission Act of 1956. There are also **15 Professional Councils** managing various aspects of accreditation and coordination.

Central universities also follow the **Central Universities Act of 2009**, which outlines their purpose, powers, and governance, and led to the creation of **12 new universities.** As of June 2023, the UGC lists **56** central universities.

Central Universities:

- **University of Delhi (DU)** - New Delhi
- **Jawaharlal Nehru University (JNU)** - New Delhi
- **Banaras Hindu University (BHU)** - Varanasi, Uttar Pradesh
- **Aligarh Muslim University (AMU)** - Aligarh, Uttar Pradesh
- **University of Hyderabad (UoH)** - Hyderabad, Telangana
- **Jamia Millia Islamia (JMI)** - New Delhi
- **Pondicherry University** - Puducherry
- **Central University of Rajasthan** - Ajmer, Rajasthan
- **Central University of Punjab** - Bathinda, Punjab
- **Central University of Gujarat** - Gandhinagar, Gujarat

Delhi has the most central universities, with **seven**. Every Indian state has at **least one central university except Goa.** Among the union territories, central universities are located in Delhi, Jammu and Kashmir, Ladakh, and Puducherry.

The President of India serves as the visitor of these central universities.

- **JNU – Jawaharlal Nehru University**
    - Location: New Delhi, Delhi
- **DU – University of Delhi**
    - Location: New Delhi, Delhi
- **BHU – Banaras Hindu University**
    - Location: Varanasi, Uttar Pradesh
- **JMI – Jamia Millia Islamia**
    - Location: Jamia Nagar, Delhi
- **AMU – Aligarh Muslim University**
    - Location: Aligarh, Uttar Pradesh
- **UoH – University of Hyderabad**
    - Location: Hyderabad, Telangana
- **Dr. Rajendra Prasad Central Agricultural University**
    - Location: Pusa, Bihar
- **Pondicherry University**
    - Location: Pondicherry, Puducherry
- **CUP – Central University of Punjab**
    - Location: Bathinda, Punjab
- **CURAJ – Central University of Rajasthan**

- Location: NH-8, Ajmer, Rajasthan

Question

Statement I: Central University is established under an act of Parliament.
Statement Il: The Prime Minister of India acts as the visitor of the Central University.

In light of the above statements, choose the most appropriate answer from the options given below

1. Both Statement I and Statement Il are Correct
2. Both Statement I and Statement Il are Incorrect
3. Statement I is Correct but Statement Il is Incorrect
4. Statement l is Incorrect but Statement Il is Correct

Explanations:
Answer: 3. Statement I is Correct but Statement Il is Incorrect

Statement I is Correct: Central universities in India are indeed established by an act of Parliament.

Statement II is Incorrect: The President of India, not the Prime Minister, acts as the visitor of central universities.

Question

Central Universities are:

A. established by the UGC
B. established by an act of the Parliament
C. established by the Department of Education, Government of India
D. funded by the Central government
E. Funded by the 'Niti Ayog'

Choose the correct option:

1. A and D only
2. C and E only
3. B and D only
4. B and E only

Explanations:
Answer: 3. B and D only

Central universities in India are established by an act of Parliament and are funded by the Central government. These universities are created to serve as prominent institutions of higher learning directly under the purview of the central government.

Question

Given below are two statements: one is labelled as Assertion (A) and the other is labelled as Reason (R).

Assertion (A): Central Universities are considered elite higher education institutions in
India.
Reason (R): Despite their elitist image, these institutions do not find place in the top order of international ranking.

In the light of the above two statements choose the correct answer from the options given below

1. Both (A) and (R) are true and (R) is the correct explanation of (A)
2. Both (A) and (R) are true, but (R) is NOT the correct explanation of (A)
3. (A) is true. but (R) is false
4. (A) is false, but (R) is true

Explanations:
Answer: 2. Both (A) and (R) are true, but (R) is NOT the correct explanation of (A)

Assertion (A) is True: Central Universities in India are highly regarded for their quality of education, research output, and overall academic standards. They are often considered elite institutions within the country.

Reason (R) is True: It is accurate that many of these institutions, despite their high reputation within India, often do not feature prominently in global university rankings.

However, the reason provided (R) does not explain why central universities are considered elite within India. The elitist image is based on their national reputation, quality of education, and the role they play in the Indian higher education system, rather than their international rankings.

Question

Generally, who is the visitor of central universities of India?

1. Prime Minister of India
2. President of India
3. Minister, MHRD
4. UGC Chairman

Explanations:
Answer: 2. President of India

In India, the President of India is the visitor of central universities. This means that the President has a formal and ceremonial role, including the power to address convocation ceremonies, appoint key officials, and ensure the universities are functioning according to their charters.

Question

Match the column:

A. Muir Central College	I. Lucknow University
B. Oriental College	II. Allahabad University
C. University College	III. Aligarh University
D. Canning Collège	IV. Panjab University

1. A-I, B-II, C-III, D-IV
2. A-II, B-III, C-IV, D-I
3. A-III, B-IV, C-I, D-II
4. A-IV, B-I, C-II, D-III

Explanations:
Answer: 2. A-II, B-III, C-IV, D-I

A. Muir Central College → II. Allahabad University: Established in **1872**, later became part of **Allahabad University**.

B. Oriental College → III. Aligarh University: Initially focused on **Oriental studies**, later merged into **Aligarh Muslim University (AMU)**.

C. University College → IV. Panjab University: Associated with **Panjab University**, focusing on **liberal arts and sciences**.

D. Canning College → I. Lucknow University: Founded in **1864**, merged into **Lucknow University in 1921**.

Question

Choose the correct statements.

A. Lal Bahadur Shastri National Academy of Administration trains future IASs
B. Polytechnics are mandated to award MBBS degree.
C. Sardar Vallabh Bhai Patel Academy trains future IPSs.
D. Jawahar Lal Nehru University, New Delhi has 89 affiliated colleges.
E. IIMC, New Delhi is a premier institution of management counseling.

1. AC
2. BDE
3. ABD
4. CE

Explanations
Answer: 1. AC

Lal Bahadur Shastri National Academy of Administration (LBSNAA) trains future IAS officers, making statement **A correct.**

Polytechnics **offer diploma courses in engineering and technology, not MBBS degrees**, making **B incorrect.**

Sardar Vallabhbhai Patel National Police Academy **(SVPNPA) trains future IPS officers,** making **C correct.**

Jawaharlal Nehru University **(JNU),** New Delhi is **a central university** and does not have 89 affiliated colleges, **making D incorrect.**

IIMC (Indian Institute of Mass Communication), New Delhi is not a management institution but a premier institute for media and journalism, **making E incorrect.**

State University

In India, state universities are managed and **funded** by **the state governments** of each state. After the adoption of the **Constitution of India in 1950**, education became a state responsibility. However, a constitutional amendment in **1976 made it a joint responsibility of both the state and central governments.**

As of 23 August 2022, the UGC lists **456** state universities.

State Universities

- **University of Mumbai** - Mumbai, Maharashtra
- **University of Calcutta** - Kolkata, West Bengal
- **University of Madras** - Chennai, Tamil Nadu
- **Osmania University** - Hyderabad, Telangana
- **Punjab University** - Chandigarh
- **University of Mysore** - Mysore, Karnataka
- **Gauhati University** - Guwahati, Assam
- **Annamalai University** - Chidambaram, Tamil Nadu
- **University of Rajasthan** - Jaipur, Rajasthan
- **Andhra University** - Visakhapatnam, Andhra Pradesh

According to Section 12(B) of the **UGC Act of 1956, the UGC has the authority to "allocate and disburse**, out of the Fund of the Commission, grants to Universities." Consequently, the UGC categorizes state universities as either "declared fit to receive Central/UGC assistance under Section 12(B) of the UGC Act–1956" or not, and this status is noted in the published lists. Updates to these declarations are made during UGC meetings and are documented in the minutes. The latest list, published by the UGC on 17 May 2021, includes **252 universities that are deemed fit to receive Central/UGC assistance.**

Question

Assertion A: Universities play a key role in building a symbiotic relationship between the nation, state and society
Reason R: Universities are centres for creation and transmission of knowledge

In light of the above statements, choose the most appropriate answer from the options given below

1. Both A and R are correct and R is the correct explanation of A
2. Both A and R are correct but R is NOT the correct explanation of A
3. A is correct but R is not correct
4. A is not correct but R is correct

Explanations:
Answer: 2. Both A and R are correct but R is NOT the correct explanation of A

Assertion (A) is Correct: Universities indeed play a crucial role in fostering a strong relationship between the nation, state, and society by contributing to the social, economic, and cultural development.

Reason (R) is Correct: Universities are fundamentally centers for the creation and dissemination of knowledge through teaching, research, and community engagement.

However, while Reason (R) is true and supports the importance of universities, it does not directly explain the specific role of universities in building a symbiotic relationship between the nation, state, and society. The creation and transmission of knowledge is a part of the broader contributions of universities, but it is not the direct explanation for the assertion.

Question

Who among the following was the principal of Bengal National College, established in 1906?

1. Motilal Ghosh
2. Aurobindo Ghosh
3. Satish Chandra Mukharjee

4. Bipin Chandra Paul

Explanations:
Answer: 2. Aurobindo Ghosh

Bengal National College was established in **1906** as part of the **Swadeshi movement**, aimed at providing **nationalist education** free from British control. **Aurobindo Ghosh** was appointed as its **first principal**. He was a **freedom fighter, philosopher, and nationalist leader**, who later became a spiritual thinker and founded **Sri Aurobindo Ashram**.

Other Options:

Motilal Ghosh - Editor of *Amrita Bazar Patrika*, but not associated with the college.

Satish Chandra Mukherjee - A nationalist educator who promoted Swadeshi education but was not the principal.

Bipin Chandra Pal - A major nationalist leader but not associated with the college's administration.

Private University

Private universities and colleges are higher education institutions **not run, owned, or primarily funded by the government**. However, they often benefit from tax breaks, public student loans, and government grants. Depending on where they are located, these universities might still be regulated by the government. **Private universities differ from public and national universities** and are usually nonprofit organizations.

Private universities are run by **private entities and get their funding from tuition fees,** investments, and **private donations.** Unlike state-run institutions, **the degrees awarded by private colleges might come from an affiliated university that sets the curriculum**.

State universities are managed by the state government of each Indian state or territory and are typically established by an act of the local legislative assembly. India's higher education system includes both private and public universities. Public universities receive support from the Indian central and state governments, while private universities rely mostly on private funding.

All universities in India are recognized by the University Grants Commission (UGC), which operates under the UGC Act of 1956. There are also 15 Professional Councils that oversee different aspects of accreditation and coordination. **State private universities in India are regulated by the UGC under the Establishment and Maintenance of Standards in State Private Universities Regulations, 2003.** According to these regulations, state private universities are established through an act of a local legislative assembly and listed by the UGC in the Gazette once the act is passed. As per a ruling by the Supreme Court of India, UGC recognition is necessary for these universities to operate. **The UGC also sends committees to inspect state private universities and publishes their reports**.

The UGC regularly updates the list of state private universities. As of 25 November 2022, there are **430 state private universities listed by the UGC.** The first to be notified was Sikkim Manipal University on 11 October 1995. State private universities have been established in 26 of the 28 Indian states, but none in the 8 union territories.

Private Universities

- **Amity University** - Noida, Uttar Pradesh
- **OP Jindal Global University** - Sonipat, Haryana
- **Ashoka University** - Sonipat, Haryana
- **Shiv Nadar University** - Greater Noida, Uttar Pradesh
- **SRM Institute of Science and Technology** - Chennai, Tamil Nadu
- **Lovely Professional University (LPU)** - Phagwara, Punjab
- **KIIT University** - Bhubaneswar, Odisha
- **Chandigarh University** - Mohali, Punjab
- **Azim Premji University** - Bengaluru, Karnataka
- **Jain University** - Bengaluru, Karnataka

India is home to numerous esteemed private universities known for their academic excellence and diverse programs. Here are some of the most prominent:

Birla Institute of Technology and Science (BITS), Pilani: Established in 1964, BITS Pilani is renowned for its engineering and science programs. It has campuses in Pilani, Goa, Hyderabad, and Dubai.

Manipal Academy of Higher Education (MAHE): Founded in 1953, MAHE offers a wide range of programs across various disciplines and has campuses in Manipal, Mangalore, Bangalore, and international locations like Dubai and Malaysia.

Vellore Institute of Technology (VIT): Established in 1984, VIT is known for its engineering programs and has campuses in Vellore, Chennai, Bhopal, and Amaravati.

Amrita Vishwa Vidyapeetham: Founded in 1994, this university offers programs in engineering, medicine, and social sciences, with campuses in Coimbatore, Amritapuri, Bengaluru, Kochi, and Mysuru.

Symbiosis International University: Established in 2002, Symbiosis offers diverse programs and has campuses in Pune, Noida, Bengaluru, Hyderabad, and Nagpur.

O.P. Jindal Global University: Founded in 2009, it is recognized for its law, business, and international affairs programs, located in Sonipat, Haryana.

Ashoka University: Established in 2014, Ashoka is known for its liberal arts and sciences programs, located in Sonipat, Haryana.

Shiv Nadar University: Founded in 2011, it offers interdisciplinary programs in engineering, humanities, and management, located in Greater Noida, Uttar Pradesh.

Christ University: Established in 1969, Christ University offers programs in humanities, social sciences, science, commerce, and management, with campuses in Bengaluru, Delhi NCR, and Pune.

Amity University: Founded in 2005, Amity offers a wide range of programs and has campuses across India and abroad.

Question

Which of the following is a private university?

1. Anna University
2. BITS pilani
3. Burdwan University
4. HIT

Explanations:
Answer: 2. BITS pilani

Among the options given, BITS Pilani (Birla Institute of Technology and Science, Pilani) is a private university. It is a well-known private institution of higher education in India, particularly famous for its engineering and technology programs. The other universities listed are either public or state universities.

Deemed University

A "Deemed University" or "Deemed-to-be-University" in India is a status given to higher education institutions that **perform exceptionally well in specific areas of study.** This special status is granted by the Department of Higher Education based on the advice of the UGC (University Grants Commission), under **Section 3 of the UGC Act, 1956**.

An institution other than a traditional university, which excels in a specific field, can be declared a "Deemed-to-be-University" by the Central Government on the recommendation of the UGC. The first institute to receive this status was the Indian Institute of Science on 12 May 1958. Importantly, deemed universities have the **authority to award degrees**, providing them the academic status and privileges of a university.

In India, both private and public universities make up the higher education system. Public universities get support from the central and state governments, while private universities are funded by various private bodies and societies. The UGC, empowered by the UGC Act of 1956, recognizes universities in India. Besides the UGC, there are 15 Professional Councils that oversee different aspects of accreditation and coordination.

Being a deemed university gives institutions full autonomy over their courses, syllabus, admissions, and fees. As of 30 November 2021, there are 126 institutions listed as deemed universities by the UGC. **Tamil Nadu has the highest number of deemed universities,** with **28 institutions** holding this status.

Section 12(B) of the UGC Act of 1956 also allows the UGC to allocate and disburse grants to universities. The UGC categorizes institutions as either "fit to receive Central/UGC assistance under Section 12(B) of the UGC Act–1956" or not and publishes these lists. Updates are made during UGC meetings and documented in the minutes. The latest list, published on 24 August 2022, includes 50 institutes deemed fit to receive Central/UGC assistance.

Deemed-to-be Universities

- **Indian Institute of Science (IISc)** - Bengaluru, Karnataka
- **Tata Institute of Social Sciences (TISS)** - Mumbai, Maharashtra
- **Birla Institute of Technology and Science (BITS)** - Pilani, Rajasthan
- **Manipal Academy of Higher Education (MAHE)** - Manipal, Karnataka
- **Vellore Institute of Technology (VIT)** - Vellore, Tamil Nadu
- **Homi Bhabha National Institute (HBNI)** - Mumbai, Maharashtra
- **Gandhigram Rural Institute** - Gandhigram, Tamil Nadu
- **Sri Sathya Sai Institute of Higher Learning** - Puttaparthi, Andhra Pradesh
- **Narsee Monjee Institute of Management Studies (NMIMS)** - Mumbai, Maharashtra
- **Symbiosis International University** - Pune, Maharashtra

Question

Statement I: The purpose of higher education is to promote critical and creative thinking abilities among
Statement II: Deemed Universities can design their own syllabus and course work but cannot grant degrees.

In light of the above statements, choose the most appropriate answer from the options given below

1. Both Statement I and Statement Il are true.
2. Both Statement I and Statement Il are false.
3. Statement I is true but Statement Il is false.
4. Statement I is false but Statement Il is true.

Explanations:
Answer: 3. Statement I is true but Statement Il is false.

Statement I is True: One of the primary purposes of higher education is indeed to foster critical and creative thinking skills in students, enabling them to analyze, evaluate, and create new ideas and solutions.

Statement II is False: Deemed Universities have the authority to design their own syllabus and coursework and also have the power to grant degrees. They enjoy full academic status and privileges similar to other universities.

Question

Which one of the following is deemed to be university?

1. Periyar University, Salem
2. Nagaland University, Kohima
3. Guru Ghasidas Vishwavidyalaya, Bilaspur
4. Gandhigram Rural University, Madurai

Explanations:
Answer: 4. Gandhigram Rural University, Madurai

Gandhigram Rural University, Madurai is a **deemed-to-be university**. It was granted deemed university status in 1976 under Section 3 of the UGC Act, 1956. It is a specialized institution focusing on rural development and Gandhian principles.

The other institutions listed are central or state universities:

- **Periyar University, Salem**: A state university.
- **Nagaland University, Kohima**: A central university.
- **Guru Ghasidas Vishwavidyalaya, Bilaspur**: A central university.

Institute under State Legislature Act

Institute under State Legislature Act is a type of university-level institution in India, established or incorporated by a state legislature act. Although such institutes do not come under the higher education department of the state and are run and funded by another department, they enjoy academic status and privileges like state universities.

Open University

An open university is a type of university that **operates with an open-door academic policy,** meaning it has **minimal or no entry requirements**. These universities often use teaching methods such as **open-supported learning or distance education**. However, it's important to note that not all open universities focus solely on distance education, and not all distance education universities have open admission policies. The term 'open learning' refers to educational approaches that aim to:

- Opening access to education and training provision.
- Freeing learners from the constraints of time and place.
- Offering flexible learning opportunities to individuals and groups of learners.

The first state open university established in India was Bhim Rao Ambedkar Open University in Hyderabad, founded in 1982. Following this, the **Indira Gandhi National Open University (IGNOU) was established on 20 September 1985.** Named after the late prime minister, **IGNOU was set up in line with the National Education Policy of 1986**.

Question

The first open university in India was established in the year

1. 1980
2. 1982
3. 1985
4. 1986

Explanations:
Answer: 2. 1982

The first open university in India, Dr. B.R. Ambedkar Open University in Hyderabad, was established in the year 1982. This university marked the beginning of the open and distance learning system in India, aiming to make higher education more accessible to a larger population.

Question

Identify the correct chronological sequence of the establishment of the following universities?

A. Bhoj Open University
B. Karnataka State Open University
C. Netaji Subhash Open University
D. Nalanda Open University
E. Yashwant Rao Chavan Open University

1. AEBDC
2. DEABC
3. BDECA
4. CDEAB

Explanations:
Answer: 2. DEABC

The correct chronological order of the establishment of the given **open universities** is:

- **Yashwantrao Chavan Maharashtra Open University (1989)**
- **Nalanda Open University (1987)**
- **Bhoj Open University (1991)**
- **Karnataka State Open University (1996)**
- **Netaji Subhas Open University (1997)**

Thus, the correct sequence is **D → E → A → B → C**.

Question

Identify the correct chronology of the following open universities:

A. Karnataka State Open University

B. Bhoj Open University
C. Rajarshi Tandon Open University
D. Netaji Subhas Open University
E. Nalanda Open University

1. ACDEB
2. BDEAC
3. CDBAE
4. EBADC

Explanations
Answer: 4. EBADC

- **Nalanda Open University (1987)**
- **Bhoj Open University (1991)**
- **Netaji Subhas Open University (1997)**
- **Karnataka State Open University (1996)**
- **Rajarshi Tandon Open University (1999)**

Question

Which of the following was the chairman of the committee constituted for the establishment of the National Open University:

1. G. Parthasarathy
2. G. Rami reddy
3. Hari Gautam
4. K.L. Shrimali

Explanations:
Answer: 1. G. Parthasarathy

G. Parthasarathy was the **chairman** of the committee that recommended the establishment of the **National Open University**, which later became **Indira Gandhi National Open University (IGNOU)** in 1985.

G. Rami Reddy – Former **Vice-Chancellor of IGNOU**, but not the committee chairman.

Hari Gautam & K.L. Shrimali – Not associated with this initiative.

Question

The first Open University established in India is:

1. Yashwantrao Chavan Maharashtra Open University, Nasik
2. Nalanda Open University, Patna
3. Bhim Rao Ambedkar Open University, Hyderabad
4. Tamil Nadu Open University, Chennai

Explanations:
Answer: 3. Bhim Rao Ambedkar Open University, Hyderabad

The first Open University established in India is the Bhim Rao Ambedkar Open University, located in Hyderabad. It was founded in 1982 and marked the beginning of open and distance learning in the country, aiming to make higher education accessible to a larger population.

Question

Select the alternative features from the following. which make open universities as non-traditional universities:

A. Innovative method of teaching and learning
B. Innovative method of admission, curriculum and evaluation
C. Modern communication techniques
D. Teacher's friendly approaches

Select the correct option

1. (b), (c) and (d) only
2. (a), (b) and (c) only
3. (a), (c) and (d) only
4. (a), (b) and (d) only

Explanations:
Answer: 2. (a), (b) and (c) only

Open universities are considered non-traditional because of several innovative approaches they use in various aspects of education:

Innovative method of teaching and learning (a): Open universities employ unique and flexible teaching methods, often using technology and self-paced learning to cater to a diverse student population.

Innovative method of admission, curriculum, and evaluation (b): They have flexible admission criteria, diverse curriculum options, and unique evaluation methods that differ from traditional universities.

Modern communication techniques (c): Open universities leverage modern communication tools such as online platforms, multimedia resources, and virtual classrooms to facilitate learning and interaction.

These features collectively make open universities non-traditional.

Question

Arrange the following open Universities according to their year of establishment in Chronological order:

A. Yashwant Rao Chavan Maharashtra Open University
B. Karnataka State Open University
C. U.P. Rajarshi Tandon Open University
D. Kota Open University
E. Madhya Pradesh Bhoj Open University

1. ABCDE
2. DAEBC
3. BCEAD
4. DABCE

Explanations:
Answer: 2. DAEBC

D. Kota Open University (1987): Now known as **Vardhman Mahaveer Open University**, it was the first open university in India.

A. Yashwant Rao Chavan Maharashtra Open University (1989): Established in 1989.

E. Madhya Pradesh Bhoj Open University (1991): Established in 1991.

B. Karnataka State Open University (1996): Established in 1996.

C. U.P. Rajarshi Tandon Open University (1999): Established in 1999.

Indira Gandhi National Open University (IGNOU)

- **Established in 1985** under the **IGNOU Act**.
- Named after **Prime Minister Indira Gandhi**.
- Headquartered in **New Delhi, India**.
- Largest **open university in the world**.
- Provides **distance and open education**.
- Offers **UG, PG, diploma, and certificate courses**.
- Regulated by **University Grants Commission (UGC)**.
- Supports **flexible and lifelong learning**.
- Uses **online, printed, and multimedia resources**.
- Recognized by **AICTE, NCTE, and DEC**.
- Caters to **millions of students globally**.
- Has **regional centers across India**.
- Focuses on **inclusive and skill-based education**.
- Provides **affordable and accessible learning**.
- Plays a key role in **higher education reforms**.

Question

Which of the following Open universities was established in accordance with the National Education policy, 1986

1. Dr. BR Ambedkar Open University, Hyderabad
2. Indira Gandhi National Open University, Delhi
3. Karnataka State Open University, Mysore
4. Yashwant Rao Chavan Maharashtra open University, Nasik

Explanations:
Answer: 2. Indira Gandhi National Open University, Delhi

The Indira Gandhi National Open University (IGNOU), Delhi, was established on 20 September 1985 and named after the late Prime Minister. It was set up in accordance with the National Education Policy of 1986. This policy aimed to democratize education and make it accessible to a larger section of the population through open and distance learning.

Question

Indira Gandhi National Open University was established in the year

1. 1975
2. 1980
3. 1985
4. 2000

Explanations:
Answer: 3. 1985

Indira Gandhi National Open University (IGNOU) was established on 20 September 1985. It was named after the late Prime Minister Indira Gandhi and was created to provide accessible, inclusive education through open and distance learning, in line with the National Education Policy of 1986.

Question

The term 'open learning' represents approaches that focus on-

A. Opening access to education and training provision
B. Freeing learners from the constraints of time and place
C. Learning and evaluation without a specified curriculum
D. Offering flexible learning opportunities to individuals and groups of learners
E. Making students free from any educational loads

Choose the correct option:

1. A, B and C only
2. A, B and D only
3. A, B and E only
4. B, C and D only

Explanations:
Answer: 3. A, B and D only

The term 'open learning' refers to educational approaches that aim to:

- Opening access to education and training provision (A)

- Freeing learners from the constraints of time and place (B)
- Offering flexible learning opportunities to individuals and groups of learners (D)

These approaches are designed to make education more accessible and adaptable to the needs of learners, providing them with the flexibility to learn at their own pace and in their own space.

Question

Which of the following modality of higher education is the example of evolution in post-independence India?

1. Teacher Education
2. Technical Education
3. Legal Education
4. Distance Education

Explanations:
Answer: 4. Distance Education

In post-independence India, distance education has significantly evolved as a modality of higher education. This approach has expanded access to education, allowing students from various geographical and socio-economic backgrounds to pursue higher education without the constraints of physical presence in traditional classrooms. Institutions like the Indira Gandhi National Open University (IGNOU) exemplify this evolution, offering a wide range of programs through distance learning methods.

Question

Which of the following statements are correct about Indira Gandhi National Open University IGNOU)? To indicate your answer, select from the code given below:

A. It is an autonomous organisation.
B. It is devoted to the promotion of open and distance education systems.
C. It conducts assessment and accredits the State Open Universities.
D. It has jurisdiction in respect of the Open and Distance learning system in India and to the study centres outside India.

Select the correct option

1. (a) and (b)
2. (b) and (d)
3. (c) and (d)
4. (d) and (a)

Explanations:
Answer: 1. (a) and (b)

Indira Gandhi National Open University (IGNOU) is an autonomous organization dedicated to promoting open and distance education systems. It has a significant role in expanding access to higher education through its innovative teaching methods and wide reach. However, it does not conduct assessment and accreditation of State Open Universities; this responsibility typically lies with bodies like the University Grants Commission (UGC) and the National Assessment and Accreditation Council (NAAC).

Distance Education in India

- **Introduced in 1962** with Delhi University's **School of Correspondence**.
- **IGNOU (1985)** is the largest **open university** in India.
- **Regulated by UGC-DEB** (Distance Education Bureau).
- Provides **flexible learning** for working professionals.
- Offers **UG, PG, diploma, and certificate programs**.
- Uses **printed materials, online resources, and virtual classes**.
- Covers **engineering, management, arts, science, and law**.
- Supports **inclusive education for rural and disabled learners**.
- Allows **self-paced learning without classroom restrictions**.
- Encourages **lifelong education and skill development**.

Question

Instructional communication in the distance education mode is:

1. unstructured
2. informal
3. self-regulatory

4. structured and interactive

Explanations:
Answer: 4. structured and interactive

Instructional communication in the distance education mode is typically structured and interactive. Distance education involves organized and systematic instructional materials and methods. Courses are designed with clear objectives, structured content, and assessment strategies. Interactive elements like forums, virtual classrooms, and multimedia resources are used to engage students and facilitate learning.

Foreign Universities Establishing Campuses in India

India has recently seen a surge in foreign universities establishing campuses within its borders, following regulatory changes that encourage international educational collaboration. Notable examples include:

Deakin University, Australia: In March 2023, Deakin University became the first foreign university to open a branch campus in India, located in GIFT City, Gujarat.

University of Southampton, United Kingdom: The University of Southampton is set to establish a campus in Gurugram, Haryana, with academic programs expected to commence by July 2025.

These developments are part of India's broader strategy to enhance its higher education landscape by integrating global academic standards and providing students with access to international curricula within the country.

Question

The first foreign university to set up its campus at GIFT City, Gujarat, is:

1. London University, Britain
2. Queen's University, Ireland

3. Deakin University, Australia
4. Moscow University, Russia

Explanations:
Answer: 3. Deakin University, Australia

Deakin University became the **first foreign university** to set up its campus at **GIFT City, Gujarat, India**. Announced in **2023**, this initiative aligns with **India's NEP 2020**, which promotes international collaborations in higher education. **GIFT City (Gujarat International Finance Tec-City)** is being developed as a global financial and education hub. Deakin University's presence will **enhance India's global education partnerships** and provide world-class academic opportunities.

Question

Which of the following norms are prescribed for foreign universities to set up their campuses in India.

A. Foreign universities must invest in the Indian manufacturing industry.
B. They should have secured a position within the top 500 in global ranking.
C. They should have secured a position within the top 500 in global ranking in the subject-wise category.
D. They should employ only Indians for teaching and non-teaching.
E. They should possess outstanding expertise in a specific area.

1. AB
2. BCD
3. CDE
4. BCE

Explanations:
Answer: 4. BCE
The norms prescribed for foreign universities to set up their campuses in India include:

- **B. They should have secured a position within the top 500 in global ranking.**

- **C. They should have secured a position within the top 500 in global ranking in the subject-wise category.**
- **E. They should possess outstanding expertise in a specific area.**

These criteria ensure that only high-quality and globally recognized institutions establish campuses in India. There is no requirement for foreign universities to invest in the Indian manufacturing industry **(A)** or to employ only Indians for teaching and non-teaching roles **(D)**.

Public Sector Universities in India with Notable Collaborations with Foreign Universities:

Indian Institute of Technology, Kanpur (IIT Kanpur)

- **Collaborations**:
  - **University of California,**
  - **Santa Cruz**
  - Focus on Computer Science, Artificial Intelligence, Machine Learning, and Bioinformatics.

Indian Institute of Science, Bengaluru (IISc Bengaluru)

- **Collaborations**:
  - **University of Adelaide,**
  - **University of Melbourne,**
  - **Nagasaki University**:
  - Joint research in various scientific and engineering disciplines.

Indian Institute of Technology Bhubaneswar (IIT Bhubaneswar):

- **Collaborations**: Partnerships with multiple international institutions, including:
  - **University of Quebec,**
  - **University of Waterloo,**
  - **Texas A&M University,**
  - **University of Edinburgh,**
  - **University of Southampton,**
  - **University of Manchester**.

Jawaharlal Nehru University (JNU), New Delhi:

- **Collaborations**: Engaged in academic collaborations with foreign institutions, including a twinning arrangement with a German university.

Banaras Hindu University (BHU), Varanasi:

- **Collaborations**: Initiated steps to regularize existing academic collaborations as per new regulations.

Jamia Millia Islamia, New Delhi:

- **Collaborations**: Engaged in academic collaborations with foreign institutions.

Tezpur University, Assam: Collaborations:

- Engaged in academic collaborations with foreign institutions.

Pondicherry University, Puducherry: Collaborations: Offers twinning, joint degree, and dual degree programs in collaboration with foreign institutions, including **Indiana University, USA**.

Maulana Azad National Urdu University, Hyderabad:

- **Collaborations**: Engaged in academic collaborations with foreign institutions.

Hemvati Nandan Bahuguna Garhwal University, Uttarakhand.

Question

Identify the public sector universities from the following that have the highest number of collaboration with foreign universities.

A. Indian Institute of Technology, Kanpur
B. Indian Institute of Science, Bengaluru
C. Pondicherry University, Pondicherry
D. North-Eastern Hill University, Shillong
E. Gujarat Vidyapeeth, Gujarat

1. ABC
2. BCD
3. CDE

4. ADE

Explanations:
Answer: 1. ABC

Based on the information available, among the listed public sector universities, the **Indian Institute of Technology, Kanpur (IIT Kanpur)** and the **Indian Institute of Science, Bengaluru (IISc)** have notable collaborations with foreign universities.

Indian Institute of Technology, Kanpur (IIT Kanpur): IIT Kanpur has signed a memorandum of understanding with the University of California, Santa Cruz, focusing on areas such as Computer Science, Artificial Intelligence, Machine Learning, and Bioinformatics.

Indian Institute of Science, Bengaluru (IISc): IISc has established partnerships with international institutions, including the University of Adelaide, University of Melbourne, and Nagasaki University, facilitating research and academic exchanges in various scientific and engineering disciplines.

While **Pondicherry University, Pondicherry** has engaged in collaborations with foreign institutions, such as the University of Tours and the University of Warsaw, these partnerships are fewer in comparison.

There is limited publicly available information regarding significant international collaborations for **North-Eastern Hill University, Shillong**, and **Gujarat Vidyapeeth, Gujarat**.

Stand-Alone Professional Universities in India

- **Law Universities**
  - National Law School of India University (NLSIU), Bangalore
  - NALSAR University of Law, Hyderabad
  - National Law University, Delhi
- **Health Science Universities**
  - All India Institute of Medical Sciences (AIIMS), New Delhi

  - Postgraduate Institute of Medical Education and Research (PGIMER), Chandigarh
  - King George's Medical University (KGMU), Lucknow
- **Technical Universities**
  - **Indian Institutes of Technology (IITs)**
    - IIT Bombay
    - IIT Delhi
    - IIT Madras
  - **National Institutes of Technology (NITs)**
    - NIT Trichy
    - NIT Surathkal
  - **Indian Institutes of Information Technology (IIITs)**
    - IIIT Allahabad
    - IIIT Bangalore
- **Indian Institute of Mass Communication (IIMC)**
  - **(IIMC)** was established in **1965**.
  - Founded by the **Ministry of Information and Broadcasting, Government of India**.
  - Aims to **train professionals in journalism, advertising, and public relations**.
  - Headquarters located in **New Delhi**, with regional centers across India.

Question

Which of the following come under the category of stand-alone professional universities?

A. Universities of Journalism
B. Law Universities
C. Health Science Universities
D. Technical Universities
E. Homeopathy Universities

1. ABC
2. ABD
3. CDE
4. BCD

Explanations:

Answer: 4. BCD

Stand-alone professional universities are institutions that specialize in a specific field of study rather than offering a broad range of disciplines. The following categories qualify as stand-alone professional universities:

Law Universities (B) – Dedicated to legal education and research (e.g., NLSIU, NALSAR, NLU Delhi).

Health Science Universities (C) – Focus on medical, dental, pharmacy, and allied health sciences (e.g., AIIMS, PGIMER, KGMU).

Technical Universities (D) – Primarily offer engineering, technology, and applied sciences (e.g., IITs, NITs, IIITs).

Excluded Categories:

Universities of Journalism (A) – While journalism programs exist, they are typically part of broader institutions or media schools rather than stand-alone universities.

Homeopathy Universities (E) – Though they exist, they fall under AYUSH (Ayurveda, Yoga, Unani, Siddha, and Homeopathy) rather than the traditional category of professional stand-alone universities.

Thus, the correct answer is **BCD (Law Universities, Health Science Universities, and Technical Universities).**

Question

Indian Institute of Mass Communication was established in the year-

1. 1964
2. 1965
3. 1967
4. 1970

Explanations:
Answer: 2. 1965

- **Indian Institute of Mass Communication (IIMC)** was established in **1965**.
- Founded by the **Ministry of Information and Broadcasting, Government of India**.
- Aims to **train professionals in journalism, advertising, and public relations**.
- Headquarters located in **New Delhi**, with regional centers across India.

CHAPTER IV

Oriental, Conventional, Non-conventional, Professional, Technical, Skill Based, Value Education and Environmental Education

Oriental Education of Learning:

Oriental learning refers to the study and **understanding of traditional knowledge, philosophies, languages, and cultures primarily from East Asian countries** such as China, Japan, Korea, and Vietnam.

Oriental studies is the academic field that encompasses the study of Near Eastern and Far Eastern societies and cultures, including their languages, peoples, history, and archaeology. Indology is defined as the study of Indian history, literature, philosophy, and culture.

Oriental Research Institutes contribute to these fields by collecting, editing, and publishing manuscripts related to religion, philosophy, literature, grammar, art, and science.

These colleges are recognized by various government bodies in India, including the AICTE (All India Council for Technical Education), the Pharmacy Council of India, and the National Council for Teacher Education. The degree courses offered are affiliated with the University of Mumbai.

Question

"I never teach my pupils; I only attempt to provide the conditions in which they can learn" **is a statement by:**

1. Swami Vivekananda
2. Albert Einstein
3. Sri Aurobindo
4. Aristotle

Explanations:
Answer: 2. Albert Einstein

The statement **"I never teach my pupils; I only attempt to provide the conditions in which they can learn"** is attributed to **Albert Einstein**. This reflects his **constructivist approach** to education, emphasizing **experiential learning** rather than rote memorization. Einstein believed that **curiosity, exploration, and self-discovery** are key to meaningful learning.

ORIENTAL RESEARCH INSTITUTES:

Oriental Education Society

- **Established in 1992** by **Javed Khan**.
- Aims to provide **higher education in Mumbai & Navi Mumbai**.
- Operates **13 institutes across 4 campuses**.
- Educates **over 8000 students annually**.
- Functions as a **Public Charitable Trust**.

Asiatic Society

- **Founded in 1794** by **Sir William Jones**.
- Houses **manuscripts in Sanskrit, Arabic, Persian, and more**.
- Recognized as an **Indological research center**.
- Holds **historical, linguistic, and cultural studies**.
- Preserves **rare Indian and foreign texts**.

Question

A British official of the East India company who was interested in higher learning in India was.

1. Francis Gladwin
2. William Ward
3. William Adam
4. William Jones

Explanations:
Answer: 4. William Jones

Sir William Jones (1746–1794) was a British **orientalist, philologist, and a judge of the Supreme Court of Bengal**. He was deeply interested in **Indian higher learning, literature, and languages**. In **1784**, he founded the **Asiatic Society of Bengal**, which played a crucial role in the study of Indian history, languages, and culture. He is famous for his discovery of the relationship between **Sanskrit, Greek, and Latin**, which contributed to the field of comparative linguistics.

Adyar Library and Research Center (Chennai)

- **Established in 1882**, focuses on **ancient texts**.
- Possesses **175,000 printed books and 18,600 manuscripts**.
- Publishes **a series of 108 Upanishads**.
- Specializes in **Indian philosophy and theosophy**.
- Serves as a **major Indological research center**.

Oriental Institute (Baroda)

- **Founded in 1893** by **Sayajirao Gaekwad**.
- Holds **789 Sanskrit volumes and multilingual texts**.
- Preserves texts in **Hindi, Gujarati, and ancient scripts**.
- Specializes in **Vedic and historical research**.
- Supports **translation and publication of classical works**.

Question

The education imported through institutions of higher learning in India such as 'Sanskrit Vidyapith' is an example of

1. Non-conventional learning programmes
2. Value Education Programmes
3. Oriental learning Programmes
4. Professional education programmes

Explanations:
Answer: 3. Oriental learning Programmes

Institutions like 'Sanskrit Vidyapith' focus on the study and promotion of traditional Indian knowledge systems, languages, and cultures, which align with Oriental learning programmes. These programmes emphasize classical subjects such as Sanskrit, ancient Indian philosophy, and traditional literature, making them distinct from non-conventional learning, value education, and professional education programmes.

Oriental Research Institute (Mysore & Tirupati)

- **Mysore institute was established in 1891**, Tirupati in **1941**.
- Focuses on **religion, philosophy, and Sanskrit studies**.
- Preserves **ancient Telugu and Kannada manuscripts**.
- Conducts research in **Indian history and culture**.
- Promotes **academic studies in classical literature**.

Conventional and Non-conventional Learning

Conventional Learning

Conventional learning refers to traditional educational methods characterized by in-person classroom instruction, textbooks, lectures, and structured curricula. This approach follows a linear model where teachers impart knowledge to students, often emphasizing memorization and standardized assessments.

It is an instructor-centered model that includes all the elements of traditional teaching and learning, such as crowded classrooms, instant information sharing, an impersonal approach to students, and materials like black/white boards, desks, and pencils.

Conventional teaching, also known as traditional teaching, is a one-way approach where the teacher is the active participant, and students are passive listeners. This lecture-based method primarily relies on the use of a chalkboard for instruction.

As the name suggests, conventional learning involves traditional classroom settings where teachers and students are physically present together. This method focuses on oral recitation and imparting knowledge about values, religion, customs, traditions, and cultures. Technology does not play a role in conventional learning, and it is not accessible to everyone. Conventional Learning includes:

- **Traditional classroom-based education** with structured curriculum.
- **Teacher-centered approach** with direct instruction.
- **Fixed syllabus** approved by educational authorities.
- **Regular assessments** through exams and grading systems.
- **Degree-oriented learning** in schools and universities.
- **Emphasis on theoretical knowledge** over practical skills.
- **Limited flexibility** in course structure and pace.
- **Follows standardized textbooks** and learning materials.
- **Face-to-face interaction** between students and teachers.
- **Recognized globally** for academic and professional qualifications.

Examples of Conventional Learning

- **Schools and Universities** – Structured education with fixed curricula.
- **Engineering and Medical Colleges** – Degree programs with theoretical and practical components.
- **Law Schools** – Traditional legal education with classroom lectures.
- **Teacher Training Institutes** – Formal teacher certification programs.
- **Military Academies** – Rigid, discipline-based educational training.

Question

Which of the following are not the characteristics of conventional learning?

A. Emphasis on self directed learning and independent study
B. Students learn through listening and observation
C. No fixed curriculum
D. Leamer oriented
E. Require regular attendance

Select the correct option:

1. BE
2. AE
3. ACD

4. BC

Explanations:
Answer: 3. ACD

Conventional Learning Characteristics:

Emphasis on self-directed learning and independent study: This is not a characteristic of conventional learning, as it typically involves structured teacher-led instruction rather than self-directed learning.

Students learn through listening and observation: This is a characteristic of conventional learning, where students primarily learn by listening to lectures and observing demonstrations.

No fixed curriculum: Conventional learning usually has a fixed curriculum, so this is not a characteristic of conventional learning.

Learner-oriented: Conventional learning is often more teacher-centered rather than learner-oriented.

Require regular attendance: This is a characteristic of conventional learning, which typically requires students to attend classes regularly.

Conventional learning typically involves a fixed curriculum, is teacher-oriented rather than learner-oriented, and does not emphasize self-directed learning or independent study.

Non-conventional Learning

Non-conventional learning refers to educational approaches that deviate from traditional classroom-based instruction. It often emphasizes self-directed, experiential, and interdisciplinary learning. These approaches prioritize individual interests, foster autonomy, and encourage continuous learning beyond formal academic settings. Examples include courses in pet grooming, spa management, ethical hacking, and online learning.

Community College or Learning Falls Under Non-Conventional Education

Community Colleges and **Community Learning** fall under **Non-Conventional Education** because they offer **flexible, skill-based, and career-oriented learning**. These institutions focus on **practical training, vocational education, and open learning**, making them distinct from **formal, degree-oriented education systems**.

- **Skill-Based Learning** – Focus on **job-oriented programs**.
- **Flexible Curriculum** – Adapt to **industry needs and student pace**.
- **Open to All Learners** – No rigid **eligibility criteria** like conventional education.
- **Short-Term Certification Programs** – Offer **certificates, diplomas, and associate degrees**.
- **Blended Learning Approach** – Use of **online, offline, and practical methods**.

However, some community colleges also offer conventional degree programs, creating an overlap between conventional and non-conventional learning. **Objectives of Community College:**

- **Provide skill-based education** for higher studies.
- **Make education relevant** to local communities.
- **Ensure vertical mobility** in higher education.
- **Offer employment-oriented, industry-driven courses**.
- **Support flexible learning** for diverse students.
- **Integrate hands-on training** with theory.
- **Encourage lifelong learning** and career growth.
- **Provide education for working professionals**.
- **Collaborate with industries** for internships.
- **Bridge academics with practical skill training**.
- **Improve accessibility** in rural and urban areas.
- **Empower economically disadvantaged groups**.
- **Enhance entrepreneurship skills** for self-employment.
- **Provide alternative pathways** beyond formal degrees.
- **Promote innovation** in education methods.
- Life skill engagement

- Lateral entry into higher education system
- Educational opportunities for rural students

Question

According to UGC, which of the following are the objectives of community colleges ?

A. To provide skill-based education to the students of higher education.
B. To make higher education relevant to the learner and communities.
C. To provide vertical mobility for pursuers of higher education.
D. To open vistas of employment.
E. To train youngsters in traditional skill sectors

Select the correct option:

1. A, B, C only
2. B, C, D only
3. C, D, E only
4. A, D, E only

Explanations:
Answer: 1. A, B, C only

According to UGC, the objectives of community colleges include providing skill-based education to students of higher education (A), making higher education relevant to the learners and their communities (B), and providing vertical mobility for students pursuing higher education (C). These objectives focus on integrating practical skills with academic learning and ensuring that education aligns with the needs of both students and the wider community. While opening vistas of employment and training youngsters in traditional skill sectors are important, they are not specifically highlighted as objectives of community colleges according to UGC.

Question

The concept of community college ensures which of the following?

A. Life skill engagement

B. Lateral entry into higher education system
C. Educational opportunities for rural students
D. Providing employment to the educated unemployed
E. Expansion of local colleges
F. Preparing the youth for lower level employment market

Choose the correct answer from the options given below

1. Only (a), (b) and (c)
2. Only (b), (c) and (d)
3. Only (c), (d) and (e)
4. Only (d), (e) and (f)

Explanations:
Answer: 1. Only (a), (b) and (c)

The concept of community colleges is designed to engage students with life skills (a), provide lateral entry into the higher education system (b), and offer educational opportunities for rural students (c). These colleges aim to make education accessible and relevant to local communities, enabling students to develop practical skills and seamlessly transition into further higher education or the job market. While providing employment opportunities and preparing youth for lower-level employment are related goals, they are not the primary focus of community colleges according to this concept.

Question

Which of the following categories of colleges is primarily intended for creating work ready manpower on a large scale?

1. Autonomous college
2. Community college
3. Agriculture college
4. Technical college

Explanations:
Answer: 2. Community college

Community colleges are primarily designed to create work-ready manpower on a large scale. They focus on providing practical, skill-based education that prepares students for immediate employment in various trades and professions. The programs offered at community colleges are often tailored to meet the needs of local industries and communities, making them an effective avenue for developing a workforce that is ready to enter the job market with the necessary skills and training.

Non-conventional education focuses on developing skills related to science and technology. This type of learning involves activities such as writing, visualizing, imagining, and critical thinking. It is interactive, accessible to everyone, and relies heavily on technology to enhance the learning experience. Non-conventional Learning includes:

- **Flexible and innovative education models**.
- Does **not** adhere to a **fixed curriculum.**
- **Student-centered approach** with self-paced learning.
- **Focus on skill-based and experiential learning**.
- **Online, distance, and open schooling methods**.
- **Use of multimedia, e-learning, and virtual tools**.
- **No strict syllabus**; evolves based on industry needs.
- **Emphasizes creativity, critical thinking, and research**.
- **Project-based, peer-to-peer, and hands-on learning**.
- **Accessible to diverse learners**, including professionals.
- **Alternative certifications** rather than traditional degrees.

Examples of Non-Conventional Learning

- **Distance Education (IGNOU, NIOS)** – Flexible learning without classroom attendance.
- **Online Courses (Coursera, Udemy, edX)** – Self-paced learning with digital content.
- **Skill-Based Learning (Polytechnic, ITI)** – Vocational training for job-specific skills.
- **Experiential Learning (Internships, Apprenticeships)** – Practical, hands-on industry experience.
- **Open Universities (AIU, Open Schooling)** – Alternative education models for diverse learners.

Question

Which of the following characteristics pertains to Non-conventional learning?

1. One campus education with fixed time
2. Teacher-centered learning
3. Requirement of regular attendance
4. No fixed curriculum

Explanations:
Answer: 4. No fixed curriculum

Non-conventional learning often does not adhere to a fixed curriculum, allowing for more flexibility and adaptability in the learning process. Unlike traditional education, which usually requires attendance at a specific campus, has a set timetable, and is teacher-centered, non-conventional learning emphasizes a more flexible, learner-centered approach that can take place in various environments and often involves self-directed study.

Question

Which items in the following constitute the non-conventional learning programmes?

(i) Tea sommelier
(ii) Oriental languages
(iii)Spa management
(iv) Museologs
(v) Comparative languages

Select the correct answer from the options given below:

1. (i), (ii), and (iv)
2. (ii), (iii) and (v)
3. (i), (iii) and (iv)
4. (ii), (iv) and (v)

Explanations:
Answer: 3. (i), (iii) and (iv)

Non-conventional learning programs are those that deviate from traditional academic subjects and focus on specialized, often vocational or emerging fields.

Tea sommelier (i) involves the study of tea varieties, tasting, and pairing, which is a specialized vocational program.

Spa management (iii) pertains to the management and operation of wellness and spa facilities, another specialized vocational field.

Museology (iv) is the study of museums and their role in society, focusing on curation, management, and educational roles within museums, which is non-traditional compared to mainstream academic disciplines.

These programs emphasize practical skills and specialized knowledge, fitting the definition of non-conventional learning.

Oriental languages and comparative languages are more traditional academic disciplines focused on language studies and therefore do not fit the non-conventional category as effectively.

Question

Identify the non-conventional learning programmes:

(i) Gerontology
(ii) Psychology
(iii) Ethical hacking
(iv) Anthropology
(v) Pet Groomers

Choose the correct answer from the options given below:

1. (i), (ii) and (iii)
2. (ii), (iii) and (iv)
3. (iii), (iv) and (v)
4. (i), (iii) and (v)

Explanations:
Answer: 4. (i), (iii) and (v)

Non-conventional learning programs refer to those educational paths that deviate from traditional, academic-focused disciplines and instead focus on specialized, often vocational or emerging fields:

Gerontology (i) involves the study of aging and the issues related to it, which is a specialized field addressing the needs and care of the elderly population, fitting the non-conventional category.

Ethical hacking (iii) involves learning about cybersecurity and ethical ways to test and improve security systems, which is a modern, specialized vocational field.

Pet Groomers (v) involves the training and skills needed for grooming and caring for pets, which is a vocational training program focusing on practical skills for a specific trade.

Psychology and anthropology are more traditional academic disciplines focused on the study of the mind and human societies, respectively, and thus do not fit the non-conventional category as well as the others.

Question

Non-traditional teaching and learning strategies lay emphasis on

(i) Students need based resource materials and learning standards
(ii) Developing skills. attitude and values
(iii) Promoting In-Box thinking process
(iv) Lecture based model
(v) Acquiring knowledge necessary to respond creatively

Select your answer from the following options:

1. (i), (ii) and (v)
2. (ii), (v) and (V)
3. (ii), (iii) and (iv)
4. (i), (iv) and (v)

Explanations:
Answer: 1. (i), (ii) and (v)

Non-traditional teaching and learning strategies focus on:

(i) Students need-based resource materials and learning standards: This approach ensures that learning resources are tailored to meet the individual needs of students, fostering a more personalized and effective learning experience.

(ii) Developing skills, attitudes, and values: Non-traditional strategies aim to cultivate not just academic knowledge but also essential skills, positive attitudes, and core values that are crucial for personal and professional growth.

(v) Acquiring knowledge necessary to respond creatively: This emphasizes creative thinking and problem-solving, encouraging students to apply their knowledge in innovative ways to address real-world challenges.

Promoting in-box thinking and lecture-based models are more aligned with traditional teaching methods and do not emphasize the personalized and creative approaches that are central to non-traditional teaching and learning strategies.

Question

Which of the following is a non-conventional learning programme in higher education?

1. Swayam
2. Face-to-face teaching-learning
3. Tutorial class
4. Seminar

Explanations:
Answer: 1. Swayam

Swayam is an online platform initiated by the Government of India to offer courses from various fields of study. It is designed to reach a large audience and provides an alternative to traditional face-to-face teaching methods. It emphasizes self-paced, flexible, and accessible learning, making it a non-conventional learning programme in higher education.

Face-to-face teaching-learning, tutorial class, and seminar are traditional methods of instruction that involve direct interaction between teachers and students in a physical classroom setting. These methods do not fall under non-conventional learning programmes, which typically leverage technology and flexible learning schedules.

Professional, Technical and Skill Based education.

In the evolving landscape of education, **Professional, Technical, and Skill-Based Education** plays a crucial role in preparing students for **employment, industry demands, and entrepreneurship**. Unlike conventional academic learning, this education system emphasizes **practical knowledge, hands-on training, and industry-specific skills**. **Professional education** includes fields like **law, medicine, and management**, while **technical education** focuses on **engineering, technology, and applied sciences**. **Skill-based education** promotes **vocational training, craftsmanship, and specialized trades**, catering to a diverse workforce. The **All India Council for Technical Education (AICTE), National Skill Development Corporation (NSDC), and University Grants Commission (UGC)** regulate and promote these programs in India. Government initiatives like **Skill India, National Education Policy (NEP) 2020, and community colleges** further enhance accessibility and employability. These programs ensure that students are not just degree holders but also **job-ready professionals, contributing to economic growth and innovation**. The Indian education system covers everything from primary education to specialized research education. Here's a breakdown:

School Education and Literacy

- **Primary Schooling:** The first stage of formal education.
- **Secondary Education:** The next level after primary education.
- **Senior Secondary Education:** Prepares students for higher education or vocational training.

Higher Education (Tertiary Education)

Tertiary education refers to **higher education beyond secondary school**, including **universities, colleges, technical institutes, and vocational training centers**. It encompasses **undergraduate, postgraduate, diploma, and doctoral programs**, preparing students for **advanced knowledge, research, and professional careers**. In India, tertiary education is regulated by bodies like the **University Grants Commission (UGC), All India Council for Technical Education (AICTE), National Council for Teacher Education (NCTE), and Medical Council of India (MCI)**. The **National Education Policy (NEP) 2020** aims to enhance **access, quality, and employability** in tertiary education by promoting **multidisciplinary learning, skill development, and digital education**. With **private and public institutions offering diverse courses**, tertiary education plays a vital role in **economic growth, innovation, and global competitiveness**.

Higher Education System or Tertiary Education System Higher education, also known as the tertiary education system, is a significant part of the Indian education structure. India's higher education system is the third-largest in the world, following the United States and China, and includes academic, professional, and technical degrees. It also includes Professional, Technical, and Skill-Based Education.

- **Academic Degrees (Non-professional):** Courses like Bachelor of Arts (BA) or Master of Science (MSc).
- **Professional Degrees:** Specialized courses like Bachelor of Medicine (MBBS) or Bachelor of Law (LLB).
- **Technical Degrees:** Engineering, IT, and other technical fields.

Question

Higher Education is also known as-

1. Professional Education
2. Senior Secondary Education
3. Tertiary Education
4. Technical Education

Explanations:

Answer: 3. Tertiary Education

- **Higher Education = Tertiary Education**, which comes after secondary schooling.
- **Includes universities, colleges, and vocational institutions.**
- **Covers undergraduate, postgraduate, and doctoral studies.**
- **Professional & Technical Education** are **subsets** of higher education

Question

Statement I: NCERT is the main governing body at the tertiary level of Education in India.
Statement II: Tertiary education includes both higher education and Vocational education & training in India.

1. Both Statement I and Statement Il are correct.
2. Both Statement I and Statement Il are incorrect.
3. Statement I is correct but Statement Il is incorrect.
4. Statement I is incorrect but Statement Il is correct.

Explanations:
Answer: 4. Statement I is incorrect but Statement Il is correct.

NCERT (National Council of Educational Research and Training) primarily focuses on school education, not tertiary education. Tertiary education, on the other hand, includes both higher education (such as universities and colleges) and vocational education and training (such as polytechnics and ITIs) in India. Therefore, Statement I is incorrect, but Statement II is correct.

Vocational Education (Skill-Based): Focuses on practical skills and trades.

- **Focuses on practical skills** and industry trades.
- **Prepares students for specific careers** or jobs.
- **Includes technical, industrial, and service skills**.
- **Programs offered at ITIs, polytechnics, and colleges**.
- **Covers fields like mechanics, carpentry, and hospitality**.
- **Emphasizes hands-on training** over theoretical learning.
- **Regulated by AICTE, NSDC, and UGC**.

- **Supported by Skill India and NEP 2020.**
- **Enhances employability** in various industries.
- **Provides certifications, diplomas, and apprenticeships.**

Academic Degrees (Non-Professional Education):

Non-professional education focuses on theoretical study and is not specifically designed to prepare students for professional careers. These degree programs often lead to research opportunities, potentially conferring the title of doctor (PhD). The courses are aimed at fostering a life of scholarship within an academic discipline, rather than applying knowledge directly to professional practices. Graduates with academic qualifications may not necessarily use their degrees in their professional careers, as these programs emphasize theoretical understanding over practical application.

Examples of such degrees are Bachelor of Arts (BA), Bachelor of Science (BSc), Master of Arts (MA), Master of Science (MSc), Master of Philosophy (MPhil), and Doctor of Philosophy (PhD). These academic degrees come in various specializations like BA in Economics, BA in English, BA in Hindi, BSc in Physics, BSc in Computer Science, BSc in Applied Science, and many more.

Traditionally, degrees like BA, BSc, and BCom were seen as the standard and most established forms of higher education. They provide a deep understanding of a specific subject, allowing students to pursue a master's degree or a professional course afterward. While these traditional degrees were highly valued in the past, professional courses have gained significant popularity and are now firmly established in the job market.

Non-Professional Education:

- **Keeps More Career Options Open:** These degrees give you flexibility in choosing your career path.
- **Helps You Specialize:** You can dive deep into a specific subject area.
- **Doesn't Make You Job-Ready:** Unlike professional degrees, these programs don't necessarily prepare you directly for a job.

Professional Education:

Professional education helps students gear up for specific careers like law, pharmacy, medicine, and education. It's a structured way to get specialized training through professional schools, where you not only learn the theoretical stuff but also how to apply it practically.

Some common goals of professional education include:

Incorporating the basics: Learning the fundamental knowledge and values of a professional field.

Understanding concepts and techniques: Grasping the key concepts, principles, and techniques used in practice.

Achieving competence: Reaching a level of skill necessary for responsible entry into the professional world.

Continual development: Taking on the responsibility to keep improving and developing your skills over time.

Examples of Professional Education Degrees:

- **Surgery and Medicine:** Degrees like MBBS, MS, and MD.
- **Dentistry**: Degree like BDS.
- **Management Studies:** Degree like MBA.
- **Law**: Degrees like LLB and LLM.
- **Education**: Degrees like B.Ed. and M.Ed.
- **Finance and Accounting:** Certifications like CA, ICWA, and CS.
- These degrees are designed to get you job-ready and equipped with the specific skills needed for your chosen profession.

Question

Choose the correct statements:

A. PhD in Chemistry is a professional degree
B. PhD in education is a professional degree
C. LLM is a professional degree
D. M. Pharma is a non-professional degree

E. M.Se. Computer Science is a professional degree

1. C
2. ABD
3. E
4. CE

Explanations:
Answer: 1. C: **LLM - A professional degree** (Law specialization).

- **PhD in Chemistry- Not a professional degree** (It is a research degree).
- **PhD in Education - Not a professional degree** (It is a research-based degree).
- **M. Pharma - A professional degree** (Regulated under pharmacy education).
- **M.Sc. Computer Science - Not a professional degree** (Academic, not professional).

Technical Education (Technical Degree)

According to Britannica, technical education is all about preparing students for jobs that involve applied science and modern technology. It focuses on understanding and practically applying basic principles of science and math.

In India, technical education includes programs in engineering, technology, management, architecture, town planning, pharmacy, applied arts and crafts, hotel management, and catering technology.

The top body for technical education in India is the All India Council for Technical Education (AICTE). It was set up in November 1945 to survey the facilities available for technical education and promote its development across the country. The AICTE was later established by the AICTE Act in 1987.

Examples of Technical Education Degrees:

- **Engineering and Technology:** Diploma, B.Tech, M.Tech.

- **Architecture:** B.Arch, M.Arch.
- **Pharmacy**: B.Pharma, M.Pharma.

Skill-Based Education (Vocational Education)

Skill-based education, also known as Vocational Education or Career and Technical Education (CTE), is all about preparing learners for jobs that involve manual or practical activities. It's not your typical academic stuff; instead, it's focused on specific trades, occupations, or vocations. That's why it's called vocational education.

This type of education helps learners develop expertise in specific techniques or technologies. It's all about gaining skills through both practical and academic knowledge and is fully job-oriented for a specific field.

Examples of Skill-Based Education (Vocational Education):

ITIs: Industrial Training Institutes offer various skill-based training programs.

Pradhan Mantri Kaushal Vikas Yojana (PMKVY): A government scheme aimed at skill development.

SANKALP: Skills Acquisition and Knowledge Awareness for Livelihood Promotion.

Polytechnic Schemes: These provide diploma courses in various technical fields.
Promote Vocational Education in Schools and Higher Education: Encouraging skill development from an early age.

Question

Statement I: Skill-based education is focused on the idea that it may be learned better if it is practiced in real
life.
Statement II: Non- conventional higher education is totally based on the teaching-learning activities that are offered on campus with fixed-time classes.

1. Both Statement I and Statement II are true
2. Both Statement I and Statement II are false
3. Statement I is true but Statement II is false
4. Statement I is false but Statement II is true

Explanations:
Answer: 3. Statement I is true but Statement II is false

Statement I is true because skill-based education emphasizes practical, hands-on learning experiences that mirror real-life scenarios, enhancing the learning process. Statement II is false because non-conventional higher education typically includes flexible learning formats such as online courses, distance education, and asynchronous learning, which are not confined to on-campus, fixed-time classes. Non-conventional education often allows learners to study at their own pace and in various settings.

Question

The union government of India had in 2011 decided to establish a National Institute of Design in the states of:

A. Andhra Pradesh
B. Kerala
C. Assam
D. Goa
E. Haryana

1. ABC
2. BCD
3. ACE
4. DE

Explanations:
Answer: 3. ACE

In **2011**, the Union Government of India decided to establish **National Institutes of Design (NIDs)** in the following states:

- **A. Andhra Pradesh**

- **C. Assam**
- **E. Haryana**

These new NIDs were part of the government's plan to expand design education and promote innovation across the country. The states of **Kerala (B)** and **Goa (D)** were not included in this specific decision.

VALUE EDUCATION AND ENVIRONMENTAL EDUCATION

In the rapidly evolving world, education is not just about acquiring knowledge but also about developing **ethical values and environmental consciousness**. **Value Education** instills **moral, ethical, social, and cultural values**, shaping responsible individuals who contribute positively to society. It emphasizes **character-building, integrity, empathy, and discipline**, ensuring that students grow into responsible citizens.

Similarly, **Environmental Education** is essential in addressing **climate change, sustainability, and conservation**. It promotes **awareness about natural resources, pollution control, and eco-friendly practices**, ensuring that future generations understand their role in preserving the planet. With initiatives like **NEP 2020, Swachh Bharat Abhiyan, and global sustainability efforts**, environmental education has become a crucial part of the curriculum in schools and universities.

This book explores the **significance, implementation, and impact** of **Value and Environmental Education**, highlighting their role in **holistic learning**. By integrating these disciplines, education moves beyond academics, preparing individuals to lead with **conscience, responsibility, and a commitment to a better future**.

Question

"Education is the manifestation of perfection already in man" **is a statement by:**

1. Rabindranath Tagore
2. MK Gandhi
3. Sri Aurobindo

4. Swami Vivekananda

Explanations:
Answer: 4. Swami Vivekananda

The statement "*Education is the manifestation of perfection already in man*" is attributed to **Swami Vivekananda**. He emphasized that education is not just about acquiring knowledge but about uncovering the inherent potential and perfection within each individual.

VALUE EDUCATION

'Value' can be defined as the degree of importance of something or an action, with the aim of determining the best actions to take or the best way to live, and to describe the significance of different actions.

Value education is important because it helps individuals achieve results in the right way, maintain a balance between tradition and modernity, foster healthy relations across different communities and cultures, conserve and treat the environment correctly, and prevent unethical behavior.

RECOMMENDATIONS:

Education Commission (1966): Suggested the introduction of social, moral, and spiritual values in the school curriculum.

National Policy on Education (1986): Recommended education for values to remove intolerance, violence, and superstition while sustaining social, cultural, and scientific principles.

National Curriculum Framework for School Education (2000): Highlighted the disintegration of social, ethical, and spiritual values.

National Curriculum Framework (NCF) (2005): Prescribed values like tolerance, respect for human rights, cooperation, justice, responsible citizenship, and peaceful conflict resolution.

AIMS OF VALUE EDUCATION

Comprehensive and holistic development: Value education aims to foster the all-round development of individuals, nurturing their intellectual, emotional, social, and moral capacities.

Making people mindful of fading values: It encourages awareness and reinforcement of important values that may be diminishing in modern society, ensuring they are preserved and practiced.

Bringing in a dynamic social conscience: Value education aims to instill a sense of social responsibility, promoting active participation in community welfare and social justice.

Enhancing the quality of education: By integrating values into the curriculum, it seeks to improve the overall quality of education, making it more meaningful and relevant to real-life situations.

Connecting the heart, head, and hand: Value education strives to integrate emotional intelligence (heart), intellectual growth (head), and practical skills (hand) to create well-rounded individuals.

TYPES OF VALUE

Human value: These values emphasize the importance of compassion, empathy, and respect for human dignity, fostering interpersonal harmony and ethical behavior.

National or constitutional value: These values are derived from the principles enshrined in a nation's constitution, promoting patriotism, justice, equality, and the rule of law.

Religious value: Religious values focus on the moral and ethical teachings of various faiths, encouraging spiritual growth, ethical conduct, and respect for diverse religious beliefs.

Aesthetic value: Aesthetic values highlight the appreciation of beauty in art, nature, and culture, fostering creativity, sensitivity, and an appreciation for the finer aspects of life.

Social value: Social values emphasize the importance of cooperation, community service, and social responsibility, promoting a sense of belonging and collective well-being.

Vocational value: Vocational values relate to the importance of work ethics, professionalism, and skill development, preparing individuals for productive and satisfying careers.

Question

What is the primary aim of value education?

1. To promote economic development
2. To inculcate moral values
3. To enhance technical skills
4. To improve physical fitness

Explanation

Answer: 2) To inculcate moral values

Value education focuses on instilling ethical and moral values in individuals, shaping their character and behavior.

Question

Which of the following best describes "value crisis"?

1. A financial downturn affecting education
2. A decline in moral and ethical standards
3. An increase in cultural diversity
4. Overemphasis on traditional practices

Explanation

Answer: 2) A decline in moral and ethical standards

A "value crisis" refers to a situation where there's a noticeable decline in societal moral and ethical values, leading to various social issues.

Question

In the context of value education, which method is most effective for developing moral reasoning in students?

1. Lectures
2. Case studies
3. Memorization
4. Drills

   Answer: 2) Case studies

   Explanation: Using case studies allows students to analyze real-life scenarios, enhancing their moral reasoning and ethical decision-making skills.

Question

Which organization in India has emphasized the need for value education in its policies?

1. Reserve Bank of India
2. University Grants Commission
3. Indian Medical Association
4. Press Council of India

Explanation

Answer: 2) University Grants Commission

The UGC has highlighted the importance of value education in its guidelines to promote holistic development in higher education.

Question

Which of the following is a key component of value education?

1. Technical proficiency
2. Moral development
3. Physical strength
4. Economic acumen

Explanation

Answer: 2) Moral development

Value education primarily aims at the moral development of individuals, fostering virtues like honesty, integrity, and empathy.

Question

The purpose of value education is best served by focusing on:

1. Cultural practices prevailing in society
2. Norms of conduct laid down by a social group
3. Concern for human values
4. Religious and moral practices and instructions
   Answer: 3) Concern for human values
   Explanation: Emphasizing human values ensures that education addresses universal ethical principles, promoting harmony and understanding.

Question

Which teaching method is most suitable for imparting value education?

1. Lecture method
2. Discussion method
3. Demonstration method
4. Project method

Explanation

Answer: 2) Discussion method

The discussion method encourages students to express their views and reflect on various perspectives, facilitating deeper understanding of values.

Question

Value education in schools primarily aims to:

1. Prepare students for competitive exams
2. Develop students' technical skills
3. Instill ethical and moral values

4. Enhance physical development

Explanation

Answer: 3) Instill ethical and moral values

The main goal of value education is to nurture ethical and moral values among students, guiding their behavior and decision-making.

Question

Which of the following strategies can effectively promote value education?

1. Strict disciplinary actions
2. Incorporating value-based stories and activities
3. Increasing homework assignments
4. Emphasizing rote memorization

Explanation

Answer: 2) Incorporating value-based stories and activities

Engaging students with stories and activities that highlight moral lessons helps in internalizing values effectively.

Question

Which level of Bloom's Taxonomy involves the ability to judge the value of material for a given purpose?

1. Analysis
2. Synthesis
3. Evaluation
4. Application

Explanation

Answer: 3) Evaluation

In Bloom's Taxonomy, the evaluation level pertains to making judgments about the value of ideas or materials, which is crucial in value education.

Question

Books written by which of the following famous persons of Singh Sabha were taught in Sikh Girls College?

A. My Veer Singh
B. Lala Devraj
C. Harnam Kaur
D. Bhai Mohansingh Ved

1. ABCD
2. AD
3. AC
4. BC

Explanations:
Answer: 2. AD

Bhai Vir Singh (often written as My Veer Singh) was a prominent Sikh scholar, poet, and writer associated with the **Singh Sabha Movement**. His literary works played a significant role in **promoting Sikh education and cultural identity**. His books were used in Sikh Girls' Colleges.

Lala Devraj was also an influential figure in the **Singh Sabha Movement**, contributing to **Sikh literature and education**. His works were included in the curriculum of Sikh Girls' Colleges.

Harnam Kaur and **Bhai Mohan Singh Ved** were involved in Sikh education, but their books were not primarily part of the curriculum in Sikh Girls' Colleges.

ENVIRONMENTAL EDUCATION

OBJECTIVES OF ENVIRONMENTAL EDUCATION

Knowledge: Environmental education aims to provide individuals with a deep understanding of environmental issues, ecosystems, and the impact of human activities on the environment. It equips learners with the scientific knowledge necessary to analyze and address environmental challenges.

Awareness: This objective focuses on raising awareness about environmental issues and their significance. It encourages individuals to recognize the importance of environmental conservation and the role they can play in protecting natural resources.

Skills: Environmental education seeks to develop practical skills that enable individuals to take effective action for the environment. These skills include critical thinking, problem-solving, and the ability to implement sustainable practices in daily life.

Attitudes: It aims to cultivate positive attitudes towards the environment, fostering a sense of responsibility and stewardship. This involves promoting values such as respect for nature, empathy for living organisms, and a commitment to sustainability.

Participation: Encouraging active participation is crucial in environmental education. It motivates individuals to engage in community initiatives, conservation projects, and policy-making processes, contributing to collective efforts to address environmental issues.

EVOLUTION OF INDIAN ENVIRONMENTAL EDUCATION

42nd Amendment to the Constitution (1974): The amendment made it the state government's responsibility to preserve and improve the environment and protect forests and wildlife. This constitutional change highlighted the importance of environmental protection and laid the foundation for environmental policies in India.

The National Policy on Education (1986): This policy emphasized the need to spread awareness about safeguarding the environment. It recognized the importance of environmental education in schools and aimed to integrate environmental awareness into the educational curriculum.

Supreme Court Mandate (1991): The Honourable Supreme Court of India made environmental education compulsory, underscoring its critical role in the nation's education system. This decision mandated that environmental education be included in the curriculum at all levels of schooling, ensuring that future generations are educated about environmental issues and conservation.

Question

Environmental education encompasses the issues of:

A. Resource Consumption
B. Environmental degradation
C. Biodiversity loss
D. Economic empowerment
E. Climate change and its impact

Choose the correct answer from the options given below:

1. A, B, C, and D only
2. A, B, C, and E only
3. B, C, D and E only
4. A and E only

Explanation

Answer: 2. A, B, C, and E only

Environmental education addresses issues like resource consumption, environmental degradation, biodiversity loss, and climate change impacts. Economic empowerment, while important, is not a primary focus.

CHAPTER V

Policies, Governance, and Administration

Policies, Governance, and Administration

Policies, governance, and administration play a critical role in shaping the **education system**, ensuring its **efficiency, accessibility, and quality**. **Educational policies** provide a **framework for curriculum development, institutional regulations, and resource allocation**, while **governance** establishes **decision-making structures** at national, state, and institutional levels. Effective **administration** ensures the **smooth implementation of policies**, addressing challenges such as **equity, inclusivity, and technological advancements**.

In India, organizations like the **University Grants Commission (UGC), All India Council for Technical Education (AICTE), National Council for Teacher Education (NCTE), and National Medical Commission (NMC)** regulate different sectors of education. Key policies such as the **National Policy on Education (1968, 1986, 2020)** have played transformative roles in **modernizing education, integrating technology, and enhancing skill development**. Governance mechanisms ensure **autonomy and accountability in institutions**, while administrative bodies implement reforms to meet **global educational standards**.

This section explores the **evolution, impact, and challenges** in education policies, governance structures, and administrative frameworks, shaping India's **higher education landscape**.

Radhakrishnan Commission/University Education Commission 1948-49:

The University Education Commission was the first education commission established **post-independence in 1948.** It was led by **Dr. Sarvepalli Radhakrishnan,** who later became the President of India. The commission is also known as the Radhakrishnan Commission.

- **Formed in 1948**, chaired by **Dr. S. Radhakrishnan**.
- First **post-independence commission** on higher education.
- Aimed to reform **university education system**.
- Focused on **intellectual, cultural, and moral growth**.
- Emphasized **quality, research, and knowledge expansion**.
- Recommended **mother tongue** for undergraduate courses.
- **English** to continue for **higher education**.
- Promoted **interdisciplinary learning** and specialization.
- Encouraged **higher education for women**.
- Strengthened **teacher training** and faculty development.
- Suggested better **salaries for university teachers**.
- Advocated **university autonomy** and reduced interference.
- Proposed reforms in **examination and evaluation**.
- Emphasized **moral and value education**.
- Recommended **rural and adult education programs**.
- Encouraged **scientific and industrial research**.
- Proposed establishing **University Grants Commission (UGC)**.
- **UGC officially established in 1956**.
- Helped modernize **Indian higher education system**.
- Laid foundation for **future education policies**.

Its primary purpose was to address issues faced by colleges and universities and to suggest improvements in the higher education system.

Key Recommendations:

- **Integration of Secondary and Higher Education**
  - Recommended a **three-year bachelor's degree** program.
- **Establishment of the University Grants Commission (UGC)**
- **Setting up of rural universities**:
  - Establishment of universities in rural areas.
  - It recommended setting up **new rural universities**.
  - To promote **agriculture, rural industries, and village development**.
- **Development of research** in **agriculture, commerce, law, science, and technology**.
- **Focus on student welfare**:

    - Student support services, including **hostels, scholarships, and counseling** to ensure overall development.
- The commission **supported English for higher education**.
- It recommended the **mother tongue for undergraduate courses**.

Question

The University Education Commission (1948-49) suggested a bachelor's degree of:

1. Five years
2. Four years
3. Three years
4. Two years

Explanations:
Answer: 3. Three years

The University Education Commission (1948-49), also known as the Radhakrishnan Commission, recommended a three-year bachelor's degree program. This recommendation was part of its broader reforms to improve the quality and structure of higher education in India. The three-year degree structure was intended to provide a balanced and comprehensive education, allowing students to specialize in their chosen fields while also gaining a foundational understanding of other disciplines. This recommendation has largely been adopted in the Indian higher education system.

Question

The major recommendations of the Radhakrishnan Commission are:

A. Transfer of urban universities to rural areas
B. Setting up of rural universities
C. Development of research in agriculture, commerce, law, science and technology
D. Making English language as the medium of instruction at all levels of teaching
E. Focus on student's Welfare

1. A, B

2. B, C, D
3. C, D, E
4. B, C, E

Explanations:
Answer: 4. B, C, E

The **Radhakrishnan Commission (1948-49)** emphasized the need for **higher education reforms** in India. Among its key recommendations:

Setting up of rural universities (**B**) – The commission proposed the establishment of universities in rural areas to promote **agriculture, rural industries, and village development**.

Development of research in **agriculture, commerce, law, science, and technology** (**C**) – It stressed the importance of research-oriented education in various disciplines to modernize India's economy.

Focus on student welfare (**E**) – The commission recommended student support services, including **hostels, scholarships, and counseling** to ensure overall development.

Why not the other options?

A (Transfer of urban universities to rural areas) – The commission did not suggest relocating existing universities; instead, it recommended setting up **new rural universities**.

D (Making English the medium of instruction at all levels) – The commission **supported English for higher education**, but it recommended the **mother tongue for undergraduate courses**.

Question

Which of the following is the first Post-Independence education commission in India?

1. Indian Education Commission
2. Calcutta University Commission
3. University Education Commission
4. Indian Universities Commission

Explanations:
Answer: 3. University Education Commission

The first Post-Independence education commission in India was the University Education Commission (1948-49), also known as the Radhakrishnan Commission. It was established to examine the state of university education in India and recommend reforms to improve higher education after independence.

The other commissions listed either predate independence (e.g., Calcutta University Commission, 1917) or were established later (e.g., Indian Education Commission, 1964-66, also known as the Kothari Commission).

Question

In 1948, under whose chairmanship a University Commission was appointed with the purpose of reconstruction of university education to meet the demand for scientific, technical and other manpower needed for the socio-economic development of the country?

1. Dr. Zakir Hussain
2. Dr. S. Radhakrishnan
3. Dr. A.L Mudaliar
4. Dr. DS. Kothari

Explanations:
Answer: 2. Dr. S. Radhakrishnan

In 1948, Dr. S. Radhakrishnan chaired the University Education Commission, which was appointed with the purpose of reconstructing university education to meet the demand for scientific, technical, and other manpower needed for the socio-economic development of the country. This commission is also known as the Radhakrishnan Commission.

University Grants Commission (UGC)

The UGC is a statutory body under the Department of Higher Education, Ministry of Education, Government of India. It was established according to the UGC Act 1956. The UGC is responsible for coordinating, determining, and maintaining standards of higher education in India. It provides recognition to universities and disburses funds to recognized universities and colleges.

Recognition of Universities: The UGC grants recognition to universities across India. Disbursement of Funds: It allocates funds to recognized universities and colleges to ensure the maintenance of education standards. Doctoral Scholarships: The UGC provides doctoral scholarships to individuals who clear the Junior Research Fellowship (JRF) in the National Eligibility Test (NET). Annually, approximately ₹725 crore (US$87 million) is spent on doctoral and post-doctoral fellowships.

Headquarters and Regional Centres: The UGC headquarters is located in New Delhi.
It has six regional centres in Pune, Bhopal, Kolkata, Hyderabad, Guwahati, and Bangalore.

Future Prospects: There is a proposal under consideration by the Government of India to replace the UGC with a new regulatory body called the Higher Education Commission of India (HECI).

The University Education Commission of 1948-49 laid the groundwork for many reforms in the Indian higher education system, with the establishment of the UGC being one of its most significant contributions.

The University Grants Commission (UGC) of India has had several chairpersons since its establishment in 1956. Here is a list of notable chairpersons:

- **Dr. Shanti Swarup Bhatnagar** (1956-1957) - First Chairman of UGC.
- **Dr. D. S. Kothari** (1961-1973) - Renowned educationist and scientist.
- **Dr. V. K. R. V. Rao** (1973-1977) - Economist and founder of the Delhi School of Economics.
- **Dr. Malcolm Adiseshiah** (1977-1978) - Economist and educator.
- **Dr. Madhuri R. Shah** (1978-1983) - First woman chairperson of UGC.
- **Dr. Yash Pal** (1986-1991) - Eminent scientist and educationist.

- **Prof. Ram Reddy** (1991-1997) - Noted educationist and administrator.
- **Prof. Hari Gautam** (1997-2002) - Academic and administrator.
- **Prof. Arun Nigavekar** (2002-2005) - Educationist and former Vice-Chancellor of Pune University.
- **Prof. Sukhadeo Thorat** (2006-2011) - Economist and social scientist.
- **Prof. Ved Prakash** (2011-2016) - Educationist and former Vice-Chancellor of National University of Educational Planning and Administration (NUEPA).
- **Prof. D. P. Singh** (2018-2021) - Academic and former Director of the National Assessment and Accreditation Council (NAAC).
- **Prof. M. Jagadesh Kumar** (2022-Present) - Current Chairman of UGC, academic, and former Vice-Chancellor of Jawaharlal Nehru University (JNU).

Question

Which commission/committee recommended that the ordinary amenities and decencies of life should be provided for women in colleges ordinarily planned for men and that there should be no curtailment of opportunities for women' ?

1. Durgabai Deshmukh Committee 1959)
2. Kothari Commission (1964 - 66)
3. Bhaktavatsalam committee (1963)
4. Radhakrishnan Commission (1948)

Explanations:
Answer: 4. Radhakrishnan Commission (1948)

The Radhakrishnan Commission (1948), also known as the University Education Commission, recommended that the ordinary amenities and decencies of life should be provided for women in colleges ordinarily planned for men and that there should be no curtailment of opportunities for women. This recommendation was part of their broader vision for inclusive and equitable higher education.

Question

The chronological sequence of the following chairpersons of UGC is:

A. Armaity S. Desai
B. G. Ram Reddy
C. Manmohan Singh
D. Yashpal
E. Madhuri R. Shah

1. AEBDC
2. BCEAD
3. CDAEB
4. EDCBA

Explanations:
Answer: 4. EDCBA

- **Madhuri R. Shah (E) - 1981-1986:** First woman chairperson of UGC.
- **Manmohan Singh (D) - 1986-1991:** Later became India's Prime Minister.
- **Yashpal (C) - 1991-1994:** Known for reforms in higher education.
- **G. Ram Reddy (B) - 1994-1997:** Pioneer in distance education and Open University system.
- **Armaity S. Desai (A) - 1995-1999:** Focused on educational reforms and quality assurance.

Question

Government of India constituted a University Education Commission in November-1948 under the Chairmanship

1. Dr. Lakshmanaswamy
2. Shri Maulana Abul Kalam Azad
3. Dr. Radhakrishnan
4. Dr. Yash Pal

Explanations:
Answer: 3. Dr. Radhakrishnan

The Government of India constituted the University Education Commission in November 1948 under the chairmanship of Dr. S. Radhakrishnan. This commission was tasked with examining and suggesting improvements for university education in India to better align with the country's needs for scientific, technical, and other forms of manpower for socio-economic development. Dr. Radhakrishnan's leadership and vision were instrumental in shaping the recommendations of this commission.

Question

The University Education Commission (1948-49) laid stress on

(A) Religious education
(B) Changes in curriculum
(C) Women's education
(D) Rural universities
(E) Examination reforms

1. (A), (B) and (C) only.
2. (A), (C)and (D) only.
3. (A), (D) and (E) only.
4. (B), (C), (D) and (E) only.

Explanations:
Answer: 4. (B), (C), (D) and (E) only.

The University Education Commission (1948-49), under the chairmanship of Dr. S. Radhakrishnan, emphasized several key areas for the improvement of higher education in India. These areas included changes in the curriculum to make education more relevant and comprehensive, enhancing women's education to ensure equal opportunities, establishing rural universities to cater to the educational needs of rural areas, and implementing examination reforms to improve the assessment and evaluation process.

Question

Which was the first education commission of independent India?

1. Sargent commission
2. Kothari commission

3. Radhakrishnan commission
4. Mudaliar commission

Explanations:
Answer: 3. Radhakrishnan commission

The first education commission of independent India was the University Education Commission (1948-49), which was chaired by Dr. S. Radhakrishnan. This commission was established to examine the state of university education in India and to suggest improvements and reforms. It focused on various aspects such as curriculum changes, women's education, rural universities, and examination reforms, making it a significant step in shaping India's higher education system.

Question

Radhakrishnan Commission regarding medium of instruction in higher education?

A. The medium of higher education should be in regional language.
B. Immediate steps should be taken to prepare scientific and technical terminologies in federal lang
C. All the federal languages must be written in Devanagari script.
D. International and scientific terminological words should be avoided.
E. English should be banished from the higher education field in India immediately.

1. A, B and C only
2. B, C and D only
3. C, D and E only
4. A, D and E only

Explanations:
Answer: 1. A, B and C only

The Radhakrishnan Commission emphasized the importance of regional languages in higher education but also acknowledged the need for immediate steps to develop scientific and technical terminologies in the federal language. Additionally, it suggested that all federal languages should be written in the Devanagari script. These recommendations aimed to strengthen the use of Indian languages in higher education while ensuring that scientific and technical subjects could be adequately taught and understood.

Question

UGC was established on the recommendation of-

1. University Education Commission
2. Higher Education Commission
3. Ministry of Education
4. Planning Commission

Explanations:
Answer: 1. University Education Commission

The University Grants Commission (UGC) was established based on the recommendations of the University Education Commission (1948-49), chaired by Dr. S. Radhakrishnan. The commission emphasized the need for an organization to oversee and coordinate university education, leading to the formation of the UGC to ensure standards and quality in higher education across India.

Question

Which of the following recommendations were put forward by the University Education Commission appointed after independence by the Indian Government concerning medical education in India?

A. Medical colleges should admit a maximum number of hundred students.
B. History of medicine with special reference to Indian systems should be taught in the first degree course in medicine.
C. More importance should be attached to Public health, Engineering and Nursing.
D. There should be provision of ten beds per student admitted in the medical college.

1. AB
2. BC

3. BCD
4. ABCD

Explanations:
Answer: 4. ABCD

The University Education Commission, chaired by Dr. S. Radhakrishnan, made comprehensive recommendations concerning medical education in India. These included:

A: Limiting the number of students admitted to medical colleges to ensure quality education.

B: Incorporating the history of medicine, particularly focusing on Indian systems, into the first-degree course.

C: Emphasizing the importance of public health, engineering, and nursing as integral components of medical education.

D: Ensuring an adequate student-to-bed ratio in medical colleges to provide practical training opportunities.

Question

Which of the following presidents of India was basically an academician?

1. Gyani Zail Singh
2. Pranab Mukharjee
3. APJ Abdul Kalam
4. Sarvapalli Radhakrishnan

Explanations:
Answer: 4. Sarvapalli Radhakrishnan

Sarvapalli Radhakrishnan was fundamentally an academician, philosopher, and professor before becoming the President of India. He held various academic positions, including Vice-Chancellor of Andhra University and Banaras Hindu University, and was also a professor at the University of Oxford.

Question

Statement I: The Radhakrishnan Commission recommended to standardise university teaching in India.
Statement II: The Radhakrishnan Commission also suggested the establishment of an All India University Examination Board.

1. Both Statement I and Statement Il are true
2. Both Statement I and Statement Il are false
3. Statement I is true but Statement ll is false
4. Statement I is false but Statement Il is true

Explanations:
Answer: 3. Statement I is true but Statement ll is false

The Radhakrishnan Commission (University Education Commission) recommended standardizing university teaching in India to ensure consistency and quality across institutions. However, it did not suggest the establishment of an All India University Examination Board.

Question

The Government of India in November 1948 appointed a University Education Commission under the Chairmanship of-

1. DS Kotharl
2. Ms. Sucheta Kriplani
3. Dr. S. Radhakrishnan
4. Mrs. Annie Besant

Explanations:
Answer: 3. Dr. S. Radhakrishnan

In November 1948, the Government of India appointed the University Education Commission under the chairmanship of Dr. S. Radhakrishnan. This commission was tasked with examining the state of university education in India and suggesting improvements to meet the demands of the country post-independence.

Question

The first education commission in Independent India is:

1. Secondary Education Commission
2. The Education Commission
3. University Education Commission
4. National Knowledge Commission

Explanations:
Answer: 3. University Education Commission

The first education commission in independent India was the University Education Commission, appointed in November 1948 under the chairmanship of Dr. S. Radhakrishnan. This commission was established to address the issues facing higher education in India and to suggest reforms to improve the quality and accessibility of university education.

Question

In 1948, under whose Chairmanship a University Education Commission was set up to reconstruct University Education in India?

1. Sardar Vallabh Bhai Patel
2. Prof. P.C. Joshi
3. Dr. S. Radhakrishnan
4. Dr. Vikram Sarabhai

Explanations:
Answer: 3. Dr. S. Radhakrishnan

In 1948, the Government of India set up the University Education Commission under the chairmanship of Dr. S. Radhakrishnan. The commission was tasked with restructuring and improving the university education system in India post-independence.

Mudaliar Commission 1952-53

The Government of India established the Secondary Education Commission on 23 September 1952. The commission was chaired by Dr. Lakshmanaswamy Mudaliar and is often referred to as the Mudaliar Commission. The primary goal was to evaluate and reform secondary education in India.

Key Recommendations:

Diversifying the Curriculum: The commission recommended diversifying the curriculum to include a broader range of subjects and vocational education.

Intermediate Level: The introduction of an intermediate level between secondary and university education.

Three-Tier Undergraduate Courses: Proposed a three-tier structure for undergraduate courses to better prepare students for higher education and the workforce.

Objectives of Secondary Education:

Development of Democratic Citizenship: Educating students to be informed and active citizens in a democracy.

Improvement of Vocational Capability and Efficiency: Enhancing students' vocational skills to improve their employability and efficiency in various trades.

Education for Leadership: Fostering leadership qualities among students. Development of Personality: Emphasizing overall personality development, including moral and ethical values.

Policy for the Spread of Secondary Education:

Vocational Education: Vocational education should be integrated into secondary education, aiming for 30% of students at the lower secondary level and 50% at the higher secondary level to receive vocational training.

Equality of Opportunities: Emphasis on providing equal opportunities in secondary education, including increasing the availability of scholarships.

Special Programs for Marginalized Groups: Implementing special programs to expand secondary education among girls, scheduled castes, and tribes.

Development of Talent: Genuine efforts should be made to identify and nurture talent among students.

District-Level Plans: Plans should be made to expand secondary education in each district, with full implementation within ten years.

Educational Standards: New schools should meet required educational standards, and existing schools should be upgraded to higher standards.

The Mudaliar Commission's recommendations aimed to create a more inclusive, diversified, and practical secondary education system in India, ensuring that students are better prepared for both higher education and vocational careers. The focus was on equal opportunity, vocational training, and the overall development of students' abilities and personalities.

Question

Which one of the following groups of commission on education has been given chronologically in an order of year in which they were constituted?

1. Kothari Commission, Mudaliar Commission, Radhakrishnan Commission
2. Radhakrishnan Commission, Mudaliar Commission, Kothari Commission
3. Mudaliar Commission, Kothari Commission, Radhakrishnan Commission
4. Radhakrishnan Commission. Kothari Commission, Mudaliar Commission

Explanations:
Answer: 2. Radhakrishnan Commission, Mudaliar Commission, Kothari Commission

Question

In which year the Secondary Education Commission was appointed under the chairmanship of Dr. A.L. Mudaliar:

1. 1950

2. 1951
3. 1952
4. 1962

Explanations:
Answer: 3. 1952

The Secondary Education Commission, also known as the Mudaliar Commission, was appointed by the Government of India in the year 1952 under the chairmanship of Dr. A.L. Mudaliar. Its purpose was to examine the existing system of secondary education in India and suggest measures for its improvement.

The Kothari Commission Overview:

The National Education Commission (1964-1966), popularly known as the Kothari Commission, was an ad hoc commission established by the Government of India. It aimed to examine **all aspects of the educational sector in India.** The commission was chaired by **Daulat Singh Kothari,** who was also the chairman of the University Grants Commission at that time.

The commission submitted its report on 29 June 1966, titled "Education and National Development Report of the Education Commission." A key highlight from the commission's findings was the statement, "The destiny of India is being shaped in her classroom." The recommendations of the Kothari Commission significantly **influenced the National Policy on Education in 1968.**

Drawing on Nehru's vision, the Kothari Commission aimed to create a coherent education policy for India. The commission believed that education should:

- Increase productivity
- Develop social and national unity
- Consolidate democracy
- Modernize the country
- Develop social, moral, and spiritual values

To achieve these goals, the commission emphasized free and compulsory education for all children up to the age of 14.

Key Recommendations:

Development of Languages: Promotion of Hindi, Sanskrit, regional languages, and the implementation of the three-language formula.

Equality of Educational Opportunities: Addressing regional, tribal, and gender imbalances to ensure equal access to education.

Scientific Education and Research: Prioritizing the development of scientific education and research to meet India's development needs.

Eradication of Illiteracy: Implementing measures to eradicate illiteracy and promote adult education.

Curriculum Focus: Historically, India's curriculum has prioritized mathematics and science over social sciences or arts. The Kothari Commission actively promoted this focus, arguing that India's development would benefit more from engineers and scientists than from historians. This perception has persisted, though recently, subjects like commerce and economics have gained importance.

The Kothari Commission's work laid the foundation for many educational policies and reforms in India, aiming to build a robust and equitable education system that could support the nation's modernization and development goals.

Keys to Remember Kothari Commission

- **Established in 1964**, chaired by **D.S. Kothari**.
- **Comprehensive review** of India's education system.
- **Covered all levels** from primary to university.
- **Recommended 6% GDP spending** on education.
- **Introduced the 10+2+3 education system**.
- **Suggested senior universities for advanced research**.
- **Promoted linkage of universities** with research institutes.
- **Emphasized science education** for economic growth.
- **Advocated national-level teacher recruitment**.

- **Proposed autonomy** for universities and colleges.
- **Encouraged vocational education** at secondary level.
- **Recommended student welfare measures** in universities.
- **Suggested national evaluation standards** for education.
- **Opposed uncontrolled expansion** of higher education.
- **Proposed major universities** for academic excellence.
- **Promoted language education** under three-language formula.
- **Recommended focus on moral value education**.
- **Advocated rural university establishment** for development.
- **Integrated education and skill development** policies.
- **Recognized the importance of environmental education**.
- **Linked education with national economic needs**.
- **First policy to emphasize lifelong learning**.
- **Led to National Policy on Education (1968)**.
- **Highlighted role of technology in education**.
- **Focused on improving teacher training programs**.

Question

The Kothari Commission (1963-64) suggested spending _ of national income on education.

1. 3 percent
2. 6 percent
3. 7 percent
4. 9 percent

Explanations:
Answer: 2. 6 percent

The Kothari Commission (1964-66), also known as the **Indian Education Commission**, recommended that **6 percent of the national income** should be spent on education. This recommendation was made to ensure adequate funding for the development and expansion of the education system in India, aiming to improve access, quality, and equity in education.

Question

Which of the following recommended the linkages of Universities with outside autonomous research organisations?

1. Indian Council of Medical Research
2. Education Commission (1964-66)
3. Indian Council of Agricultural Research
4. Calcutta university Commission

Explanations:
Answer: 2. Education Commission (1964-66)

The **Education Commission (1964-66)**, also known as the **Kothari Commission**, recommended the **linkages of universities with outside autonomous research organizations**. This recommendation was aimed at promoting collaboration between universities and research institutions to enhance the quality of education and research in India. The commission emphasized the importance of integrating academic and research activities to foster innovation and development.

Question

Some of the major recommendations of the Kothari commission on Higher education are:

A. Avoid introducing new courses
B. Select teachers at the national level
C. Restrict the expansion of higher education
D. Provide autonomy to the universities
E. Abolish the continuous evaluation system

1. A, B, C only
2. B, D, E only
3. B, C, D only
4. A, D, E only

Explanations:
Answer: 3. B, C, D only

The Kothari Commission (1964-66) made several key recommendations for higher education in India, focusing on improving quality and efficiency. Among these, the commission recommended selecting teachers at the national level to ensure high standards (B), restricting the expansion of higher education to maintain quality (C), and providing autonomy to universities to enhance their functioning and decision-making capabilities (D). These measures aimed to create a more robust and effective higher education system in India.

Question

Which education commission suggested the development of some universities into senior universities?

1. Sargent commission
2. Radhakrishna commission
3. Mudaliar commission
4. Kothari commission

Explanations:
Answer: 4. Kothari commission

The Kothari Commission (1964-66) suggested the development of some universities into senior universities. This recommendation aimed to enhance the quality and standards of higher education by creating institutions with advanced facilities, research capabilities, and a higher level of academic autonomy. The idea was to establish centers of excellence that could lead the way in education and research.

Question

The first Education commission of India also adhered to

1. The one-language formula
2. The two-language formula
3. The three-language formula
4. The four-language formula

Explanations:
Answer: 3. The three-language formula

The first Education Commission of India, known as the University Education Commission (1948-49) led by Dr. S. Radhakrishnan, adhered to the three-language formula. This formula was designed to promote multilingualism and ensure that students in India learned Hindi, English, and a regional language, thus fostering national integration and providing broader linguistic skills.

Question

Some important recommendations of the Kothari Commission were :

A. Establishment of clusters of advanced centres in major universities
B. Abolition of the system of affiliate colleges
C. Abolition of continuous evaluation system
D. Establishment of six major universities
E. Improving quality and content of lecturing

1. ABC
2. BCD
3. CDE
4. ADE

Explanations:
Answer: 4. ADE

The Kothari Commission (1964-66) provided several key recommendations to reform higher education in India. These included the establishment of clusters of advanced centers in major universities to enhance research and advanced studies, improving the quality and content of lecturing to ensure effective teaching, and the establishment of six major universities to serve as models of excellence. These recommendations aimed at restructuring and elevating the standards of higher education.

Question

Which of the following education commissions of India noted that - "It is obvious that if higher education is not radically improved, our administration and technical progress, our intellectual standards and social advance, will all be most seriously handicapped"?

1. Kothari Commission
2. Radhakrishnan Commission
3. Hunter Commission
4. University Education Commission of 1948

Explanations:
Answer: 1. Kothari Commission

The Kothari Commission (1964-66) emphasized the critical role of higher education in India's overall development. It pointed out that without significant improvements in higher education, the country's administration, technical progress, intellectual standards, and social advancement would face severe limitations. This commission's comprehensive report highlighted the need for reform and expansion of the higher education system to meet national goals.

Question

Which among the following was proposed by the Kothari commission vis-a-vis language?

1. Use of mother tongue as a medium of instruction
2. Use of Hindi as a medium of instruction
3. Two language formula
4. Three language formula

Explanations:
Answer: 4. Three language formula

The Kothari Commission (1964-66) recommended the implementation of the three-language formula to promote multilingualism and national integration in India. This formula proposed that students should learn three languages: their mother tongue or regional language, Hindi, and English. The aim was to ensure that students were proficient in their native language while also gaining skills in Hindi for national communication and English for global engagement.

Question

Statement I: It is obvious that if higher education is not radically improved, our administration and technical progress, our intellectual standards and social advance will be most seriously handicapped. This is a major recommendation of the University Education Commission.

Statement II: The University Grants Commission was established in accordance with the recommendation of the National Education Commission.

1. Both Statement I and Statement Il are true
2. Both Statement I and Statement Il are false
3. Statement I is true but Statement Il is false
4. Statement I is false but Statement Il is true

Explanations:
Answer: 2. Both Statement I and Statement Il are false

Statement I: The quote "It is obvious that if higher education is not radically improved, our administration and technical progress, our intellectual standards and social advance will be most seriously handicapped" is actually a major recommendation of the Kothari Commission (1964-66), not the University Education Commission (1948-49).

Statement II: The University Grants Commission (UGC) was established based on the recommendations of the University Education Commission (1948-49), not the National Education Commission (Kothari Commission).

Question

Destiny of India is being shaped in her classrooms. This is stated in

1. NPE 1986
2. NKC report
3. Education Commission
4. University Education Commission

Explanations:
Answer: 3. Education Commission

The statement "The destiny of India is being shaped in her classrooms" was made by the Education Commission (1964-66), also known as the Kothari Commission. This commission emphasized the critical role of education in national development and the importance of improving educational standards to shape the future of the country.

Question

The Kothari Commission had recommended a certain percentage of national income to be invested in education. What was that percentage?

1. 10%
2. 8%
3. 6%
4. 5%

Explanations:
Answer: 3. 6%

The Kothari Commission (1964-66) recommended that 6% of the national income should be invested in education. This recommendation emphasized the importance of adequate funding to improve the quality and accessibility of education across India.

Question

India's first National Policy on Education was a sequel to the recommendations of which of the following committees/commissions?

1. Kothari Commission
2. Mudaliar Commission
3. Ramamurti Review Committee
4. Radhakrishnan Commission

Explanations:
Answer: 1. Kothari Commission

India's first National Policy on Education (NPE) was formulated in 1968. This policy was a direct sequel to the recommendations of the Kothari Commission (1964-66), which had extensively reviewed the Indian education system and provided comprehensive suggestions for its improvement and development.

Question

Which of the following committees/commissions in their report recommended that science Education and Research should receive high priority to accelerate the national economy?

1. Acharya Narendra Dev Committee
2. Mudaliar Commission
3. Radhakrishnan commission
4. Kothari Commission

Explanations:
Answer: 4. Kothari Commission

The Kothari Commission (1964-66) placed a significant emphasis on the development of science education and research. It recommended that science education and research should be given high priority to accelerate the national economy and ensure technological and industrial advancement. The commission believed that improving science education was crucial for national development and progress.

Question

Which of the following commission/committee in post-independent India has paid attention to all the levels of education?

1. Radhakrishnan Commission
2. Kothari Commission
3. Mudaliar Commission
4. Acharya Ramamurti Committee

Explanations:
Answer: 2. Kothari Commission

The Kothari Commission (1964-66) is the one that paid attention to all levels of education in post-independent India. It provided comprehensive recommendations covering all aspects of the education system, including primary, secondary, and higher education. The commission aimed to integrate and improve the entire education system, addressing issues and providing solutions for all levels.

Question

The report of which of the following Education Commissions carries the sub-title Education for National Development?

1. Radhakrishnan Commission
2. Mudaliar Commission
3. Calcutta University Education Commission
4. Kothari Commission

Explanations:
Answer: 4. Kothari Commission

The Kothari Commission (1964-66) report carries the subtitle "Education for National Development." This commission emphasized the role of education in national development and provided comprehensive recommendations to transform the education system in India to meet the socio-economic needs of the country.

Question

In which year the Education Commission under the Chairmanship of Dr. D.S. Kothari was set up?

1. 1952
2. 1955
3. 1960
4. 1964

Explanations:
Answer: 4. 1964

The Education Commission, also known as the Kothari Commission, was set up in 1964 under the Chairmanship of Dr. D.S. Kothari to examine all aspects of the educational sector in India and to advise the government on the development and restructuring of education.

Question

On the recommendations of which commission, 10+2+3 structure was incorporated in the statement of National Policy on Education, 1968?

1. Kothari Commission
2. Mudaliar Commission
3. Ramamurti Commission
4. Mandal Commission

Explanations:
Answer: 1. Kothari Commission

The 10+2+3 structure, which denotes 10 years of general education, followed by 2 years of higher secondary education, and then 3 years of university education, was incorporated in the National Policy on Education, 1968, based on the recommendations of the Kothari Commission. The Kothari Commission was instrumental in suggesting this structure to streamline and improve the education system in India.

Sarva Shiksha Abhiyan (SSA)

- **Launched in 2001** under **Atal Bihari Vajpayee.**
- Aims for **universal elementary education** in India.
- Supports children aged **6-14 years.**
- Linked to the **Right to Education Act.**
- **86th Amendment** made education a **fundamental right.**
- Ensures **free and compulsory education.**
- Focuses on **reducing dropout rates.**
- Targets **gender and social inclusion gaps.**
- Provides **infrastructure, classrooms, and teachers.**
- Special programs for **disadvantaged children.**
- **Mid-Day Meal Scheme** integrated for nutrition.
- Encourages **community participation in schools.**
- Covers **teacher training and development.**
- Promotes **use of technology in education.**
- Focuses on **quality and learning outcomes.**
- Bridges **rural-urban education gaps.**
- Promotes **inclusive education** for all.
- **State and Central Government** share funding.
- Targets **100% enrollment and retention.**
- Extended beyond **2010 due to slow progress.**

Mid-Day Meal Scheme (PM-POSHAN)

- **Started in Puducherry in 1930.**
- Implemented by **Tamil Nadu in the 1960s.**
- Expanded **nationwide after 2001.**
- Provides **free meals in schools.**
- Covers **primary and upper primary schools.**
- Renamed **PM-POSHAN in 2021.**
- Aims to **improve child nutrition levels.**
- Encourages **school attendance and enrollment.**
- Supports students in **Anganwadis, Madrasas.**
- **World's largest school meal program.**
- Over **120 million children benefit.**
- Funded by **Central and State Governments.**
- **Supreme Court mandated expansion in 2002.**
- Monitored by **Ministry of Education.**
- Reduces **dropout rates in rural areas.**
- Includes **fortified food for better health.**
- Covers **pre-primary students since 2022.**
- Ensures **food safety and hygiene standards.**
- Encourages **community involvement in schools.**
- Improves **learning outcomes through better health.**

School Education Quality Index (SEQI)

- **Launched by NITI Aayog in 2019.**
- Measures **education quality in schools.**
- Covers all **States and Union Territories.**
- **Kerala ranked highest** in education quality.
- **Uttar Pradesh ranked lowest** in education quality.
- Assesses **30 key education indicators.**
- Focuses on **learning outcomes.**
- Tracks **enrollment, retention, and equity.**
- Evaluates **infrastructure and teacher training.**
- Aims to **improve state education policies.**
- Encourages **competition among states.**
- Promotes **data-driven education reforms.**
- **Collaborates with the World Bank.**

- Uses **feedback for policy improvements**.
- Supports **cooperative federalism in education**.
- Focuses on **reducing learning disparities**.
- Benchmarks **best practices in education**.
- Encourages **state accountability in education**.
- Helps states **identify weaknesses and strengths**.
- Aligns with **National Education Policy (NEP) 2020**.

Global Teacher Award – Overview & Significance

The Global Teacher Prize Award, run by the Varkey Foundation in partnership with UNESCO, celebrates exceptional teachers to raise the profession's profile worldwide. Initiated in 2013 by Sunny Varkey, Chairman of the Varkey Foundation, the award aims to highlight the importance of teachers and their impact on education.

History and Growth:

- **Inaugural Year (2013):** Over 5,000 entries from 127 countries.
- **2020:** Saw 12,000 nominations and applications from over 140 countries.

Significant Milestones:

- **2020 Virtual Ceremony:** Broadcast from the Natural History Museum in London, with Stephen Fry announcing the winner.
- **Special Recognition:** COVID hero award presented to UK Maths teacher Jamie Frost, who received US$ 45,000 for his extraordinary efforts during the pandemic.

Objectives and Impact:

- **Recognition:** Enhances respect, reward, and celebration of teachers globally by spotlighting outstanding teachers and sharing their stories.
- **Inspiration:** Aims to inspire top candidates to join the teaching profession.

- **National Influence:** The prize has led to the creation of over 40 National Teacher Prizes, recognizing and celebrating teachers at the country level.

AYUSH Undergraduate Education

- AYUSH refers to **Ayurveda, Yoga, Unani, Siddha, and Homeopathy**.
- Regulated by the **National Commission for Indian System of Medicine** (NCISM).
- Bachelor's degrees include **BAMS, BHMS, BUMS, BSMS, and BNYS**.
- Admission through **NEET-UG** for AYUSH courses.
- Course duration is typically **5.5 years** (including internship).
- Emphasizes traditional medicine with modern scientific integration.
- Includes clinical training in **AYUSH hospitals**.
- Promotes **holistic health** and wellness practices.
- Government initiatives like the **National AYUSH Mission (NAM)** support it.
- Growing international recognition and research opportunities.

Question

Which of the following are the parts of AYUSH undergraduate education?

A. Siddha
B. Sowa - Rigpa
C. Yoga-Shastra
D. Homoeopathy
E. Sanjeevani

1. (A), (B) and (E) Only
2. (B), (C) and (D) Only
3. (A), (B) and (D) Only
4. (A), (C) and (E) Only

Explanations:
Answer: 3. (A), (B) and (D) Only

The **AYUSH** system of medicine includes the following disciplines, which are part of undergraduate education:

(A) Siddha: A traditional system of medicine originating in Tamil Nadu.
(B) Sowa-Rigpa: A traditional Tibetan system of medicine.
(D) Homoeopathy: A system of alternative medicine based on the principle of "like cures like."

Yoga-Shastra (C) and **Sanjeevani (E)** are not recognized as separate disciplines under AYUSH undergraduate education.

The Government of India introduced the National Skills Qualifications Framework (NSQF)

The Government of India introduced the National Skills Qualifications Framework (NSQF) in 2013. The NSQF organizes qualifications through various levels of data, knowledge, aptitude, and skills.

Key Features and Benefits of NSQF:

International Equivalency: Establishes national policies to identify skill proficiency and competencies at different levels, aligning them with international standards.

Flexible Pathways: Allows multiple entry and exit points between skill training, vocational education, job markets, and general and technical education, facilitating seamless transitions for learners.

Progressive Pathways: Provides a structured framework for skill qualifications, enabling learners to progress through different levels of competence.

Lifelong Learning: Encourages lifelong training, education, and skill development, ensuring that learners can continually upgrade their skills.

Industry Tie-ups: Collaborates with industries and markets to understand job market requirements, ensuring that the skills acquired are relevant and in demand.

Credible Mechanism: Creates a transparent, accountable, and credible mechanism for skill development across multiple sectors.

Recognition of Prior Learning: Offers better potential for recognizing and validating early learning, helping individuals build on their existing skills and knowledge.

The National Education Mission, also known as Samagra Shiksha Abhiyan

The National Education Mission, also known as Samagra Shiksha Abhiyan, is a comprehensive program launched in 2018 to address the school education sector from pre-school to class 12. It was allocated a budget of ₹385.72 billion (US$4.6 billion) in the 2019 Interim Union Budget of India. This mission includes four key schemes:

1. **Saakshar Bharat:** Aimed at providing literacy to non-literate individuals aged 15 and above, with a particular focus on women's literacy. It was launched by Prime Minister Manmohan Singh on 8 September 2009 as a centrally sponsored scheme. Saakshar Bharat is part of the Department of School Education, Ministry of Education, Government of India, and operates under the National Literacy Mission. It covers a vast number of districts with various literacy programs and has set up 'Model Adult Education Centres' in selected villages.

2. **Sarva Shiksha Abhiyan:** Focuses on the universalization of elementary education across India.

3. **Rashtriya Madhyamik Shiksha Abhiyan:** Aimed at improving secondary education.

4. **Centrally Sponsored Scheme on Teacher Education (CSSTE):** Focuses on enhancing the quality of teacher education.

In 2021, the NIPUN Bharat Mission was launched as part of Samagra Shiksha Abhiyan to ensure foundational literacy and numeracy skills by Grade 3. The 2023–24 Union Budget allocated ₹37,453.47 for the Samagra Shiksha Abhiyan.

The National Literacy Mission (NLM) was initiated in 1988 with the goal of educating 80 million adults aged 15–35 over an eighty-year period. It operates as an autonomous wing of the Ministry of HRD (now Ministry of Education) and has undertaken extensive literacy campaigns and programs across India to achieve its goals.

Question

Statement I: India spends one of the lowest amounts per student for higher education in the world.
Statement II: The percentage expenditure on university and higher education in India was 0.77 percent in 1990 - 91 and it declined to 0.66 percent in 2004 - 2005.

1. Both Statement I and Statement Il are correct
2. Both Statement I and Statement Il are incorrect
3. Statement I is correct but Statement Il is incorrect
4. Statement i is incorrect but Statement Il is correct

Explanations:
Answer: 1. Both Statement I and Statement Il are correct

Both statements highlight issues related to the financial allocation and spending on higher education in India. Statement I points out that India has one of the lowest per-student spending rates for higher education globally, indicating underinvestment in the sector. Statement II provides specific data showing a decline in the percentage of expenditure on university and higher education, from 0.77 percent in 1990-91 to 0.66 percent in 2004-2005, reflecting reduced financial commitment over time.

The STARS Project Overview

The STARS Project, which stands for Strengthening Teaching-Learning and Results for States, is a significant initiative aimed at enhancing the assessment system in schools and ensuring equal education opportunities for all students. Here are the key details related to the project:

- **Total Cost and Funding:** The project has a total cost of Rs. 5,718 crore, with partial financial support from the World Bank amounting to US$ 500 million.

- **Approval and Management:** The project was approved by the Union Government on June 24, 2020, and is managed by the Department of School Education and Literacy, Ministry of Education (MoE).
- **Alignment with NEP 2020:** The STARS Project shares similar objectives with the National Education Policy (NEP) 2020, focusing on improving educational outcomes.
- **Target States:** Six Indian states are covered under the STARS Project:
    - Himachal Pradesh
    - Rajasthan
    - Maharashtra
    - Madhya Pradesh
    - Kerala
    - Odisha
- **Implementation:** The project is implemented through the Samagra Shiksha Scheme.
- **Assessment Body:** PARAKH (Performance Assessment, Review, and Analysis of Knowledge for Holistic Development) has been established under the Department of School Education and Literacy, Ministry of Education (MoE) to oversee the education system.
- **Focus Areas:** As part of the Atmanirbhar Bharat Abhiyan, the project focuses on initiatives like PM e-Vidya, Foundational Literacy and Numeracy Mission, and the National Curricular and Pedagogical Framework for Early Childhood Care and Education.
- **Similar Project:** A parallel project, funded by the Asian Development Bank (ADB), aims to implement education reforms in five Indian states: Gujarat, Assam, Tamil Nadu, Jharkhand, and Uttarakhand.
- **PISA Participation:** The project will also fund India's participation in the Programme for International Student Assessment (PISA) survey.

India's Five-Year Plans and Higher Education

First Five-Year Plan (1951-1956)

- **Established University Grants Commission (UGC) in 1953.**
- Focused on **expanding higher education infrastructure**.
- Promoted **scientific and technical education**.
- Strengthened **teacher training programs**.
- Laid the **foundation for future policies**.

Second Five-Year Plan (1956-1961)

- Established **Indian Institutes of Technology (IITs)**.
- Introduced **three-year degree courses**.
- Improved **libraries and laboratory facilities**.
- Increased **salaries of university teachers**.
- Strengthened **technical and engineering education**.

Question

The second five-year plan for implementation included the recommendations of the following:

A. University Education Commission
B. Languages Commission of India
C. Rural Higher Education Committee
D. Committee on Establishment of New Universities Three-Year Degree Course Committee

Choose the correct answer from the Options below:

1. ABC
2. BCD
3. CDE
4. ABE

Explanations:
Answer: 4. ABE

The **Second Five-Year Plan (1956-61)** included the recommendations of the following committees/commissions:

- **A. University Education Commission (1948-49)**: Also known as the Radhakrishnan Commission, its recommendations were implemented to reform higher education.
- **B. Languages Commission of India**: Its recommendations were considered to address linguistic issues in education.
- **E. Three-Year Degree Course Committee**: Its recommendations were implemented to standardize the duration of undergraduate programs.

The **Rural Higher Education Committee (C)** and the **Committee on Establishment of New Universities (D)** were not directly associated with the implementation of the Second Five-Year Plan.

Question

Which of the following steps were taken by the university grants commission during the second five-year plan?

A. Introduction of three-year degree course.
B. Improvement in libraries and laboratories.
C. Increase in the salaries of university teachers.
D. No new departments were approved in the universities.
E. Hindi was made the optional medium of instruction besides local languages in all Indian universities.

1. (A), (B) and (C) Only
2. (B), (C) and (D) Only
3. (C), (D) and (E) Only
4. (A), (D) and (E) Only

Explanations:
Answer: 1. (A), (B) and (C) Only

During the **Second Five-Year Plan (1956-61)**, the **University Grants Commission (UGC)** took the following steps:

(A) Introduction of three-year degree course: This was implemented to standardize undergraduate education.

(B) Improvement in libraries and laboratories: Efforts were made to enhance infrastructure and resources for better academic and research facilities.

(C) Increase in the salaries of university teachers: This was done to improve the quality of teaching and attract talented individuals to the profession.

The steps **(D) No new departments were approved in the universities** and **(E) Hindi was made the optional medium of instruction besides local languages in all Indian universities** were not specific initiatives during the Second Five-Year Plan.

Third Five-Year Plan (1961-1966)

- Established **new universities and technical colleges**.
- Created **rural institutes in Wardha, Mysore**.
- Set up **examination research units**.
- Increased **funding for higher education**.
- Expanded **science and engineering programs**.

Question

An important feature of the third five-year plan was

1. Abolition of Education Commission.
2. Reduction in the number of colleges
3. Setting up examination research units in some universities
4. More emphasis on open book examination.

Explanations:
Answer: 3. Setting up examination research units in some universities

An important feature of the **Third Five-Year Plan (1961-66)** in India was the **setting up of examination research units in some universities**. These units were established to improve the examination system, conduct research on assessment methods, and ensure fairness and efficiency in evaluating students. This initiative was part of broader efforts to enhance the quality of education and address issues related to examination reforms.

Question

Which of the following were the initiatives taken during the third five-year plan?

A. Removal of the diploma course system.
B. Provision for correspondence courses.
C. Establishment of additional colleges including regional engineering colleges.
D. Appointment of a working group on technical education.
E. Less emphasis on trained manpower.

1. ABC
2. BCD
3. CDE
4. ADE

Explanations:
Answer: 2. BCD

- **Provision for correspondence courses** – Introduced for expanding access to higher education.
- **Establishment of additional colleges** – More colleges, including **Regional Engineering Colleges (RECs)**, were founded.
- **Appointment of a working group on technical education** – Aimed to improve technical education.

Incorrect Options

- **Removal of diploma course system** – Not a major initiative in this plan.
- **Less emphasis on trained manpower** – The plan **focused on manpower development**.

Question

Which of the following research institutes were established between the first and third five year plans?

A. Indian Institute of Science
B. Saha Institute of Nuclear physics
C. Lok Bharati
D. Gandhi Gram Rural Institute
E. Raman Research Institute

1. ABC
2. ADE
3. BCE
4. BCD

Explanations:
Answer: 4. BCD
The research institutes established between the **First (1951-56)** and **Third (1961-66) Five-Year Plans** include:

- **B. Saha Institute of Nuclear Physics**: Established in 1949, it falls within the timeline of the First Five-Year Plan.
- **C. Lok Bharati**: Established in 1955, it aligns with the First Five-Year Plan.
- **D. Gandhi Gram Rural Institute**: Established in 1956, it falls within the timeline of the First Five-Year Plan.

The **Indian Institute of Science (A)** was established in 1909, and the **Raman Research Institute (E)** was established in 1948, both predating the First Five-Year Plan.

Fourth Five-Year Plan (1969-1974)

- Focused on **education for marginalized communities**.
- Introduced **new policies for accessibility**.
- Expanded **technical education opportunities**.
- Strengthened **teacher training and recruitment**.
- Promoted **regional and rural higher education**.

Fifth Five-Year Plan (1974-1978)

- Developed **rural higher education institutions**.

- Established **autonomous colleges for flexibility**.
- Encouraged **community-based education models**.
- Strengthened **vocational and skill-based learning**.
- Focused on **higher education decentralization**.

Question

Match the column:

A. First five year plan	I. Autonomous colleges
B. Second five year plan	II. University grants commission
C. Third five year plan	III. specialized departments of scientific study
D. Fifth five year plan	IV. two rural institutes in Wardha and mysore

1. A-I B-II C-III D-IV
2. A-II B-III C-IV D-I
3. A-III B-IV C-I D-II
4. A-IV B-I C-II D-III

Explanations:
Answer: 2. A-II B-III C-IV D-I

A. First Five-Year Plan (1951-1956) → University Grants Commission (UGC) (II)
B. Second Five-Year Plan (1956-1961) → Specialized departments of scientific study (III)
C. Third Five-Year Plan (1961-1966) → Two rural institutes in Wardha and Mysore (IV)
D. Fifth Five-Year Plan (1974-1978) → Autonomous colleges (I)

Sixth Five-Year Plan (1980-1985)

- Strengthened **technical and vocational education**.
- Aligned education **with industrial sector needs**.
- Expanded **engineering and medical institutions**.
- Focused on **entrepreneurial and skill development**.
- Encouraged **collaboration with industries**.

Seventh Five-Year Plan (1985-1990)

- Focused on **quality enhancement in education**.
- Encouraged **research and innovation**.
- Expanded **higher education funding**.
- Strengthened **science and technology studies**.
- Improved **university governance and accountability**.

Eighth Five-Year Plan (1992-1997)

- Expanded **distance education programs**.
- Encouraged **privatization in higher education**.
- Improved **IT and management education**.
- Introduced **digital learning initiatives**.
- Focused on **higher education accessibility**.

Question

The policy of privatisation of higher education began with the introduction of :

1. Fourth five year plan
2. Sixth five year plan
3. Eighth five year plan
4. Tenth five year plan

Explanations:
Answer: 3. Eighth five year plan

The policy of **privatisation of higher education** in India gained significant momentum with the introduction of the **Eighth Five-Year Plan (1992-97)**. This plan emphasized economic liberalization, privatization, and globalization (LPG model), which extended to the education sector as well. It encouraged private participation in higher education to meet the growing demand and reduce the financial burden on the government.

Question

The policy on higher education during the eighth five-year plan was to encourage-

1. Expansion of public sector
2. Involvement of private sector
3. Establishment of foreign campuses
4. Entry of foreign Universities

Explanations:
Answer: 2. Involvement of private sector

The policy on higher education during the **Eighth Five-Year Plan (1992-97)** was to encourage the **involvement of the private sector**. This was part of the broader economic reforms and liberalization policies introduced during this period. The plan aimed to reduce the financial burden on the government and expand access to higher education by promoting private investment and participation in the education sector.

Ninth Five-Year Plan (1997-2002)

- Promoted **autonomy in higher education institutions**.
- Established **Indian Institute of Management (IIMs)**.
- Encouraged **global collaborations in education**.
- Strengthened **accountability in universities**.
- Focused on **research and technology programs**.

Question

The Indian Institute of management, Indore, was set up during:

1. Eighth five year plan
2. Ninth five year plan
3. Tenth five year plan
4. Eleventh five year plan

Explanations:
Answer: 2. Ninth five year plan

The Indian **Institute of Management, Indore (IIM Indore)** was established in **1996**, during the **Ninth Five-Year Plan (1997-2002)**.

- The **Ninth Five-Year Plan** focused on **higher education reforms, autonomy, and expansion of premier institutions**.
- As part of this initiative, **IIM Indore was set up to strengthen management education** in India.
- The plan also emphasized **accountability in higher education and the establishment of more specialized institutes**.

Tenth Five-Year Plan (2002-2007)

- Increased **higher education enrollment rates**.
- Established **14 world-class universities**.
- Strengthened **science-based higher education**.
- Provided **financial assistance to universities**.
- Encouraged **R&D in Indian universities**.
- Providing financial assistance to universities and colleges of unincorporated states.

Question

In the *Tenth Five Year Plan,* the central government's focus in the field of higher education was:

A. Establishment of 14 world class universities
B. Diversion of funds to private universities for better performance
C. Strengthening science-based higher education and research in universities.
D. Restructuring of various councils
E. To provide financial assistance to universities and colleges of unincorporated states.

1. ABC
2. ACE
3. BCD
4. DE

Explanations:
Answer: 2. ACE

The **Tenth Five-Year Plan (2002-2007)** focused on **expanding and improving higher education in India**. Among its key initiatives:

Establishment of 14 world-class universities (**A**) – The plan aimed to set up top-tier universities to **enhance research and innovation** in India.

Strengthening science-based higher education and research in universities (**C**) – It emphasized **scientific research, technology development, and innovation** in higher education.

Providing financial assistance to universities and colleges of unincorporated states (**E**) – The plan focused on **funding institutions in underdeveloped regions** to **ensure educational equity**.

Why not the other options?

B (Diversion of funds to private universities) – The plan did not prioritize funding private institutions but focused on **public universities and research development**.

D (Restructuring of various councils) – Though reforms were discussed, **major restructuring was not a central focus** of this plan.

Question

The 10th Five Year Plan acknowledged the importance of?

1. Population studies
2. Extension education
3. Information technology
4. Social work

Explanations:
Answer: 3. Information technology

The **10th Five-Year Plan (2002-2007)** emphasized the **role of Information Technology (IT)** in education and development. Focused on **digital education, e-learning, and IT infrastructure** in higher education. Promoted **research and development in science and technology**.

Population studies, Extension education, and Social work *were not primary focuses.*

Eleventh Five-Year Plan (2007-2012)

- Expanded **higher education infrastructure**.
- Established **new universities and colleges**.
- Increased **funding for research programs**.
- Focused on **inclusive education policies**.
- Encouraged **public-private partnerships in education**.

Twelfth Five-Year Plan (2012-2017)

- Encouraged **innovation in higher education**.
- Strengthened **industry-academia collaboration**.
- Promoted **skill development programs**.
- Introduced **new regulatory frameworks**.
- Emphasized **global competitiveness in education**.

National Knowledge Commission (NKC)

The National Knowledge Commission (NKC) was an advisory body established by the Government of India in 2005 with the aim of transforming India into a knowledge-based society. It was chaired by Sam Pitroda.

Key Objectives of the NKC:

- Enhancing Access to Knowledge
- Improving the Quality of Education
- Expanding Research and Innovation
- Knowledge Networks and Libraries
- Creating a Knowledge Workforce

Question

What were the National Knowledge Commission's recommendations for the minimum gross enrollment ratio to be achieved in higher education by 2015?

1. 5 percent
2. 10 percent
3. 15 percent

4. 20 percent

Explanations:
Answer: 3. 15 percent

The **National Knowledge Commission (NKC)**, established in 2005, recommended that the **minimum Gross Enrollment Ratio (GER)** in higher education should be **15 percent by 2015**. This recommendation was part of its broader vision to expand access to higher education and improve the quality and relevance of education in India.

Question

The National Knowledge Commission suggested that the proposed national universities should not have

1. Affiliated colleges
2. Public funding
3. Linkage with industries
4. Teaching departments

Explanations:
Answer: 1. Affiliated colleges

The **National Knowledge Commission (NKC)**, established in **2005**, aimed to reform the **higher education system in India**. One of its major recommendations was the establishment of **national universities** with a **focus on quality and research**.

NKC proposed that national universities should NOT have affiliated colleges (**Option 1**) because:

- **Affiliation weakens academic autonomy** and slows down decision-making.
- The **existing affiliating system was seen as outdated** and **not conducive to academic excellence**.
- NKC recommended **more autonomous universities** with **direct control over academics, curriculum, and faculty**.

Why not the other options?

- **Public funding (Option 2)** – NKC supported a **mixed funding model** (government and private sources).
- **Linkage with industries (Option 3)** – NKC encouraged **stronger industry-academia collaboration** for research and innovation.
- **Teaching departments (Option 4)** – National universities were **expected to have specialized teaching departments**.

Question

The National Knowledge Commission recommended needs-blind admissions' for

1. National universities
2. State universities
3. Private universities
4. Foreign universities operating in India

Explanations:
Answer: 1. National universities

The **National Knowledge Commission (NKC)** recommended **"needs-blind admissions"** for **national universities**. This means that admissions to these universities should be based solely on merit, without considering the financial background of the students. The aim was to ensure equal opportunities for all students, regardless of their economic status, and to promote inclusivity in higher education.

Question

Which of the following are the administrative reforms in universities suggested by the National Knowledge Commission?

A. Appointment of vice-chancellors based on their academic and administrative credentials
B. De-politicisation of appointments
C. Centralised control of universities
D. Restrictions on academic freedom
E. Creation of a good research environment

1. ABC
2. BCD

3. CDE
4. ABE

Explanations:
Answer: 4. ABE

The **National Knowledge Commission (2005)** suggested:

- **A) Appointment of vice-chancellors** based on **academic and administrative credentials**.
- **B) De-politicization of appointments** to ensure **merit-based selection**.
- **E) Creation of a good research environment** to enhance **innovation and academic excellence**.

Options C (Centralized control) and **D (Restrictions on academic freedom)** were **not recommended**, as NKC advocated for **university autonomy**.

Question

Which of the following commissions suggested the establishment of National Universities in India?

1. Kothari commission
2. Radhakrishnan commission
3. Knowledge commission
4. Planning commission

Explanations:
Answer: 3. Knowledge commission

The **Kothari Commission (1964-66)**, also known as the **Education Commission**, suggested the establishment of **National Universities** in India. These universities were envisioned as institutions of excellence that would set high academic standards and serve as models for other universities in the country.

Question

Statement I: The Indian universities to reach global standards need sustained support for programmes in research and development.
Statement II: The "knowledge economy', as envisaged by the Knowledge Commission, does not need government involvement in higher education.

1. Both Statement I and Statement Il are true.
2. Both Statement I and Statement Il are false.
3. Statement I is true but Statement Il is false.
4. Statement I is false but Statement Il is true.

Explanations:
Answer: 3. Statement I is true but Statement Il is false

Statement I (True): Indian universities **require sustained support** for **research and development** to reach **global standards**. The **National Knowledge Commission (NKC)** emphasized **investment in R&D** to boost **higher education quality**.

Statement II (False): The **"knowledge economy"** envisioned by NKC **requires government involvement** in higher education for **policy support, funding, and regulation**. NKC advocated for a **balanced public-private partnership**, not complete withdrawal of government support.

Question

The national knowledge commission was established in the year-

(1) 1998
(2) 2000
(3) 2005
(4) 2007

Explanations:
Answer: (3) 2005

Question

Identify the correct set of key mandate areas of the National Knowledge Commission

A. Access
B. Concepts
C. Delivery
D. Applications
E. Services

1. A, B, C and D only
2. B, C, Dand E only
3. A, B, D and E only
4. A, C, D and E only

Explanations:
Answer: 3. A, B, D and E only

The **National Knowledge Commission (NKC)** focused on key mandate areas to **enhance India's knowledge economy**:

- **A) Access** – Ensuring **wider reach** of knowledge and education.
- **B) Concepts** – Developing **new frameworks for knowledge creation**.
- **D) Applications** – Encouraging **practical implementation** of knowledge.
- **E) Services** – Improving **knowledge-based services** in various sectors.

Question

Which of the following are the main recommendations of the Knowledge Commission' with regard to higher education in India?

a. More regulatory institutions
b. Closure of private universities
c. Massive expansion of higher education.
d. Focus on affirmative action
e. Efforts to achieve excellence
f. Nationalisation of higher education

1. abc
2. bdf
3. cde

4. def

Explanations:
Answer: 3. cde

The **National Knowledge Commission (2005)** recommended:

- **C) Massive expansion of higher education** – Suggested **more universities** to increase **enrollment and accessibility**.
- **D) Focus on affirmative action** – Ensured **inclusion of marginalized communities** in higher education.
- **E) Efforts to achieve excellence** – Emphasized **quality improvement, research, and faculty development**.

Options A (More regulatory institutions), B (Closure of private universities), and F (Nationalization of higher education) were **not recommended** by NKC. Instead, it **advocated autonomy and public-private collaboration**.

Major Educational Committees and Policies in India (1953-1993)

Committee on Differentiation of Curricula for Boys and Girls (1953)

- **Formed in 1953** to design gender-based curricula.
- **Recommended practical skills** for girls' education.
- **Encouraged home science** and handicrafts training.
- **Boys focused on science, commerce, industry.**
- **Criticized for reinforcing gender stereotypes.**

National Commission on Teachers (1983-85)

- Chaired by **D. P. Chattopadhyay**.
- Focused on **teachers' professional development**.
- Recommended **better salary and service** conditions.
- Emphasized pre-service, in-service training.
- Stressed teacher accountability, ethics.

National Policy on Education (1986)

- Aimed at universalizing **elementary** education.
- Introduced **Operation Blackboard** for primary schools.
- Emphasized teacher **education and training**.
- Promoted open, **distance learning** systems.
- Encouraged research, technological education.

Acharya Ramamurti Committee (1990)

- Reviewed **National Policy on Education (1986).**
- Recommended **people-centric** education reforms.
- Suggested **vocational training** at all levels.
- Emphasized **value-based**, inclusive education.
- Focused on **decentralization** in governance.

Yashpal Committee - Learning Without Burden (1993)

- **Chaired by Yashpal in 1993.**
- Aimed at reducing **students' academic burden**.
- Suggested reducing **rote memorization.**
- Promoted joyful, **concept-based learning**.
- Encouraged **interdisciplinary, holistic** education.

Question

A. National Commission on Teachers
B. Acharya Ramamurti Committee
C. Yashpal Committee - Learning without Burden
D. Committee on Differentiation of Curricula for Boys and Girls
E. National Policy on Education

1. BCDAE
2. EBCDA
3. CDAEB
4. DAEBC

Explanations
Answer: 4. DAEBC

- Committee on Differentiation of Curricula for Boys and Girls (1953)
- National Commission on Teachers (1983-85)
- National Policy on Education (1986)
- Acharya Ramamurti Committee (1990)
- Yashpal Committee - Learning Without Burden (1993)

Question

Which of the following is not an institution of higher education?

1. Fergusson College
2. National Institute of Technology
3. Rashtriya Indian Military College
4. Indian School of Mines

Explanations
Answer: 3. Rashtriya Indian Military College

Rashtriya Indian Military College (RIMC) is **not** an institution of higher education. It is a **military school** that prepares young cadets for entry into the **National Defence Academy (NDA)** and other armed forces training institutions.

On the other hand:

- **Fergusson College** offers undergraduate and postgraduate education.
- **National Institute of Technology (NIT)** is a premier engineering institution.
- **Indian School of Mines (ISM), now IIT Dhanbad**, is a higher education institution specializing in engineering and applied sciences.

NEP 2020

The National Education Policy (NEP) 2020 is a significant reform in the Indian education system, marking the first major policy change in the 21st century. It is built on five foundational pillars: Access, Equity, Quality,

Affordability, and Accountability. The policy aims to align with the 2030 Agenda for Sustainable Development.

Foundational Pillars:

1. **Access:** Ensuring that all children have access to education from early childhood through higher education.
2. **Equity:** Addressing disparities in education access and outcomes, ensuring inclusive and equitable quality education for all.
3. **Quality:** Focusing on improving the quality of education at all levels.
4. **Affordability:** Making education affordable for all sections of society.
5. **Accountability:** Establishing mechanisms to ensure accountability in the education system.

NEP on Vocational Education

Integration with Higher Education:

- A National Higher Education Qualification Framework (NHEQF) will be developed in sync with the National Skill Qualification Framework (NSQF). This aims to facilitate the seamless integration of vocational education into the higher education system.

National Committee for the Integration of Vocational Education (NCIVE):

- The Ministry of Human Resource Development (MHRD) will establish the NCIVE, which will consist of experts in vocational education and representatives from various ministries.
- The committee will collaborate with industry stakeholders to oversee the integration of vocational education within the broader education system.

Objectives:

- To make vocational education an integral part of the curriculum from school to higher education.

- To ensure that students gain practical skills that enhance their employability.
- To bridge the gap between academic learning and practical job-oriented training.

The NEP 2020 aims to revolutionize the Indian education landscape by making it more inclusive, holistic, and geared towards the needs of the 21st century. The integration of vocational education with higher education will provide students with multiple pathways to success, fostering a skilled and competent workforce ready to meet the challenges of the modern world.

Key Focus Areas of NEP 2020 in Higher Education

Expansion & Gross Enrollment Ratio (GER)

- **Target GER of 50% by 2035.**
- **Multidisciplinary universities by 2040.**
- **Integration of vocational education in HEIs.**

Research & Innovation

- **National Research Foundation (NRF) to boost R&D.**
- **MERUs – top-tier multidisciplinary universities.**
- **Encourages disruptive technology adoption in HEIs.**

Internationalization & Global Recognition

- **India to be a global study destination.**
- **Promotes Vishwa Guru vision in education.**
- **Ensures high-quality education in Indian languages.**

Question

The National Education Policy 2020 recommended moving towards.

1. Suburban Universities
2. Single discipline Universities
3. Multi-disciplinary Universities
4. Specialised Universities

Explanations
Answer: 3. Multi-disciplinary Universities

The **National Education Policy (NEP) 2020** recommended moving towards **multi-disciplinary universities**. This approach aims to provide students with a broader and more flexible education by integrating multiple disciplines, fostering innovation, critical thinking, and holistic learning. The policy emphasizes the importance of breaking down rigid boundaries between disciplines to create well-rounded individuals.

Value-Based & Inclusive Education in NEP 2020

Value-Based Education & Ethical Learning

- **Focuses on universal values & scientific temper.**
- **Includes life skills and constitutional values.**

Global Citizenship Education (GCED)

- Promotes tolerance, peace, and inclusivity.
- Encourages sustainability and global responsibility.

Accessibility & Affirmative Action

- **Ensures education for marginalized communities.**
- **Free quality education for disadvantaged groups.**

Question

Statement I: According to NEP 2020, value-based education shall include universal values and scientific temper.
Statement II: Value-based education did not include life skills and constitutional values as per the NEP document.

1. Both Statement I and Statement II are true.
2. Both Statement | and Statement Il are false
3. Statement I is true but Statement I is false
4. Statement I is false but Statement Il is true

Explanations:
Answer: 3. Statement I is true but Statement I is false

Statement I is accurate as NEP 2020 emphasizes value-based education that includes universal values and scientific temper. However, Statement II is incorrect because the NEP 2020 also stresses life skills and constitutional values as part of value-based education.

Question

According to National Education Policy 2020, which of the following universal human values will be considered as an integral part of holistic education?

A. Truth
B. Sympathy
C. Righteous conduct
D. Nonviolence
E. Scientific temper

1. CE
2. BDE
3. ACDE
4. ABCD

Explanations
Answer: 3. ACDE
According to the **National Education Policy (NEP) 2020**, the universal human values considered integral to **holistic education** include:

- **A. Truth**
- **C. Righteous conduct**
- **D. Nonviolence**
- **E. Scientific temper**

These values are emphasized to promote ethical, moral, and rational thinking among students, aligning with the goal of holistic development.

Question

Which of the following fundamental principles of education are highlighted under New National Education Policy?

(A). Higher education as a fundamental right
(B). Multidisciplinarity and holistic education.
(C). Outstanding research as part of higher education
(D). Promotion of multilingualism in teaching and learning.
(E). Setting up of another knowledge commission

1. (A), (B) and (C) only.
2. (B), (C) and (D) only.
3. (C), (D) and (E) only.
4. (A), (D) and (E) only.

Explanations:
Answer: 2. (B), (C) and (D) only.

The New National Education Policy (NEP) highlights the following principles:

- Multidisciplinarity and holistic education.
- Outstanding research as part of higher education.
- Promotion of multilingualism in teaching and learning.

However, it does not state higher education as a fundamental right or propose the setting up of another knowledge commission.

Question

The New Education Policy of 2020, suggested degree courses in:

A. Development Communication
B. Logic
C. Art and Museum Administration
D. Graphic Design
E. Web Design

1. ABC
2. BCD

3. CDE
4. BDE

Explanations:
Answer: 3. CDE

The **New Education Policy (NEP) 2020** emphasized **multidisciplinary education** and introduced **diverse degree programs**, including:

- **C) Art and Museum Administration** – Focused on **heritage management and curation**.
- **D) Graphic Design** – Encouraged **creative and digital arts education**.
- **E) Web Design** – Integrated **technology with visual communication**.

Options A (Development Communication) and B (Logic) were **not explicitly highlighted** in NEP 2020's-degree course recommendations.

NEP 2020 on Higher Education

The National Education Policy (NEP) 2020 outlines several ambitious goals and structural changes to transform higher education in India.

Goals and Objectives:

1. **Increasing Gross Enrolment Ratio:** The NEP aims to increase the Gross Enrolment Ratio (GER) in higher education, including vocational education, from 26.3% (2018) to 50% by 2035.
2. **Multidisciplinary Institutions:** By 2040, all higher education institutions (HEIs) will aim to become multidisciplinary institutions, offering a wide range of courses and disciplines.

Higher Education Commission of India (HECI)

Higher Education Commission of India (HECI): HECI will be established as a single overarching umbrella body for the entire higher education system, excluding medical and legal education. It will have four verticals:

- **National Higher Education Regulatory Council (NHERC):** This will be the regulatory body for higher education.
- **National Accreditation Council (NAC):** A meta-accrediting body responsible for overseeing the accreditation of institutions.
- **Higher Education Grants Council (HEGC):** This body will handle funding and financing of higher education based on transparent criteria.
- **General Education Council (GEC):** It will frame the expected learning outcomes for higher education programs, also referred to as 'graduate attributes.'

Role of Each Vertical

- **NHERC regulates higher education institutions (HEIs).**
- **NAC is responsible for accreditation of HEIs.**
- **HEGC manages funding and financial support.**
- **GEC sets academic standards and frameworks.**

University Autonomy & Self-Governance

- **All HEIs aim for self-governance in 15 years.**
- **Graded accreditation ensures institutional autonomy.**

Question

According to NEP 2020, the first vertical of Higher Education Commission of India (HECI) will be the

1. National Accreditation Council (NAC)
2. National Education Regulatory Council (NHERC)
3. General Education Council (GEC)
4. Higher Education Grants Council (HEGC)

Explanations:
Answer: 2. National Education Regulatory Council (NHERC)

According to NEP 2020, the Higher Education Commission of India (HECI) will be established as an overarching regulatory body for higher education in India. The first vertical of HECI will be the National Higher Education

Regulatory Council (NHERC), which will be responsible for the regulation of higher education institutions.

Question

The National Education Policy. 2020, recommended certain verticals Under Higher Education Commission of India. They are

A. NHERC (National Higher Education Regulatory Council)
B. NAC (National Accreditation Council
C. HEGC (Higher Education Grants Council)
D. GEC (General Education Council)
E. OLC (Open Learning Council)

1. ADE
2. ABCD
3. BCDE
4. ABCE

Explanations:
Answer: 2. ABCD

- NHERC (National Higher Education Regulatory Council)
- NAC (National Accreditation Council
- HEGC (Higher Education Grants Council)
- GEC (General Education Council)

Question

The Government of India has in the year 2024 allocated six percent of GDP to education.

A. The Education cess goes to the central government.
B. The Government of Karnataka and Tamil Nadu have established respective state Education Policy Commissions.
C. Education is a subject matter of central list
D. The SDG-4 (Sustainable Development Goal-4) pertains to Education.

1. BCE
2. ADE

3. BCD
4. AD

Explanations:
Answer: 1. BCE

The Education cess goes to the Central Government – Correct: Education cess is collected as an additional tax by the **Central Government** to fund education-related initiatives.

The Government of Karnataka and Tamil Nadu have established respective State Education Policy Commissions – Correct: Both Karnataka and Tamil Nadu have **formulated their own education policies**, separate from the National Education Policy (NEP) 2020.

Education is a subject matter of the Central List – Incorrect: Education is in the Concurrent List, meaning both **Central and State Governments** can legislate on it.

The SDG-4 (Sustainable Development Goal-4) pertains to Education – Correct: SDG-4 aims to **ensure inclusive and equitable quality education** and promote **lifelong learning opportunities for all**.

Question

Statement (I): According to NEP 2020, one of the verticals of Higher Education Commission of India (HECI), General Education Council (GEC) will be responsible for accreditation of Higher Education Institutions (HEISs)

Statement (II): According to NEP 2020, through a suitable system of graded accreditation and graded autonomy, and in a phased manner over a period of 15 years, all HEis in India will aim to become independent self-governing institutions.

1. Both Statement I and Statement Il are correct
2. Both Statement I and Statement Il are incorrect
3. Statement I is correct but Statement Il s incorrect
4. Statement I is incorrect but Statement Il is correct

Explanations:
Answer: 4. Statement I is incorrect but Statement Il is correct

According to NEP 2020, the General Education Council (GEC) is not responsible for the accreditation of Higher Education Institutions (HEIs). Instead, the National Accreditation Council (NAC) will handle accreditation. Therefore, Statement I is incorrect. Statement II is correct as NEP 2020 outlines a plan where HEIs will gradually gain independence and self-governance through a system of graded accreditation and autonomy over a 15-year period.

Question

Statement I: Financing higher education in a country like India depends upon availability of resources and other financial implications.
Statement II: According to NEP 2020, funding and financing of higher education will be carried out by the second vertical of Higher Education Commission of India i.e, Higher Education Grants Council.

1. Both Statement (I) and Statement (Il) are correct.
2. Both Statement (1) and Statement (Il) are incorrect.
3. Statement (I) is correct but Statement (Il) is incorrect
4. Statement (I) is incorrect but Statement (Il) is correct

Explanations:
Answer: 3. Statement (I) is correct but Statement (Il) is incorrect

Financing higher education in India indeed depends on the availability of resources and other financial implications, making Statement I correct. However, according to NEP 2020, the Higher Education Grants Council (HEGC) is the third vertical of the Higher Education Commission of India (HECI), not the second. The second vertical is the National Accreditation Council (NAC).

Question

According to NEP 2020, All Higher Education Institutions (HEIs) shall aim to become multidisciplinary institutions and shall aim to have larger student enrolments by the year.

1. 2040

2. 2035
3. 2025
4. 2045

Explanations:
Answer: 1. 2040

According to the National Education Policy (NEP) 2020, all Higher Education Institutions (HEIs) in India are encouraged to transform into multidisciplinary institutions by the year 2040. This initiative aims to provide a more holistic and flexible education system, fostering a diverse set of skills and knowledge among students. The policy also envisions larger student enrollments to ensure that higher education is accessible to a broader segment of the population.

National Commission for Higher Education and Research (NCHER)

- **Proposed under the National Education Policy (NEP) 2010.**
- Aimed to **replace UGC, AICTE, and NCTE.**
- Designed to **streamline higher education governance.**
- Focused on **academic autonomy and regulatory efficiency.**
- Proposed to act as **a single higher education regulator.**

Objectives of NCHER

- Ensure quality and excellence in higher education.
- Promote innovation, research, and global competitiveness.
- Encourage multidisciplinary education and flexibility.
- Facilitate seamless credit transfers and mobility.
- Strengthen university autonomy and accountability.

Proposed Functions of NCHER

- Regulate standards for higher education institutions.
- Accredit and evaluate universities and colleges.
- Set policies for research and academic growth.
- Monitor faculty recruitment and development.
- Promote public-private partnerships in education.

NCHER vs. Existing Regulatory Bodies

- NCHER intended to replace UGC, AICTE, NCTE.
- Would remove redundant overlapping regulatory functions.
- Aimed at reducing bureaucratic delays in approvals.
- Proposed a single-window clearance system.
- Designed to bring uniformity across institutions.

Challenges & Status of NCHER

- Faced opposition from existing regulatory bodies.
- Concerns over autonomy of universities.
- Proposed structure not fully implemented.
- HECI (Higher Education Commission of India) replaced NCHER.
- NEP 2020 incorporated similar reforms under HECI

Question

Match the column:

A. First vertical of HECI	I. General education council (GEC)
B. Second vertide of HECI	II. National Higher Education Regulatory Council (NHERC)
C. Third ventricle of HECI	III. National Accreditation council (NAC)
D. Fourth vertical HECI	IV. Higher education grants council (HEGC)

1. A-II B-III C-IV D-I
2. A-III B-II C-IV D-I
3. A-II B-IV C-III D-I
4. A-III B-IV C-II D-I

Explanations:
Answer: 1. A-II B-III C-IV D-I

According to NEP 2020, the Higher Education Commission of India (HECI) will have four verticals:

- The first vertical is the National Higher Education Regulatory Council (NHERC).
- The second vertical is the National Accreditation Council (NAC).

- The third vertical is the Higher Education Grants Council (HEGC).
- The fourth vertical is the General Education Council (GEC).

Question

The professional organisation that opposed the inclusion of its educational discipline under NCHER was.

1. Education Council of India
2. Dental Council of India
3. Architectural Council of India
4. Bar Council of India

Explanations:
Answer: 4. Bar Council of India

National Committee for the Integration of Vocational Education (NCIVE)

- Proposed under NEP 2020 for vocational education reform.
- Aims to integrate vocational education into mainstream curricula.
- Ensures skill-based learning at all education levels.
- Focuses on industry-academia collaboration for employability.
- Develops competency-based training modules.
- Introduces multiple entry and exit options in courses.
- Encourages entrepreneurship and hands-on learning.
- Supports digital and blended learning for skill training.
- Targets 50% participation in vocational education by 2035.
- Aligns vocational programs with global education standards.

Question

What is the full form of 'NCIVE'?

1. Non-Governmental course for the Initiation of Vocational Enhancement
2. National Committee for the Integration of Vocational Education
3. Non-Governmental Council for the Integration of Veterinary Education
4. National Commission for the Information of Veterinary Education

Explanations:
Answer: 2. National Committee for the Integration of Vocational Education

The full form of 'NCIVE' as per the National Education Policy (NEP) 2020 is "National Committee for the Integration of Vocational Education." This committee is constituted to integrate vocational education into mainstream education, promoting skill development and employability among students.

Bar Council of India (BCI):

- The BCI will continue to specify standards of higher education concerning the practice in courts.
- There has been some contention regarding the Bill that was seen as restricting the BCI's power to set standards for legal education.

Multiple Entry and Exit System (MEES):

MEES allows students to exit a program at any point with a relevant certificate, diploma, or degree and re-enter the same or a different program at a later time. This provides flexibility and caters to the diverse needs of learners, facilitating lifelong learning and skill acquisition.

Key Features of NEP 2020 on Higher Education:

Emphasis on Flexibility: With the MEES, students have the flexibility to choose their educational path and adapt it to their needs and circumstances.

Multidisciplinary Approach: Encouraging a broad-based, holistic education that integrates the arts, humanities, and sciences.

Transparent and Accountable Funding: Through HEGC, funding will be allocated based on transparent and merit-based criteria.

Focus on Learning Outcomes: The GEC will ensure that programs are designed to achieve clear learning outcomes and prepare students for the workforce.

These reforms aim to create a more inclusive, flexible, and robust higher education system in India, aligning with global standards and preparing students for the challenges of the future.

Multidisciplinary Education and Research Universities (MERU)

- **Proposed under NEP 2020** to set global education standards.
- Aims to be **on par with IITs, IIMs, and top universities.**
- Focuses on **holistic and multidisciplinary education.**
- Encourages **research, innovation, and skill development.**
- Designed to **promote flexibility in course selection.**
- Will offer **interdisciplinary programs across multiple fields.**
- Supports **industry-academia collaboration for practical learning.**
- Ensures **inclusivity, accessibility, and affordability.**
- Aims to **improve India's global ranking in education.**
- Expected to **enhance employability and entrepreneurship.**

Question

Which of the following will model Public Universities for holistic and multidisciplinary education, at par with ITs, IIMs with the aim to attain the highest global standards in quality education?

1. MERUs (Multidisciplinary Education and Research Universities)
2. MVEUs (Multidisciplinary Vocational Education Universities)
3. MPEUs (Multidisciplinary Pedagogical Educational Universities)
4. MVOUs (Multidisciplinary value oriented Universities)

Explanations:
Answer: 1. MERUs (Multidisciplinary Education and Research Universities)

MERUs (Multidisciplinary Education and Research Universities) are envisioned in the NEP 2020 as model public universities for holistic and multidisciplinary education, aiming to attain the highest global standards in quality education, comparable to institutions like IITś and IIMs.

Question

Statement I: The National Policy on Education (1986) was intended to encourage interdisciplinary research in the social sciences.
Statement Il: According to the National Policy on Education (1986), the idea of rural universities was illogical.

1. Both statement (I) and statement (Il) are correct.
2. Both statement (I) and statement (Il) are wrong.
3. Statement (I) is correct but statement II) is wrong
4. Statement (I) is wrong but statement (Il) is correct

Explanations:
Answer: 3. Statement (I) is correct but statement II) is wrong

The National Policy on Education (1986) indeed aimed to encourage interdisciplinary research in the social sciences. However, it did not consider the idea of rural universities illogical. On the contrary, it supported the concept to address educational needs in rural areas.

Question

An IT giant company has its Global Education Centre at:

1. Medak
2. Ratnagiri
3. Mysore
4. Agartala

Explanations:
Answer: 3. Mysore

The IT giant company referred to **here is Infosys,** which has its **Global Education Centre in Mysore, Karnataka**. This center is one of the largest corporate training facilities in the world and is used to train new recruits and employees of Infosys.

National Educational Technology Forum (NETF)

- **Proposed under NEP 2020** to integrate technology in education.
- Aims to **enhance digital learning and online education.**
- Focuses on **AI, blockchain, virtual labs, and EdTech tools.**
- Encourages **research and innovation in educational technology.**
- Provides **a platform for knowledge sharing on digital education.**
- Supports **teacher training in modern technological methods.**
- Helps in **policy-making for tech-based learning solutions.**
- Ensures **inclusivity in digital education access.**
- Bridges **the digital divide in rural and urban education.**
- Works with **universities, EdTech companies, and policymakers.**

Question

Statement (I): The National Education Policy (2020) foresees a wide use of disruptive technologies in the higher education system.
Statement (II): The National Educational Technology Forum is expected to prepare a roadmap for integrating the disruptive technologies into the education system.

1. Both Statement (I) and Statement (II) are correct.
2. Both Statement (I) and Statement (II) are incorrect.
3. Statement (I) is correct but Statement (II) is incorrect
4. Statement (I) is incorrect but Statement (II) is correct

Explanations:
Answer: 1. Both Statement (I) and Statement (II) are correct.

The National Education Policy (2020) indeed anticipates the wide use of disruptive technologies in the higher education system to improve teaching, learning, and administration. The National Educational Technology Forum (NETF) is expected to develop a roadmap for the integration of these technologies into the education system.

Question

Statement I: Technical education is that which emphasises on the learning of techniques as technical procedures and necessary skills and aims at preparing technicians usually above the secondary level.
Statement II: There is no distinction between vocational education, industrial education and technical education.

1. Both Statement I and Statement Il are true.
2. Both Statement I and Statement Il are false.
3. Statement I is true but Statement Il is false.
4. Statement I is false but Statement Il is true.

Explanations:
Answer: 3. Statement I is true but Statement Il is false.

Statement I is true because technical education focuses on teaching students specific techniques, procedures, and skills necessary to perform technical tasks and prepare them as technicians, usually above the secondary level.

Statement II is false because there is a distinction between vocational education, industrial education, and technical education. Vocational education is broader and includes training for a wide range of jobs and skills. Industrial education focuses more on preparing individuals for employment in industrial sectors, while technical education is specifically aimed at developing technical skills and knowledge.

National Research Foundation (NRF):

To boost quality research in India, NEP 2020 envisions the establishment of the National Research Foundation (NRF). This body will provide a strong impetus for research across disciplines.

- Proposed under NEP 2020 to strengthen research.
- Aims to enhance research funding and innovation.
- Encourages multidisciplinary and cross-sectoral research.
- Supports both fundamental and applied research.
- Facilitates collaboration between universities and industries.
- Promotes international partnerships in research.
- Bridges gap between academia and real-world applications.
- Provides grants for faculty and student research projects.
- Focuses on STEM, social sciences, and humanities research.
- Ensures research contributes to national development.

Question

Statement I: As per NEP-2020, National Research Foundation (NRF) will constitute a National Committee for the Integration of Vocational Education (NCIVE)-

Statement Il: As per NEP-2020, Model Public Universities for holistic and multidisciplinary education, at par with IITs, IlMs, called MERUS (Multidisciplinary Education and Rescarch Universities) will be set up to attain the highest global standards in quality education.

1. Both Statement I and Statement II are correct.
2. Both statement I and Statement Il are incorrect.
3. Statement I is Correct but Statement Il is incorrect.
4. Statement I is incorrect but Statement Il is correct.

Explanations:
Answer: 4. Statement I is incorrect but Statement Il is correct.

Statement I is incorrect because the National Research Foundation (NRF) does not constitute a National Committee for the Integration of Vocational Education (NCIVE). Instead, the NEP-2020 mentions that the Ministry of Human Resource Development (MHRD) will constitute the NCIVE.

Statement II is correct because, according to NEP-2020, Model Public Universities for holistic and multidisciplinary education, called MERUs (Multidisciplinary Education and Research Universities), will be set up to attain the highest global standards in quality education, comparable to IITs and IIMs.

National Curriculum Framework for Teacher Education (NCTF)

- **Proposed under NEP 2020** to improve teacher training.
- **Aims to standardize teacher education curricula.**
- **Focuses on competency-based teacher training.**
- **Ensures alignment with multidisciplinary education goals.**
- **Emphasizes holistic and experiential learning methods.**
- **Promotes digital learning and technology integration.**

- **Encourages research and innovation in pedagogy.**
- **Supports continuous professional development for teachers.**
- **Introduces four-year integrated B.Ed. programs.**
- **Aims to elevate teaching as a high-quality profession.**

National Higher Education Qualification Framework (NHEQF)

- Proposed under NEP 2020 to standardize qualifications.
- Aims to align Indian education with global standards.
- Introduces credit-based learning and flexibility.
- Supports multiple entry and exit options in degrees.
- Ensures mobility between vocational and academic education.
- Defines qualification levels from undergraduate to Ph.D.
- Enhances employability through skill-based learning.
- Promotes outcome-based education and assessment.
- Encourages interdisciplinary and multidisciplinary learning.
- Facilitates easy recognition of Indian degrees worldwide.

Question

Which of the following are recommendations of the NEP2020 for improving the quality of higher education in India?

A. Introduction of National Research Foundation.
B. Accreditation of all higher education institutions
C. Integration of Vocational education into mainstream education.
D. Establishment of National Higher Education Qualification Framwork.

1. A & B only
2. C & D only
3. A.B & D only
4. A, B, C, & D

Explanations:
Answer: 4. A, B, C, & D

The National Education Policy (NEP) 2020 outlines several recommendations aimed at improving the quality of higher education in India:

Introduction of National Research Foundation (NRF): To promote quality research in higher education institutions.

Accreditation of all higher education institutions: To ensure quality and standards in higher education.

Integration of vocational education into mainstream education: To make education more relevant to employment opportunities and skills development.

Establishment of National Higher Education Qualification Framework (NHEQF): To align qualifications across the higher education system.

These recommendations are comprehensive and address multiple aspects of enhancing the quality and relevance of higher education in India.

Indian Institute of Translation and Interpretation (IITI):

India aims to expand its translation and interpretation efforts, making high-quality learning materials accessible in various Indian and foreign languages. For this purpose, an Indian Institute of Translation and Interpretation (IITI) will be established.

Adult Education:

A new and well-supported constituent body of NCERT dedicated to adult education will develop an outstanding adult education curriculum framework. This effort aims to provide lifelong learning opportunities to adults. The **National Education Policy (NEP) 2020** includes a strong focus on **adult education** as part of its broader vision for lifelong learning. Under the curriculum framework for adult education, the following components are emphasized:

1. **Foundational Literacy and Numeracy**: Ensuring that adults acquire basic reading, writing, and numeracy skills.
2. **Critical Life Skills**: Including financial literacy, digital literacy, and vocational skills.
3. **Continuing Education**: Opportunities for adults to continue learning and upgrading their skills.
4. **Community Engagement**: Encouraging participation in community-based learning programs.
5. **Use of Technology**: Leveraging digital tools and platforms to deliver adult education programs.

These components aim to empower adults, reduce illiteracy, and promote lifelong learning opportunities for all.

Question

According to NEP-2020, which is/are not under the curriculum framework of adult education?

A. A Critical Life Skills
B. Vocational Skills Development
C. Continuing Education
D. Art in Education
E. Basic Education

1. A
2. BC
3. D
4. ADE

Explanations
Answer: 3. D. Art in Education

Holistic Education and MERUs:

NEP 2020 focuses on holistic education through the establishment of model public universities called Multidisciplinary Education and Research Universities (MERUs). These institutions will aim to reach the highest global standards in quality education, similar to IITs and IIMs.

Global Citizenship Education (GCED):

GCED will equip learners with the knowledge, skills, values, and attitudes needed to fully participate in a globalized society and economy. It aims to support initiatives that promote a just, secure, peaceful, tolerant, inclusive, and sustainable world.

Question

According to NEP 2020 as a response to contemporary global challenges 'Global Citizenship Education' will be provided to learners to become active promoters of_

A. societies.
B. tolerant
C. peaceful
D. inclusive
E. secure
F. sustainable

1. BCE
2. AC
3. ABCDE
4. BDE

Explanations:
Answer: 3. ABCDE

Global Citizenship Education (GCED) under NEP 2020 aims to equip learners with the knowledge, skills, values, and attitudes needed to become active promoters of societies that are tolerant, peaceful, inclusive, secure, and sustainable. This holistic approach addresses the broad spectrum of global challenges and emphasizes the importance of preparing students to contribute positively to the global community.

Question

The National Education Policy 2020, envisaged that the new education system in India should aim at

1. Nationalist education

2. Regional education
3. Conventional education
4. Global citizenship education

Explanations:
Answer: 4. Global citizenship education

The National Education Policy (NEP) 2020 emphasizes the importance of preparing students to be active promoters of more inclusive, peaceful, and sustainable societies globally. It aims to equip learners with the knowledge, skills, values, and attitudes needed to thrive in an interconnected world. Therefore, it focuses on Global Citizenship Education rather than nationalist, regional, or conventional education. This approach is designed to foster understanding, tolerance, and cooperation among students from diverse backgrounds.

Value-based Education:

The policy emphasizes inculcating values for the holistic development of young personalities, encompassing physical, mental, emotional, and spiritual aspects. This includes instilling life skills and constitutional values in students.

Consolidation and Expansion of Institutions:

NEP 2020 also focuses on the consolidation and expansion of educational institutions to ensure optimal utilization of resources and broaden access to education.

Teacher Training:

The policy highlights the importance of continuous training and professional development for teachers to improve teaching quality and student outcomes.

Question

Statement (I): According to the National Education Policy 2020, teaching duties will be more, and student-teacher ratio will be high, and faculty will be generally transferable across institutions in the country.

Statement (II): According to the NEP, 2020, faculty will be given the liberty to design their pedagogical approaches for innovative teaching and research

1. Both Statement (I) and Statement (II) are correct.
2. Both Statement (I) and Statement (Il) are incorrect.
3. Statement (I) is correct but Statement (Il) is incorrect
4. Statement (I) is incorrect but Statement (Il) is correct

Explanations:
Answer: 4. Statement (I) is incorrect but Statement (Il) is correct

According to the National Education Policy (NEP) 2020, Statement I is incorrect because NEP 2020 emphasizes improving the student-teacher ratio and does not advocate for higher teaching duties or frequent faculty transfers across institutions. Instead, it focuses on better teacher-student interactions and manageable workloads for faculty. Statement II is correct as NEP 2020 does grant faculty the liberty to design their pedagogical approaches, promoting innovative teaching and research methods.

Question

Statement I: According to the National Education Policy document, the teacher must be the locus of basic reforms in the country's educational reforms.
Statement II: Historically marginalised or the disadvantaged student sections of the society should get paid quality education irrespective of their place of residence.

1. Both Statement I and Statement Il are true.
2. Both Statement I and Statement Il are false.
3. Statement l is true but Statement Il is false.
4. Statement I is false but Statement Il is true.

Explanations:
Answer: 3. Statement l is true but Statement Il is false.

Statement I is correct because the National Education Policy 2020 emphasizes that teachers should be central to educational reforms. They are seen as pivotal in implementing changes and improving the quality of education.

Statement II is incorrect because, according to the NEP 2020, historically marginalized or disadvantaged student sections of society should receive quality education free of cost, not paid, irrespective of their place of residence. The policy focuses on providing free and compulsory education to all children, ensuring inclusivity and equity in education.

Development of Autonomous Colleges:

The policy encourages the development of autonomous colleges to enhance academic freedom and innovation in higher education institutions.

Strengthening Research:

Strengthening research capabilities and infrastructure is a key priority, ensuring that India becomes a global leader in producing high-quality research output.

Question

The National Education Policy, 2020, also focuses on

1. Coastal area education
2. Hill area education
3. Foreign education through Indian languages
4. High quality education in Indian languages

Explanations:
Answer: 4: High quality education in Indian languages

The National Education Policy (NEP) 2020 places significant emphasis on promoting high-quality education in Indian languages. This includes efforts to develop and promote learning materials and resources in multiple Indian languages, ensuring that students can receive education in their mother tongue or regional language, particularly at the foundational stage.

The Aim of NEP 2020 – Increasing Gross Enrolment Ratio (GER) in Higher Education

- Target GER of 50% by 2035.
- Expansion of higher education institutions (HEIs).
- Integration of vocational education into mainstream education.
- Promotion of online and distance learning.
- Establishment of multidisciplinary institutions (MERUs).
- Encouraging private and public sector partnerships.
- Providing financial aid and scholarships.
- Strengthening research and innovation programs.
- Inclusion of marginalized communities and gender equity.
- Flexibility in course structures and multiple entry-exit options.

Question

The Aim of National Education Policy. 2020, is to increase the Gross Enrollment Ratio in higher education by

1. 35%
2. 26.3%
3. 50%
4. 40%

Explanations:
Answer: 3. 50%

The National Education Policy (NEP) 2020 aims to increase the Gross Enrollment Ratio (GER) in higher education, including vocational education, from 26.3% (as of 2018) to 50% by 2035.

Question

As per NEP 2020 Gross Enrolment Ratio (GER) is sought to be achieved to the extent of 50% by

1. 2030
2. 2035
3. 2040
4. 2047

Explanations:
Answer: 2. 2035

According to the National Education Policy (NEP) 2020, India aims to achieve a Gross Enrolment Ratio (GER) of 50% in higher education by the year 2035. This target is part of a broader initiative to make higher education more accessible and inclusive, encouraging more students to pursue higher studies and thereby improving the overall educational standards in the country.

Question

Statement I: The idea of abolition of regulatory bodies of education like UGC, AICIE and NCTE is based on the assumption that such multiple bodies are redundant.

Statement Il: The Bar Council of India has opposed the idea of abolition of regulatory bodies as it would affect its role as the apex regulatory body of legal professionals in India

1. Both Statement I and Statement II are true.
2. Both Statement I and Statement Il are false.
3. Statement I is true but Statement Il is false.
4. Statement I is false but Statement Il is true.

Explanations:
Answer: 1. Both Statement I and Statement II are true.

The idea behind the abolition of regulatory bodies like UGC, AICTE, and NCTE is indeed based on the assumption that having multiple bodies creates redundancy and inefficiency. The Bar Council of India has opposed the abolition of such regulatory bodies, fearing it would undermine its authority as the apex regulatory body for legal professionals in India.

NEP 2020 and GDP

- **NEP 2020 recommends 6% of GDP for education.**
- **Aims to increase public investment in education.**
- **Focuses on funding higher education and research.**

- **Supports vocational and skill-based education programs.**
- **Enhances financial aid for marginalized communities.**
- **Encourages public-private partnerships in education.**
- **Strengthens digital learning infrastructure.**
- **Invests in teacher training and development.**
- **Improves school and higher education accessibility.**
- **Ensures sustainable and equitable education growth.**

Question

Statement I: According to NEP 2020. at present the investment in research and innovation in India is only <1% of GDP

Statement II: NEP 2020 recommends the establishment of a National curriculum framework for Teacher.

1. Both Statement I and Statement II are true
2. Both Statement I and Statement II are false
3. Statement I is true but Statement Il is false
4. Statement T is false but Statement IT is true

Explanations:
Answer: 1. Both Statement I and Statement II are true

Statement I: According to NEP 2020, the current investment in research and innovation in India is indeed less than 1% of the GDP. This indicates that the nation recognizes the need for increased funding and resources dedicated to research and development to foster innovation and growth.

Statement II: NEP 2020 does recommend the establishment of a National Curriculum Framework for Teacher Education. This framework is aimed at improving the quality of teacher education, ensuring that teachers are well-prepared and continuously updated with the latest educational practices and methodologies.

Vishwa Guru in NEP 2020

- **NEP 2020 aims to restore India as Vishwa Guru.**
- **Focuses on making India a global education hub.**
- **Encourages attracting international students to Indian HEIs.**

- **Promotes high-quality education in Indian languages.**
- **Emphasizes research, innovation, and multidisciplinary learning.**
- **Supports collaboration with top global universities.**
- **Encourages export of Indian knowledge and traditions.**
- **Strengthens India's position in global education rankings.**
- **Aims to provide affordable yet world-class education.**
- **Fosters holistic, ethical, and skill-based learning.**

Question

According to NEP 2020, India will be promoted as a global study destination providing premium education at affordable costs thereby helping to restore its role as

1. Economic power
2. Knowledge Economy
3. Vishwa Guru
4. Shiksha Guru

Explanations:
Answer: 3. Vishwa Guru

According to the National Education Policy (NEP) 2020, India aims to be promoted as a global study destination offering high-quality education at affordable costs. This initiative seeks to attract international students and enhance India's global standing in education, thus helping to restore its historical role as "Vishwa Guru" (World Teacher).

National Credit Framework (NCrF) – 20 Key Points

Introduction to NCrF

- **Proposed under NEP 2020 for credit-based learning.**
- **Integrates school, vocational, and higher education.**
- **Aims to unify general and skill education.**
- **Enables credit accumulation and transfer across levels.**

Structure and Implementation

- **Applicable to all levels of education, including HEIs.**
- **Defines learning outcomes in terms of credit points.**
- **Maps qualification levels to NSQF, NHEQF, and NSEQF.**
- **Supports competency-based and outcome-based learning.**

Flexibility and Mobility

- Facilitates multiple entry and exit options.
- Allows credit banking through the Academic Bank of Credits (ABC).
- Promotes lifelong learning and upskilling.
- Encourages mobility between formal and non-formal education.
- A **three-year undergraduate Bachelor's degree** accumulates **5.5 credit levels**.
- A **Doctoral degree (Ph.D.)** is assigned **credit level 8** in the framework.

Role in Vocational and Skill Education

- Bridges academic and vocational training pathways.
- Encourages industry participation in skill-based learning.
- Supports apprenticeship and work-integrated learning models.
- Enhances employability and job readiness.

Global Alignment and Future Impact

- Aligns Indian education with global qualification standards.
- Enables seamless credit transfer across institutions.
- Encourages digital and blended learning models.
- Aims to create a robust, flexible, and inclusive education system.

Question

According to National Credit Framework (NCrF). the credit level earned after obtaining Bachelor's degree (three years of undergraduate programme) will be-

1. 7
2. 5.5

3. 6.5
4. 5

Explanations
Answer: 2. 5.5

Under the **National Credit Framework (NCrF), each level corresponds to a certain credit value** based on learning duration and competency. A **three-year undergraduate Bachelor's degree** accumulates **5.5 credit levels. This framework integrates academic, vocational, and skill-based learning** to ensure seamless transitions across education pathways.

Question

According to the National Credit Framework (NCrF) the credit level eamed after Doctoral degree (Ph.D.) will be:

1. 7
2. 8
3. 9
4. 10

Explanations
Answer: 2. 8

Under the **National Credit Framework (NCrF), credit levels increase progressively with higher education qualifications**. A **Doctoral degree (Ph.D.)** is assigned **credit level 8** in the framework. **NCrF integrates academic, vocational, and skill-based learning**, ensuring flexibility in credit accumulation and transfer.

Question

Match the column:

A. Academic year	I. A unit by which the course work is measured. It defines the number of hours of instruction required per week
B. Credit Point	II. Papers taught under the programme duly defining the learning objectives and outcomes
C. Credit	III. Two consecutive (one odd and one even)

	semesters
D. Course	IV. The product of grade point and number of credits for a course

1. A-III, B-II, C-IV, D-I
2. A-IV, B-I, C-III, D-II
3. A-III B-IV, C-I, D-II
4. A-Il, B-III, C-IV, D-I

Explanations
Answer: 3. A-III B-IV, C-I, D-II

A. Academic Year → III. Two consecutive (one odd and one even) semesters.
B. Credit Point → IV. The product of grade point and number of credits for a course.
C. Credit → I. A unit by which the coursework is measured, defining the required hours of instruction per week.
D. Course → II. Papers taught under the program, defining learning objectives and outcomes.

Abbreviations and Key Terminologies in Indian Education System

- **AICTE** - All India Institute of Technical Education
- **CBCS** – Choice Based Credit System
- **CBSE**- Central Board of Secondary Education
- **CITS**: Craftsman Instructor Training Scheme
- **CTS** - Craftsman Training Scheme
- **DGT** - Directorate General of Training
- **HEIs**: Higher Education Institutes
- **MSDE** - Ministry of Skill Development and Entrepreneurship
- **NAC**- National Apprenticeship Certificate
- **NCERT** - National Council for Educational Research and Training
- **NCrF** – National Credit Framework
- **NCVET** - National Council for Vocational Education and Training
- **NEP** - National Education Policy
- **NSEQF**- National School Education Qualification Framework
- **NHEQF** - National Higher Education Qualification Framework

- **NIOS** - National Institute of Open Schooling
- **NSQF** - National Skill Qualifications Framework
- **NTA** - National Testing Agency
- **NTC** - National Trade Certificate
- **SAMVAY** - Skill Assessment Matrix for Vocational Advancement of Youth
- **SDG** - Sustainable Development Goals
- **UGC** - University Grants Commission
- **VET** – Vocational Education and Training

University Administration and Academic Structure

The Vice-Chancellor: The vice-chancellor serves as the administrative and academic head, effectively the Chief Executive Officer (CEO) of the university. Responsibilities include maintaining discipline among teachers, staff, and students, and overseeing the overall functioning of the university.

The Syndicate/Executive Council: This is the principal management organ and the highest executive authority within the university. The Syndicate is responsible for the effective administration of the university, managing daily operations, and ensuring that all administrative functions run smoothly.

The Registrar: The registrar leads the university's civil service, acts as the custodian of all university records, and represents the university in its dealings with the outside world. Typically appointed by the Executive Council (Syndicate) based on the recommendation of a Selection Committee chaired by the Vice-Chancellor, the registrar plays a crucial role in administrative functions.

Academic Council: As the university's principal academic organ, the Academic Council coordinates and supervises the university's academic policies. Its role includes raising the standards and quality of teaching and research, strengthening ties with regional and national development, and prescribing methods of instruction, evaluation, and other academic norms.

Board of Studies: The Board of Studies is responsible for monitoring and reviewing existing program structures and course syllabi. It compares these with programs from other institutes, assesses teaching and evaluation methodologies, considers market requirements, observes modern trends, and updates courses and programs accordingly. It also makes suggestions for any necessary amendments.

Question

Statement-I: The Governor of the State is the Chancellor of deemed universities.
Statement-II: Deemed universities can design their own syllabus and course work.

1. Both Statement I and Statement Il are correct.
2. Both Statement I and Statement Il are incorrect.
3. Statement I is correct but Statement Il is incorrect.
4. Statement I is incorrect but Statement Il is correct.

Explanations:
Answer: 4. Statement I is incorrect but Statement Il is correct.

Statement I: The Governor of the State is the Chancellor of deemed universities.

This statement is incorrect. The Chancellor of deemed universities is usually appointed by the sponsoring body of the deemed university and not by the Governor of the State. The Governor is typically the Chancellor of state universities, not deemed universities.

Statement II: Deemed universities can design their own syllabus and course work.

This statement is correct. Deemed universities in India have the autonomy to design their own syllabus and coursework, providing them the flexibility to innovate and cater to specific educational and industry needs.

Question

In a State government university or Central University, recommendation of the Selection Committee for the recruitment of the faculty is approved by the

1. Academic Council
2. Executive Council
3. Finance Committee
4. Chancellor of University

Explanations:
Answer: 2. Executive Council

In both State government universities and Central Universities, the recommendation of the Selection Committee for the recruitment of faculty members is typically approved by the Executive Council. The Executive Council, also known as the Board of Governors or Syndicate in some universities, is the highest executive authority responsible for the administration and management of the university. It oversees various important functions, including faculty appointments, and ensures that the recommendations made by the Selection Committee are in line with the university's policies and standards.

Question

Given below are two statements:

Statement I: Board of studies is the basic unit of the academic system of the University.
Statement II: The responsibilities of the Board of studies include planning. coordination
and review of the academic programmes of the university.

In the light of the above statements, choose the correct answer from the options given below:

1. Both Statement I and Statement II are true
2. Both Statement I and Statement II are false
3. Statement I is correct but Statement Il is false
4. Statement I is incorrect but Statement II is true

Explanations:
Answer: 3. Statement I is correct but Statement Il is false

Statement I: Board of Studies is indeed considered the basic unit of the academic system of the university. It is responsible for the academic framework and quality of the academic programs within its jurisdiction.

Statement II: While the Board of Studies plays a crucial role in planning and reviewing the academic programs, the overall coordination and comprehensive review of all academic programs at the university level is typically the responsibility of higher academic bodies such as the Academic Council.

Question

Given below are two statements:

Statement I: The vice-chancellor of a University is an executive head who is vested with
administrative as well as academic responsibilities.
Statement II: For a charismatic leadership attribute in a vice chancellor both transactional as well as transformational leadership competencies are needed.

In the light of the above statements, choose the correct answer from the options given below:

1. Both Statement I and Statement II are true
2. Both Statement I and Statement II are false
3. Statement I is correct but Statement II is false
4. Statement I is incorrect but Statement II is true

Explanations:
Answer: 1. Both Statement I and Statement II are true

Statement I: The vice-chancellor is indeed the executive head of a university and is responsible for both administrative and academic functions, ensuring the smooth running of the institution.

Statement II: Effective vice-chancellors often need to exhibit both transactional and transformational leadership qualities. Transactional leadership involves managing day-to-day operations and maintaining the status quo, while transformational leadership involves inspiring and motivating staff and students towards innovation and improvement.

Question

In the university education system as prevalent now, which of the following bodies/committees looks after formal approval of curriculum and courses of study?

1. University Executive Council/Board of Management
2. Academic council of the concerned university
3. Board of studies
4. University Court

Explanations:
Answer: 2. Academic council of the concerned university

The Academic Council of a university is primarily responsible for the approval of curriculum and courses of study. It serves as the chief academic body of the university, overseeing academic policies, standards, and programs, including the approval of new courses and curricula.

Question

In university governance, who is the executive head?

1. The Chancellor
2. The Vice-Chancellor
3. The Registrar
4. The Education Secretary

Explanations:
Answer: 2. The Vice-Chancellor

In university governance, the Vice-Chancellor is the executive head. The Vice-Chancellor holds administrative and academic responsibilities and is responsible for the overall management and leadership of the university. They act as the chief executive officer of the institution, ensuring that the university operates smoothly and meets its educational objectives.

Question

The principal responsibilities of Academic Council in a University include

(A) Maintenance of quality and standards of academic programmes.
(B) Planning, coordination, development, oversight and review of academic programmes of University.
(C) Laying down the essential qualifications for recruitment of faculty in various disciplines.
(D) Framing and revising/updating the contents of courses of various academic programmes.
(E) Approval of fee structure for various academic programmes

Choose the correct answer from the options given below:

1. (A) and B) only
2. (A), (B), (C) and (D) only
3. (A), (B), (D) and (E) only
4. (A), (B), (C) and (E) only

Explanations:
Answer: 1. (A) and B) only

The principal responsibilities of the Academic Council in a University primarily include:

- Maintenance of quality and standards of academic programmes.
- Planning, coordination, development, oversight, and review of academic programmes of the University.

These responsibilities focus on ensuring the academic integrity and excellence of the university's educational offerings. While the Academic Council may provide input on qualifications for faculty recruitment, course content, and fee structure, these are often under the purview of other specific committees or bodies within the university governance structure.

Question

Which statutory body of a university has the power to accord formal approval to the programmes and courses of studies?

1. Senate
2. Academic Council
3. Syndicate
4. Board of Studies

Explanations:
Answer: 2. Academic Council

The Academic Council of a university is the principal academic body responsible for the maintenance of standards of education, teaching, and training. It has the authority to accord formal approval to the programmes and courses of study, ensuring they meet the necessary academic standards and align with the university's educational objectives.

Question

For the day-to-day administration of university, which of the following bodies is responsible?

1. Senate
2. Syndicate/Executive council
3. Student council
4. Academic council

Explanations:
Answer: 2. Syndicate/Executive council

The Syndicate/Executive Council is the highest executive authority in a university. It is responsible for the day-to-day administration and management of the university, ensuring that the institution runs smoothly and efficiently. This body makes decisions regarding the implementation of policies, management of resources, and overall governance of the university.

Question

In the institutions of higher education in India which of the following has the formal authority to approve the courses and programmes of studies?

1. The University Court / Senate
2. Departmental Council
3. Board of Studies
4. Academic Council

Explanations:
Answer: 4. Academic Council

The Academic Council is the principal academic body of a university. It has the formal authority to approve the courses and programs of studies. This council is responsible for maintaining standards of instruction, education, and examination within the university, ensuring that the academic framework aligns with educational goals and objectives.

Question

The leadership and executive role in higher education system in respect of state universities of India is assigned to:

1. Chancellor of the University
2. Vice-Chancellor of the University
3. Deans of Faculties
4. Dean of Studies

Explanations:
Answer: 2. Vice-Chancellor of the University

The Vice-Chancellor of the University holds the leadership and executive role in the higher education system for state universities in India. The Vice-Chancellor is responsible for the overall administration, both academic and non-academic, and acts as the chief executive officer of the university, ensuring the implementation of policies and the smooth functioning of the institution.

Question

The formal authority for approving the University level courses vests in:

1. The Academic Council
2. The University Court

3. The Executive Council
4. The Research Degree Committee

Explanations:
Answer: 1. The Academic Council

The Academic Council is the principal academic body of the university and has the authority to approve courses, curricula, and academic programs. It is responsible for maintaining the standards of instruction, education, and examination within the university.

Question

The Gross Enrolment Ratio (GER) measures the number of students enrolled in higher education as a percentage of the eligible population aged between

1. 18 to 24 years
2. 19 to 25 years
3. 18 to 23 years
4. 17 to 23 years

Explanations:
Answer: 3. 18 to 23 years

The Gross Enrolment Ratio (GER) for higher education typically measures the number of students enrolled in higher education, regardless of age, expressed as a percentage of the eligible population within a specific age group. For higher education, this age group is commonly defined as 18 to 23 years.

Question

Which of the following are the National Coordinators appointed for SWAYAM courses?

A. Indian Institute of Management, Bangalore (IMB)
B. National Programme on Technology Enhanced Learning (NTEL)
C. National Institute of Open Schooling (NIOS)
D. Block Institute of Teacher Education (BITE)
E. Consortium for Educational Communication (CEC)

Choose the most appropriate answer from the options given below :

(1) B and D only
(2) C, D and E only
(3) A, B and C only
(4) A, B, C and E only

Explanations:
Answer: 4. A, B, C and E only

The SWAYAM (Study Webs of Active Learning for Young Aspiring Minds) platform has several National Coordinators responsible for creating and delivering various courses. Some of these coordinators include prestigious institutions like the Indian Institute of Management, Bangalore (IIMB), the National Programme on Technology Enhanced Learning (NPTEL), the National Institute of Open Schooling (NIOS), and the Consortium for Educational Communication (CEC).

End

Usage Policy for NerdSchool Notes

Created by: Instructors from NerdSchool
Owned by: NERDSTABLE PVT LTD

The following notes are the intellectual property of **NERDSTABLE PVT LTD** and are made available exclusively to students who have paid for access. By using these notes, you agree to the terms and conditions outlined below:

Policy of Usage:

Personal Use Only: These notes are intended for your **personal study and exam preparation**. You are permitted to **read** and **print** them for your own reference.

No Unauthorized Distribution or Sale: You **may not sell, distribute**, or **replicate** these notes in any form, whether digitally or physically. This includes sharing copies with others, regardless of the medium (online platforms, printed materials, etc.).

No Plagiarism: You **may not claim** the contents of these notes as your own. Any form of direct publication or submission under your name, without proper citation, is strictly prohibited.

Non-Transferable Access: Access to these notes is restricted to the individual purchaser. **Sharing your login credentials** or any other means of access to these materials with others is a violation of this policy.

Additional Guidelines:

For Educational Use Only: These notes are designed to help students succeed in their academic exams and should be used responsibly. They are meant to supplement your learning, not to replace the guidance of instructors or textbooks.

No Commercial Use: The content in these notes cannot be used for **commercial purposes**. This includes using the material in any form of paid tutoring or educational courses that you offer without the explicit permission of NERDSTABLE PVT LTD.

www.ingramcontent.com/pod-product-compliance
Ingram Content Group UK Ltd.
Pitfield, Milton Keynes, MK11 3LW, UK
UKHW061133310726
14090UKWH00036B/986

9 798897 443246